W9-CIF-684

Judging Victims

Social Problems, Social Constructions

Joel Best and Scott R. Harris, series editors

JUDGING VICTIMS

Why We Stigmatize Survivors, and How They Reclaim Respect

Jennifer L. Dunn

LYNNE
RIENNER
PUBLISHERS

BOULDER
LONDON

Published in the United States of America in 2010 by
Lynne Rienner Publishers, Inc.
1800 30th Street, Boulder, Colorado 80301
www.rienner.com

and in the United Kingdom by
Lynne Rienner Publishers, Inc.
3 Henrietta Street, Covent Garden, London WC2E 8LU

Library of Congress Cataloging-in-Publication Data
Dunn, Jennifer L., 1957–
  Judging victims : why we stigmatize survivors, and how they reclaim
respect / Jennifer L. Dunn.
      p. cm. — (Social problems, social constructions)
  Includes bibliographical references and index.
  ISBN 978-1-58826-702-3 (hbk. : alk. paper)
  1. Victims of crimes—Psychology. 2. Victims of crimes—Public opinion.
I. Title.
  HV6250.25.D86 2009
  362.88—dc22
                                                          2009036831

British Cataloguing in Publication Data
A Cataloguing in Publication record for this book
is available from the British Library.

Printed and bound in the United States of America

⊗   The paper used in this publication meets the requirements
     of the American National Standard for Permanence of
     Paper for Printed Library Materials Z39.48-1992.

  5 4 3 2

To the Leverett boys,
who are all very kind to women and children

Contents

Acknowledgments

This book took a long time to write, which means that there are now a great many people who have helped along the way. Things really got going when I was granted a sabbatical and, via this, the opportunity to read far more than I had been able to up to that point. For this, I thank the College of Liberal Arts at Southern Illinois University in Carbondale (SIUC). Some of the books, including several of those from which I draw data, were paid for with a grant from the SIUC office of University Women's Professional Advancement (UWPA) and the Women's Studies Department. The university also provided the funds enabling me to present portions of the work at annual meetings of the Society for the Study of Symbolic Interaction and the Midwest Sociological Society, where countless people offered feedback on early drafts. Finally, I am especially appreciative of the invaluable aid of graduate assistants Melissa Powell-Williams, Danielle Estes, and Michelle Henton. Each of these young scholars worked incredibly hard to help me gather sources, and they provided insights I would not have gotten elsewhere.

I value the people whose work has been the inspiration for my own and who have been so generous with their advice and suggestions. Joel Best got me thinking about social problems from a constructionist per-spective and taught me two important things: how to write and how to make writing a (usually) daily practice. Although he left SIUC just as I was arriving, I made him promise to be my mentor for life or my tenure there (whichever was longer), and so far he has more than kept that promise. Doni Loseke has been the soul of kindness (tactfully never mentioning how my latest "discovery" was something she had written about years before, for example) even as she has been candid about the ideas and the writing that needed improvement. Her early work on battered women has been the foundation for virtually everything I have been thinking about lately, and her recent careful scholarship on narrative identity has been an intellectual "gift basket" as well as a challenge to think harder, more thoroughly, with greater precision, and to further effect. Rob Benford has been my chair, my mentor, and my colleague. He sparked my interest in social movements, but more important, he also nurtured it. And he has done everything in his power as head of our department to enable me to do research and writing, as have Darren Sherkat and Tom Calhoun. Along with our wonderful administrative assistants, Judy Brown and Sue Treece, they have helped more than they might realize, in innumerable large and small ways.

A lot of people were good enough to read and comment on various parts of my manuscript, some of which appeared in different forms (Dunn 2004, 2005). These folks include Rob Benford, Tom Calhoun, Ruth Chananie, Joseph Davis, Charles E. Faupel, Patricia Gagne, James Holstein, Gay Kitson, Sharon Lamb, Doni Loseke, M. Joan McDermott, Matthew Renfro-Sargent, Paul Rock, and all of the anonymous reviewers. *Judging Victims* is far better for the advice I took.

I don't think you would be holding this book in your hands if it weren't for Andrew Berzanskis. One day he e-mailed me to ask if a paper I was presenting was part of a larger project and, if so, would I like to discuss it with him. In my efforts to convince him that I had a book in me, I somehow managed to convince myself. Andrew has been patient, supportive, and encouraging and all along has shown me that he "gets it," which has been thrilling. He let me try out ideas, as did several years worth of students in my undergraduate and graduate courses in social problems and my course on victims of crime, as well as my colleagues Michelle Miller and Rachel Whaley. I am indebted to them all. I am also fortunate enough to have been mentored by Kathy Charmaz, John Hall, Mary Jackman, and Lyn Lofland. There is something of each of them in this "sociological story" (as Lyn would put it).

Then there are "the boys," to whom this book is dedicated and with whom I share my living quarters. Tom, Justin, Noah, Elias, and Corey have put up with a lot: stress, anxiety, mood swings, exhaustion, and, mostly, extended periods of inattention. I'm glad that they love me enough to bear with me, and for that (and many other reasons) I love them back. Good friends, especially Janet Fuller and Kim Asner-Self, have helped me keep things in perspective. I am glad that I also have the fellowship of Alcoholics Anonymous to remind me to stay grateful and the Southern Illinois Society of Friends to hold me in the Light. Finally, my deepest gratitude goes to all the nameless victims and survivors brave enough to tell their stories. I hope the book does them justice.

—Jennifer L. Dunn

1

Vocabularies of Victimization: Sympathy, Agency, and Identity

W hy now write a book about victims, and what do I mean by "judging victims," "stigmatizing," and "reclaiming respect"? In 1992,
Charles Sykes disparagingly called the United States a "nation of victims" (in a book by that name). Recently others have argued that more
people than ever before are claiming to be victims, facilitated by an
ever-expanding "victim industry" that makes it possible for new categories of victims to continually emerge (Best 1997; Loseke 2003). At
the same time, increasing numbers of people who might legitimately
assert their victimization instead insist that they are *not* victims but,
rather, "survivors." Victims have come to play an important role in our
society, but it is an uneasy one. In what follows, I explore the rise of one
type of victim identity, the victim of (usually) gendered violence, and
the struggles for meaning that accompany this emergence. Images of
these victims have not been static but have changed over time: How so,
and why?

Starting in 1971, rape victims, battered women, incest survivors,
and, relatively recently, clergy abuse survivors have all come to our collective attention. This is not by chance but is due to the concerted activities of groups of people who sought and seek to bring these problems
into our national consciousness. In order to do this, they have needed
more than statistics; they have had to personalize the issues by creating
evocative representations of the types of people harmed by these problems. This book focuses primarily on the efforts of the second and third
"waves" of the women's movement to construct women and children as
victims of sexual violence. This collective identity creation began as a
struggle to alter what feminists argued were widespread popular and
even social scientific conceptions of the time. These "myths," in their

1

words (Armstrong 1978; Burt 1980; Martin 1976), included ideas that women "precipitated" (Amir 1971) or somehow encouraged rape and battering and even child sexual abuse. This simple beginning has had a number of interesting consequences for how we currently think about victims.

As I will show, people who are perceived as responsible in any way for their own victimization are not readily designated or treated as victims (Christie 1986; Loseke 1999, 2003; Dunn 2002, 2004, 2005). If we think that a person must take some of the blame for what happened to him or her, we do not feel quite as sympathetic toward the person as we might otherwise (Clark 1987, 1997).

Lacking sympathy, we may be disinclined to offer help, whether we are working in law enforcement or are simply friends of the person claiming victimization. In fact, we may even be reluctant to use the term *victim* for someone who does not meet our expectations of blamelessness. When we *judge* victims, we hold them up to a standard of innocence, and if they fall short, we treat them accordingly. And the "feeling rules" (Hochschild 1979) that govern the inextricable relationship between our emotions and our actions have deep roots in our culture; change in this regard has been slow in coming and difficult to effect.

This means that the task for feminists and other activists has been to show that rape victims, battered women, and even incest survivors do not bring their injuries upon themselves. This has also been true for at least some survivors of clergy abuse. In rapid succession, the social movements associated with sexual abuse and gender violence have created images of victims and survivors that counter the myths. Drawing on lessons learned from the civil rights movement and an emergent psychological vocabulary of the self, activists in what I am calling "survivor movements" have portrayed women and children as suffering long-lasting effects of victimization and of the powerful societal forces arrayed against them. But their victimization is not their fault! It cannot be, if we are to care about what happens to them or do anything to help.

To establish (and reestablish) this necessary and fundamental claim of innocence, especially in the early stages of a survivor movement, activists and scholars and journalists portray victims as relatively helpless. Victims are trapped in their rape encounters by overwhelming physical force or in violent relationships by equally daunting sociological and psychological constraints. The images of powerlessness you will read are quite moving and continue to evoke strong emotions in audiences. As a result, we now have rape crisis centers, battered women's shelters, therapists trained in dealing with the long-term consequences of childhood sexual abuse, changes in the way the criminal justice system deals with crime victims, and changes in religious institutions.

Not everyone has been happy with how victims of sexual abuse and gender violence have been portrayed, however, and from the very beginning some of the survivor movements' characterizations have yielded criticism from within the movements and without, as well as ongoing controversy. Some feminists have argued that images of victims produced a kind of "victimism"—a portrait of victimization that is inconsistent with real women's agency and sexuality (Barry 1979; Lamb 1996). Others (e.g., Sykes 1992; Roiphe 1993; Paglia 1994), cultural critics, and those writers whom some have called the "media feminists" (Atmore 1999) have asserted that claims about the nature and prevalence of victimization are exaggerated, misleading, and ultimately confusing. The critics have created images of their own, which are not very sympathetic.

Survivor movements have responded to different counterimages in various ways. Victims of battering, and their advocates, struggled to explain the persistent phenomenon of women who returned to or remained in violent relationships. An explosion of public interest in incest was followed by doubts about the legitimacy of one of the sources of the increase: recovered memories of childhood abuse. Antirape activists have had to explain that "date rape" is "real rape," and how. Then, when the seriousness of various forms of women's violent victimization appeared to verge on being taken for granted, a new kind of abuse came to the fore, abuse by clergy. It is interesting that the typical victims of clergy are symbolized by men more than women, who are also victimized. As a social problem, clergy abuse has taken a new, but nonetheless contentious, course.

Why have these images been so hotly debated and so malleable? Images of victims are produced in the process of what Best (1987) and others in the sociology of social problems have called "claims-making." When seeking to persuade audiences to care about social issues such as violence against women and children, activists in social movements, for example, tell emotion-laden and melodramatic stories about the problems on which they are attempting to focus public attention. In these stories, which tend to be rather formulaic, appealing victims can elicit sympathy for the cause, provoke outrage at the harm being done to them, recruit new members to the social movement, and, ultimately, generate help in the form of public policy. Victims are so important in the construction of social problems and the work of social movements that it is hard to imagine claims-making without them (Loseke 2003).

Successful creation of *sympathetic* victims is complicated, though. To begin, like all the elements of the story being told, images of victims must be consistent with what we think we know about the world and how it works, with what we believe is right or wrong, just or unjust. They must draw upon widely shared understandings and values within a culture to be emotionally moving. Among these understandings, as I noted above, are the feeling rules that instruct people when, how, and toward whom to feel sympathy (Hochschild 1979; Clark 1987, 1997). As part of our socialization into our families, playgroups, schools, churches, and workplaces, we are taught to feel outrage toward what we see as injustice and compassion for those who appear to us to be unjustly harmed. Activists and other claims-makers can use what we have learned to elicit our feelings and spur us into action.

For victims, this can become a problem when there are conflicting cultural and emotional expectations. For example, what happens when a norm for directing sympathy, the "rule" that victims should be powerless to prevent their victimization, conflicts with a broader societal value, the privilege we grant to the ideals of autonomy, strength, resistance, individualism, and free will? We blame victims if they are not helpless, but sometimes we do not respect helpless people very much or identify with them. And sometimes, the situations of actual victims are murkier and more confusing than the stories we hear and the images we hold. How do movements, audiences, and individuals reconcile sometimes ambiguous and complex behaviors, identities, and experiences with relatively simple stereotypes? If we create new images of victims, will they still be effective? For example, if we start to think of victims as "survivors," will we still see them as needing our help (Loseke 2003)?

This book is an effort to understand such contradictions and their effects on individual and collective images of victims and victimization in survivor movements over time. In the activities and storytelling of activists fighting and victims struggling to make sense of rape, battering, incest, and clergy abuse, there is an ongoing interplay between labeling victims deviant when they do not conform to our stereotypes and the production of personal and collective identities that counter these negative and stigmatizing representations. These "victim contests" (Holstein and Miller 1997) also reveal ways in which changing representations of victims reflect larger cultural codes, especially those that draw upon what I call a *cultural code of agency.*

Sociologists view culture in a number of different ways: in her review Lyn Spillman characterizes them as emphasizing "meaning-making processes along three specific dimensions; meaning-making in everyday action, the institutional production of meaning, and the shared mental frameworks along which are the tools of meaning-making" (2002, p. 2). In what follows, I will examine images of victims and victimization in each of these realms, but here I refer to the "mental frameworks," what Swidler early on illuminated as part of our "toolkit" (1986) both for understanding the world and for acting on those understandings. These frameworks can concern the relatively trivial in our lives or constitute the profound, core beliefs about which we feel most strongly (Loseke 2007). Sometimes they are salient, but most of the time they are so deeply embedded we probably take them for granted.

Sociologists as well as scholars in other disciplines have given this idea many names, among them "symbolic codes, signifiers and sign systems, categorical schemas, genre, and narrative" (Spillman 2002, p. 8), and have also come up with other useful terms: semiotic codes, cultural coherence systems, symbolic repertoires, and meaning systems (cited in Loseke 2007, p. 665). According to Donileen Loseke, all these terms "reference densely packed, complex, and interlocking visions of how the world works, and of how the world *should* work" (2007, p. 665; emphasis added). I have chosen the term *cultural code* because it conveys the way in which culture *instructs* us to feel and act in particular ways according to what Alexander and Smith (1993) call a given "cultural logic." Codes provide rules, and there are consequences for breaking them, as I will show. As Loseke says, they "surround cultural narratives of identities because they contain images of the rights, responsibilities, and normative expectations of people in the world, and of the expected affective responses to these people" (2007, pp. 665–666).

The *cultural code of agency* is central to how we understand and react to victims and victimization. When sociologists discuss "agency," we often define it as that component of human action that is not determined by social forces and structures, that part of what we do that is our choice. Like philosophers, we debate whether there is such a thing and how much of it we really enjoy, or whether it is merely a social construction (Wallerstein 1997). The cultural code of agency, on the other hand, is based on the assumption that *all* individuals *do* have free will. According to the cultural logic associated with this code, it follows that we are *always* accountable for our actions.

The problem for victims is that because the code is foundational, and part of "background expectations" (Garfinkel 1964) that are rarely salient, we hold them to its standard as a sort of default. It is a version of "guilty until proven innocent," an a priori judgment. It is this cultural code that we are employing when we require victims to be innocent of any part in their own victimization, an expectation I will take up in detail in the chapters that follow. It is this code that inspires us to question any behaviors or attributes that suggest victims' agency. It is thus the source of pervasive images of victims that foster victim-blaming and a related lack of sympathy and an inability to identify with victims (Dunn 2004, 2005). I will argue that because we believe so deeply that we always "have a choice," we have a very powerful tendency to discount victims' claims and to think that they somehow "brought it on themselves." This leads us to think of them as deserving of their fate, and therefore undeserving of our compassion, and even as somehow essentially different from us.

For this reason, when people in survivor movements tell stories about victimization (the stories intended to encourage us to feel for victims and to care about what happens to them), they explain the transgressions of victims. These explanations take a particular form and make use of specific cultural codes. Mills (1940) calls this conjoining of explanation and code a "situated vocabulary of motive"—in this project (and elsewhere) I call them *vocabularies of victimization* (Dunn forthcoming). We find them in what Loseke (2001) calls "formula stories" and Davis (2005b) "victim narratives," the melodramatic, eventually well-known stories about victims and victimization told by victims, their advocates, and their opponents. Vocabularies of victimization are important because they reveal the myriad ways in which victims violate the expectations we have of them, and they show how social movements excuse or justify victimization and deflect stigma in much the same way that individuals do (Dunn 2005). Like all "aligning actions," the verbal responses potentially deviant people make when we question their motives (Stokes and Hewitt 1976), they also tell us more about the culture that is the source of the code and the source of the victim-blaming.

So too, does a different kind of story: the counternarratives told by cultural critics of the increasing numbers of people identifying as victims and the survivor movements that have facilitated victim claims. These authors emphasize the *debilitating* characteristics associated with victimization, yet they also rely on vocabularies that are built on the cultural code of agency. The critics are able to do this because there is another important component of the code: not only do we assume that people always have agency, but we place an extraordinary *value* upon it, so much so that we may lose all respect for people who claim to be helpless. This is especially true if we believe that the claim is false, but we also have a tendency to denigrate even "legitimate" victims. "There must be something wrong with them," we think. "I would not let that happen to me; I'm stronger than that."

The survivor movements I report on here use vocabularies of victimization in stories about victims or told by victims to ensure that audiences will care about rape, battering, incest, and clergy abuse and, especially, about the people who serve to represent victims of these assaults. Survivor movements also use a (different) kind of rhetoric to encourage people's identification *as* victims and thus to recruit new members who see themselves in the stories the movements tell. These social constructions might better be termed *vocabularies of surviving*, as we will see. The critics use what I call a *vocabulary of victimism* to discredit the claims of victims and their advocates and to discourage identification as victims. All of these vocabularies follow similar rules; they all find their source and their impact in the cultural code of agency. I have found these vocabularies in stories about and by victims in a wide variety of media: in the documentation of early speak-outs, in collections of stories published by activists, in victims' interview excerpts that scholars use to represent types of victimization and account for victims' deviance, in popular media such as books written with mass appeal, and most recently, in the case of clergy abuse, in tales of victimization and surviving posted to the Internet.

Finally, because victim narratives (Davis 2005b) are "formula stories"—that is, they adhere closely to the expectations we hinge upon the cultural code of agency—they have "stock characters." Loseke writes of these in her analysis of the stories she heard in a battered women's support group: "the battered woman as victim, the abusive man as villain" (2007, p. 110). I found recurring victim *types,* almost archetypes, in the stories told in the antirape movement, the battered women's movement, the incest survivor movement, the cultural countermovement, and the clergy abuse survivor movements. Thus, there are images of *blameless* victims that oppose and contrast with images of *blameworthy* victims. There are critical counterimages constructing what I call *pathetic* victims, and in response, there are survivor stories that tell us about *admirable* victims. The ways in which movements and countermovements use these images and ideas show how victims, advocates, and critics draw upon widely shared cultural understandings for their emotional and cultural resonance. The vocabularies of victimization and surviving in these stories show how victims and their advocates respond to the cultural code of agency. Victim narratives (Davis 2005b) also show how the cultural code can be appropriated by countermovements to construct a very different kind of victimization, one less at the hands of victims' assailants than through the efforts of those who claim to help.

In the remaining chapters of this book, I will first provide a brief historical introduction to each of the movements and try to "flesh out" the storytellers who, although they are individuals with various aims and skills, use the same language in the various stories from which I take my illustrations of vocabulary and infer the code of agency. Then, I will closely examine the four types of victim images, mostly using one of the survivor movements to illustrate each archetype but sometimes supplementing with data from the other movements (because each type of victim appears in more than one movement). To begin, however, I discuss the social constructionist theoretical approaches to deviance, identity, social problems, and social movements that inform my analysis. Although some readers may be familiar with these perspectives, others may benefit from some introduction to the lenses through which I view my topic. I also explain a little about how I have selected and analyzed texts and, last, provide a brief map of the rest of the book.

Blaming, Claiming, and Framing: Analytical Tools

The sociological story that I am telling about the stories people tell in survivor movements is rooted in several substantive areas tied together theoretically by scholars' common interest in the social construction of reality (Berger and Luckmann 1966). When we say that reality is "constructed," we allude to the ways in which human beings collaborate, using language and culture (and storytelling) to come to shared understandings of what the world is like, what is important in that world, and how to respond to what "really" matters. The sociological social psychologists who call themselves "symbolic interactionists" and many people interested in social problems and social movements have focused their attention on the ways in which people do this work. We actively interpret situations—and we define ourselves and situations for others (Thomas and Thomas 1929).

These situations can be brief encounters between individuals (Goffman 1983) or social problems affecting millions of people and inspiring widespread social protest (e.g., Altheide 2006). There is a lot of overlap among the sociologists in these different areas, just as there are interrelationships among the stories people tell to construct themselves, social problems, and what to do about them. For now, however, I will briefly treat the conceptualizations that are key to my analysis one at a time, beginning with the most individual and personal and moving outward from there to increasingly larger collectivities—all of which are linked to yet more encompassing societal and cultural sets of under-standings.

Beginning with an examination of emotions and norms that dictate their socially appropriate distribution, I consider the relevance of the feeling rules that govern sympathy for understanding how victims are named as such and treated accordingly. I then turn to the sociology of deviance, specifically the ideas that help us understand how some vic-tims may violate the normative expectations for this identity, what can happen as a result, and what they can do to bring themselves back into the good graces of the people from whom they are seeking help. There is a brief discussion of the literature in social problems that shows how the claiming of victim identities can be a collaborative as well as an individ-ual endeavor. I then articulate each of these key ideas with the framing perspective in social movements theory, as well as a consideration of how the "narrative turn" in the latter area can inform what I am doing. I follow this with a methodological note on how I chose the narratives in which vocabularies of victimization are embedded. This serves as prepa-ration for a somewhat more detailed description of the victim typology in terms of how the book is organized.

Emotions: Feeling Rules and Sympathy Margins

Emotions are important in the study of survivor movements because they are implicated in all social movements: when people are "moved" by the images of things that need to be changed, of injustice, and of suf-fering, they respond in part on the basis of their cognitions but more so owing to how they are feeling (Goodwin, Jasper, and Polletta 2001). Loseke points out that because we "often have deep feelings about the immorality and injustice of specific social problems conditions . . . feel-ing words such as 'outrage' about a social problem condition or 'sympa-thy' for victims are staples of social problems talk" (2000, p. 43). Because talk provides the data for social constructionist analyses, increasingly social movements and social problems scholars have been turning their attention to the role of emotions, emotion talk, and "emo-tions work" (Hochschild 1979).

Emotions work refers to the activity of evoking, suppressing, and otherwise managing one's own and others' emotions, and activists and claims-makers engage in a great deal of this in order to get and keep people involved. Some of it is directed toward audiences, such as efforts to recruit strangers to support or join social movements by inducing a "sense of crisis, shock, and outrage" (Jasper and Poulsen 1995, p. 499). Others use emotions to foster a sense of belonging, of being transformed, of having a new, collective identity; Lory Britt and David Heise, for example, write of how social movements redefine stigmatized identities from a deviance framing to an oppression framing. Emotions work converts shame into anger, not only at the oppression, but at the prior shaming, and through this process, movements "transform sequestration into solidarity" (2000, p. 262).

In the case of survivors as victims, the relevant emotion is sympathy. If audience members are to do anything about a problem, they have to believe that, whether it is global warming or child abuse, it is causing harm to people toward whom they can feel sympathetic. Thus, social movement activists become what Candace Clark has called "sympathy brokers" at the level of individuals and "sympathy entrepreneurs" at the collective level. The latter especially have had considerable success shifting public perceptions of problems that previously have been considered personal issues (Clark 1997). Social movements mobilize audiences, in part, by constructing sympathy-worthy victims of social problems.

This is not always a simple task, however, because of culturally derived feeling rules (Hochschild 1979) telling us to whom we should direct which emotions and when. Feeling rules, in Hochschild's formulation, are norms dictating the appropriateness of affect and its display. We learn feeling rules the same way we learn the other expectations and requirements people hold, through socialization into our culture and subcultures and their associated systems of stratification. We are taught what kinds of emotions are acceptable to reveal and which are necessary and suitable to be experiencing, in given situations and toward specific people and *types* of people. Activists and claims-makers thus draw upon what Loseke calls "emotional discourse." This is claims-making that, to be effective, needs to be consistent with "culturally circulating ideas about how audience members should feel about particular types of conditions and particular types of people" (Loseke 2000, p. 44).

Clark's argument is that in order for us to potentially judge people as deserving of our sympathy, we assess their moral worthiness first, making sympathizing itself a "morality-constructing act" (1997). One crucial determinant of sympathy is blamelessness—"Is the person at fault or a victim? Does he or she deserve affirmation and reprieve, or not?" (Clark 1997, p. 22). Loseke similarly asserts that even though victims are a necessary prerequisite for social problems to exist, in order to be perceived as victims, they must meet certain conditions. "We tend to reserve the status of victim for people we feel sympathy toward, and we feel sympathy when morally good people are greatly harmed through no fault of their own," she claims (1999, p. 77). The job of the sympathy entrepreneur, then, becomes one of constructing the virtue of victims and restoring audiences' positive emotions toward them. This can create "a halo of worth and morality around the unfortunates who fall into certain plights, or at least offer a way of understanding them that absolves them from blame" (Clark 1997, p. 125).

Thus, one of my objectives here is showing that activists in the anti-rape, battered women's, and incest survivor movements, as well as other kinds of claims-makers, have told the stories of victims in ways that appear calculated to evoke our sympathy and get us to care about what happens to people in the victimizing situations they describe. Often, the images they evoke are shocking and horrifying (Jasper and Poulson 1995; Johnson 1995). But, and this is a very large qualification, the images must also be of people for whom we genuinely care. If sympathizing reflects and signifies moral value, its lack indicates the presence of some factor that devalues a person.

Put differently, a victim whom we hold accountable for what happens to her, whose circumstances neither mitigate nor extenuate our judgment that she is somehow "bringing it on . . . herself" (Clark 1997, p. 84), has violated the expectation of innocence that is a crucial part of the feeling rule for sympathy. When this happens, we do not think of her as a victim, and we may label her something else entirely. She evokes rather different emotions, blame among them. This norm violation brings us to the contribution of the sociology of deviance to understanding survivor movements' (and cultural critics') stories of victims of rape, battering, incest, and clergy abuse.

Deviance: Labeling, Stigma, and Identity Work

I started my social constructionist look at victims by examining the emotions they might evoke, arguing that these are not inherent in victimization but are culturally shaped and assigned according to how we define people and interpret their behavior. It should be clear from the preceding discussion that being perceived as a victim depends less on what has happened to a person than on how the person herself is interpreted by others. That is, "victim" is a label and so, too, is "not really a victim." As Holstein and Miller (1997) put it in their "rethinking" of victimization, the identity is not a necessary product of any act but is an assignation. Drawing on early labeling theory (Tannenbaum 1938), they argue: "If 'deviants' are constituted through public definition and 'dramatization of evil' . . . then we might also view the production of victims as the public articulation and dramatization of injury and innocence" (Holstein and Miller 1997, p. 28).

Labeling theory is a social constructionist approach toward "deviance," a term we put between quotation marks to signify that it is historically and culturally relative, a matter of definition rather than of "fact" or the inherent qualities of an actor or action. From this perspective, a deviant is a person whom others have successfully labeled as such (Becker 1963), and the processes of conferring meaning and the social significance of this labeling are what is most sociologically interesting and important. The objective act is of less interest, and less consequential, than the stories people tell about it. If we apply this idea to the labeling of victims, it directs us to attend more closely to the stories of activists, claims-makers, and victims than to an "objective condition" of victimization and a victim identity that follows automatically or necessarily.

When people hear a victim narrative (Davis 2005b), the character who has been harmed only becomes a victim when the hearers of the story decide that he or she meets the criteria for being a victim. Like Clark (1997) and Loseke (1999), Holstein and Miller describe the social construction of victims as inextricable from "deflecting responsibility" (1997). This means that when a person is perceived as less than innocent in his or her injury, there is what Goffman, writing about stigma, has called a "discrepancy" between the stereotype and the actual person (1963). Our ideas about stereotypical victims, "real" victims, are pretty specific and include the expectations that they not have caused or even contributed to their own victimization.

So if a victim or her or his actions deviate from how we think victims are or ought to be, we conclude that she or he is not "really" a victim after all. The claim to victimization has been discredited. When the victim identity is lost, maligned, or clouded, our sympathy evaporates. For this reason, whenever victims and survivors are or can potentially be blamed for their own mishaps, their task is to explain whatever is problematic for their claim. In Goffman's terms, they must engage in processes of identity "management" (1963). Among these are the stories they tell about their victimization; when relating them, they must *account* for anything that casts doubt on their blamelessness.

There is a vast literature in sociology on accounts (see Orbuch 1997 for a review). The central concept in the classical accounting literature is that when people deviate from norms, they will be asked about it, and they must provide explanations or risk social disapproval or condemnation. In 1940, C. W. Mills called these the "reasons [people] give for their actions" or "vocabularies of motive" (1940, p. 904). These reasons, Mills argues, are culturally and historically specific, conventional, learned, and widely accepted. Because they "line up conduct with norms," Mills implies that they function to permit or remedy deviant behavior (1940, p. 908).

The idea of accounts is built on this foundation, what Marvin Scott and Stanford Lyman have termed the forms of talk people use "whenever an action is subject to valuative inquiry" (1968, p. 46). Accounts and other "techniques of neutralization" (Sykes and Matza 1957) are employed to preserve normal or repair deviant identities. They resolve problematic situations by showing that deviant actors recognize the norms they are violating. They make the deviance consistent with cultural expectations and thus are a type of "aligning action" (Stokes and Hewitt 1976). When providing accounts, people who risk being interpreted as deviant must come up with excuses and justifications.

Of most importance to sociologists, people must choose their accounts carefully on the basis of their social appropriateness. There is an available "vocabulary of motive" that people can draw upon, but this is cultural and historically specific, or "situated" (Mills 1940). Successful accounts indicate that the deviant recognizes the norms and how to make his or her behavior consistent with expectations; for this reason, this class of definitional phenomena is sometimes called "aligning actions" (Stokes and Hewitt 1976).

Somewhat more recently, building on Goffman's (1963) idea of "identity management" among the stigmatized, sociologists have used the term *identity work* to capture what happens when the "demeaned" in a society "attempt to generate identities that provide them with a measure of self-worth and dignity." They define identity work as "the range of activities individuals engage in to create, present, and sustain personal identities that are congruent with and supportive of the self-concept." Identity talk is one of the vehicles through which identity construction can take place (Snow and Anderson 1987, pp. 1336, 1348). That is, the homeless tell stories that are like accounts; Snow and Anderson have called this "salvaging the self" (1993). Victims and survivors do this too, as I will show.

Because salvaging is so specific, we can often deduce the norms from the identity work and accounts that appear in narratives and learn about cultural meaning this way. So when rape victims repeatedly explain why they did not sufficiently resist their attackers, we can guess that in our culture, we expect them to resist (Burt 1980). When social scientists come up with multitudinous hypotheses for battered women's "unexpectable" behavior of remaining with their abusive partners, this suggests that we consider leaving the best or only solution to violence (Loseke and Cahill 1984; Dunn 2005; Dunn and Powell 2007). When adults who relate that they recover memories of experiencing incest as children (or women who tell others about being raped by people whom they know) become fodder for social critics' characterizations of them as deluded or overreacting, we might presume that we have norms that distinguish real victims from people who are merely the victims of unscrupulous or overzealous therapists (or feminists). In the process of examining how victims and their advocates create sympathy, we will also attend to what they do when their claims and identities are called into question and to what this reveals about ourselves as a people.

Social Problems Work and the Accomplishment of Victimization

In addition to considerations of sympathy and of accounts that foster positive or deflect negative attributions and emotions, my analysis is helped by ideas that link the identity work of individuals to the significant audiences in their lives and that serve as a bridge from the particular victim to a collective victim identity. Turning again to Holstein and Miller's discussion of victim identities, they refer to victimization as "interactionally constituted" (1997). The construction of victims is a collaboration, a joint practice, a social process, and when successful, it is something we "accomplish" with the help of others. In an earlier essay, Miller and Holstein (1993) call this process "social problems work," because as a form of identity work, it is active and interpretive, it involves claims-making, and it results in the production of victims. Holstein and Miller point out that this is a categorizing or "typifying" process (to use the terminology of Best 1995). Loseke describes a kind of matching up of the actual person with the stereotype; this work occurs, she says, "when we evaluate and categorize *unique* experiences, conditions, and people as instances of *types* of experiences, conditions, and people" (2003, p. 20; emphases in original).

Social problems work occurs whenever victims of any kind seek help from people whom I think of as "eligibility workers." If a person is too poor to manage the expenses of daily life, he might apply for public assistance. If the social worker reviewing his circumstances is able to determine that he meets the criteria for eligibility for this kind of aid, that is, that he represents the type of person (poor) and social problem (poverty) for whom the aid is intended, the assistance will be forthcoming. This becomes collaboration when the social worker elicits the right information from the applicant, perhaps suggesting what to include and what to leave out of the application. The victim advocates in the prosecutor's office where I researched intimate stalking victimization did social problems work of this kind when they directed their resources toward the stalking victims whom they found the most "credible." These victims were the ones who conformed to advocates' ideas about "genuine" stalking victims (women who had left abusive relationships, obtained restraining orders, and tried to enforce them, for example).

What happens if the match is not easily made? Holstein and Miller talk about "victim contests," in which "victim status is openly negotiated, contested, and even imposed," adding that "both injury and responsibility may be at stake in such disputes" (1997, p. 37). In other words, just as there can be a discrepancy between the actual and the expectation (Goffman 1963), a deviation from norms requiring an account (Scott and Lyman 1968), and identity work that takes place when selves need salvaging from the realms into which we cast the lowest among us (Snow and Anderson 1993), there can be forms of social problems work that people direct toward accomplishing victimization in the face of questioning, skepticism, and even opposition. Importantly, this happens when group identity as well as individual identities are at stake. The ways in which social movement actors tell stories about victims are sometimes social problems work of this type.

Social Movement Framing, Collective Identity Work, and the "Narrative Turn"

Thinking about victims and vocabularies of victimization from a social problems perspective encourages the inclusion of a variety of claimsmakers in identity work. Activists and mass media as well as individual victims tell stories accounting for victims' deviance, that is, that construct the morality of collective representations as well as of particular people. Thus, in what follows, we will also think of victim narratives (Davis 2005b) as intended to foster interpretations of rape, battering, incest, and clergy abuse as social problems. Narratives produce instances of the problems and exemplify the problems, and they are stories that establish and dramatize not only the harm done to victims but especially the "exoneration from responsibility [that] accompanies victimization" (Holstein and Miller 1997, p. 43).

Victimization is a claim, and its vocabulary serves to bolster claims, especially in the face of counterclaims and other kinds of contesting. Victimization is also a collaboration in which not only victims, but also their advocates, play an active role. And because advocates can have such a significant effect—and more so when they are part of social movements with intensity and impact, such as the ones this book is about—I make use of theory in the sociology of social movements related to framing, collective identity work, and the "narrative turn."

Social movement framing and victimization. When social movement activists are trying to convince their audiences that a social problem exists, their success depends upon the power of the stories they tell about it. In terms of mobilizing actors, the presentation of the problem, or the way in which activists "frame" it (Goffman 1974; Benford and Snow 2000), is as important as or even more significant than the objective characteristics of the problem. Frames tell us what type of problem a condition is, why we should care, who should be blamed, and what to do about it. For example, if stalking is something that happens mostly to celebrities, it is a "fame problem" associated with deranged fans, and we need to make it harder for them to get access to the objects of their obsessions. Because it is rare and affects people with many resources, we may not care a great deal about it or do much if anything to intervene. But if stalking happens mostly to women trying to leave abusive relationships, it is a "domestic violence problem," and we are likely to assign responsibility, feel sympathy, and take action in the ways similar to how we have responded to activism for battered women.

Frames are thus strategic versions of reality for mobilizing people to help or join the movement, and frames that move audiences are those that draw artfully from the culture in which they are situated. When they resonate with their intended targets, they do so in part because they are consistent with the feeling rules that govern the emotions (including sympathy) that activists seek to evoke. In this way, they are like aligning actions, which work best when they are carefully chosen from appropriate vocabularies of motive. The "cultural resonance" of frames occurs when they make effective use of cultural "repertoires" using symbols whose meanings are widely shared (Williams 1995; Williams and Williams 1995; Benford and Snow 2000). In order for survivor movements to accomplish victimization, especially when the people who are in need of champions do not nicely fit our preconceptions of what they should be like in order to qualify as victims, they must frame victims in ways that generally incline people to forgive them their transgressions. Cultural resonance and emotions are linked: Loseke says that the "cultural coherence system producing 'victims' . . . is the same as the feeling rules producing 'sympathy'" (2000, p. 49).

Collective identity work in social movements. This brings us again to the topic of identities, which Robert Benford and David Snow argue are inherent and central to framing processes. A number of social movement theorists focus on how critical the construction of a collective identity—"the shared definition of a group that derives from members' common interests, experiences and solidarity"—is for recruitment and, according to Taylor and Whittier, for *"all* forms of collective action" (1992, p. 104; emphasis added). Examples of collective identities that social movements have constructed are of oppressed minorities (e.g., blacks, women, homosexuals, fat people), activists (feminists, antiwar protesters, pro-lifers, environmentalists), and victims of abuse (children, animals, the elderly). The collective identities of "rape victims," "battered women," "victims of incest," and "clergy abuse survivors" are the focus of this book, along with the counteridentity I call the "pathetic victim."

In research and theorizing on new social movements, scholars have noted that collective identities are sometimes "transformative," because activists "work to resist negative social definitions and demand that others value and treat oppositional groups differently." Victims are one such category, and this study examines how an effect of the survivor movements has been to, as Taylor and Whittier put it, "reconstitute the experience of victimization" (1992, p. 115). Collective identity work is like individual identity work; it too provides us with excuses and justifications and with reasons for the seemingly inexplicable.

Like other elements of frames (and emotions, and accounts, and social problems work), collective identities must have "narrative fidelity," the degree to which frames "resonate with the targets' cultural narrations" (Benford and Snow 2000, p. 622). This is an important factor in their appeal to potential members, to larger public audiences, and, ultimately, to people with the power to create and implement policy. Collective identity work takes place in stories that respond to the cultural code of agency, a "cultural narration" that threatens to discredit victims' claims, denies victimization, or diverts responsibility back to claimants.

Another interesting feature of collective identity work is that it cre-

ates commitment and solidarity among members of a social movement
(Hunt and Benford 2004), in part through how it encourages victims of
stigma and oppression to see themselves as victims—not because of
who they are as individuals but because of the categories to which they
belong (Taylor and Whittier 1992; Gagne 1998; Taylor 2001; Whittier
2001). When this is done meaningfully and well, it also serves to usefully engage the emotions of others. Collective identities move members
"from shame to pride" (Britt and Heise 2000) but are constructed in
public as well as within social movement organizations. Vocabularies of
victimization in social movements' narratives facilitate "victim work"
(Holstein and Miller 1997), especially when, as I will show, they redefine victims as "survivors" (Dunn 2005).

This last is important because in addition to ways in which victims
may deviate from the blamelessness and innocence we require of the
true victim, they must sometimes answer to a whole other set of cultural
expectations—those that make being a victim *itself* deviant. People may
need to be seen as victims, but they may not want to be defined or to
define themselves as weak, passive, or diminished in the process. The
same is true for the uses to which images of victims are put, and as it
happens, there are more emotions than simple sympathy at stake, more
expectations than blamelessness to meet, more aligning to do, and additional stereotypes with which to contend. The cultural code of agency
and its offshoot, vocabularies of victimization, spring from a larger story
and engender a set of stories, or narratives. Another component of the
perspective I am taking toward the social construction of victims and
victimization is inspired by recent sociological attention to the importance of narrative when studying social movements and identity.
Although my own emphasis is on the language people use when telling
stories and constructing themselves, their "grammar of motives" (Burke
1969), this rhetoric is of course situated (Mills 1940), and the concept of
narrative is helpful here.

The "narrative turn" in social movements theory. There is a natural
fit between social constructionist theoretical approaches such as the
ones I develop in this book and narrative analysis, because reality construction necessitates the telling of stories (Berger and Luckmann 1966).
It has been almost twenty years since Laurel Richardson examined the
role of narrative in sociology, arguing that "*narrative* is the primary way
through which humans organize their experiences into temporally mean-
ingful episodes" (1990, p. 118; emphasis in original). Thus, it provides
access to the things in which sociologists are most interested, including

personal biographies such as the stories rape victims tell at speak-outs, "cultural stories" like the ones informing and upon the cultural code of agency, and the transformative "collective stories" in which social movements "resist the cultural narratives about groups of people and 'tell' alternative stories" (Richardson 1990, p. 128). Vocabularies of victimization are important at each of these levels, and because the personal stories of victims are the source of the collective story of victimization and of surviving, narratives are the setting for the analysis I undertake.

The emphasis on narratives in social movements has been recently taken up by Joseph Davis, who says that "social movements are dominated by stories and storytelling" (2002, p. 4) and who has argued that their use is strategic, emotional, and persuasive. Davis goes on to argue that narrative overcomes the cognitive bias of framing theory and that in some contexts "stories precede frames, stories make frames compelling, and stories overshadow frames in mobilizing power and as a political resource" (2002, p. 25). And like Richardson (1990), Davis points to the oppositional character of movement narratives that counter larger cultural and institutional narratives.

Linking social movement theory and the sociology of emotions, using narratives as a site of inquiry, is particularly appropriate for the task I am undertaking. I wish to show the ways in which elements of victim narratives (Davis 2005b) told in the context of social movement framing and claims-making can deflect blame and evoke sympathy, pity, contempt, or admiration. Francesca Polletta has tied narratives to movements' "emotional resonance," for example:

> Stories are used strategically by activists to elicit emotions, say, the righteous indignation that propels someone into a march, or the anguish that generates financial contributions. At the same time, people make sense of their experience, and respond to it emotionally, based on familiar narratives. (2002, p. 48)

It is this *familiarity* that is of key importance in the formulation I am presenting, and it stems from the ways in which how people talk about victims creates images and explains behaviors we understand and to which, on that basis, we know how to react. Jeffery Tatum suggests that narratives do not have to be rational but instead "can bestow moral legitimation through pathos," making them all the more persuasive for wider audiences (2002, p. 182). For Joshua Yates and James Hunter, narrative links frames and emotions; it "bridges the social and emotional distance between framing . . . and the striking of a collective nerve" (2002, p. 128).

Also important for my purposes are the ways in which narratives in social movements "constitute" and "create" identities (Davis 2002; Loseke 2007). The stories people tell about themselves, especially the accounts they provide for attributes and behaviors that might result in the imputing of deviant identities, are self-constructions and therefore part of their presentations of self (Goffman 1959). But the vocabularies people employ in narratives extend beyond the personal to shape the meanings attached to individuals *and* to types of people. Loseke, for example, has recently discussed not only personal narrative identity at the microlevel, but "organizational," "institutional," and "cultural" narrative identities as well, even going so far as to argue for better understanding of the relationships "between and among" levels of narrative, or what she terms their "reflexivity" (2007, p. 675). We can work toward an understanding of this reflexivity by first examining what the narratives have in common, that is, their shared vocabularies and the cultural logic that constrains them.

People draw upon cultural narrative identities when they do the kinds of accounting and countering I am analyzing, and social movements sometimes begin with the stories of individuals, which can become collective identities through claims-making and framing. This is a theme for Davis (2005a) too, and one I will take up in Chapter 7. For now, I will note that narrative identity at all levels can be created, maintained, and transformed through the offering of accounts, through social problems work, through identity work. Rape victims, social scientists dramatizing the plight of battered women, social critics decrying "victim feminism," and clergy abuse survivors redefining the sanctity of the church all work from the same script and take up the same props. Their rhetorical tools come from a shared "toolkit" (Swidler 1986). The cultural narrative identity of the victim comes already endowed with agency, and the language of the stories reflects this. Ultimately, perhaps, the storytellers may succeed in modifying the script, or shaping the conditions under which it exerts its power (Ewick and Silbey 1995) (something else to consider as my story concludes).

In *Telling Sexual Stories: Power, Change, and Social Worlds,* Ken Plummer examines, among other things, rape stories and "recovery" stories, arguing that such stories are "successful" and in order for them to be, "there needs to be a strong community of support waiting to receive them," and if so, the stories "perform political tasks" (1995, pp. 16–17). For Plummer, these stories constitute a genre because of their common features: their focus on what Plummer calls "sexual suffering, surviving, and surpassing" (1995, p. 50). Initially secret, the suffering is told and through the telling, creates change in the individual, who becomes a survivor and in some cases identifies politically (the "surpassing").

Plummer is interested in the way the stories function as consciousness raising and argues that as private suffering is made public, these stories may then serve, although not necessarily, as the basis of collective identity and political action. Plummer talks about a "survivor world," a world "waiting to hear" a new story that, however radical, nonetheless fits into "the most accepted narratives of that society: the dominant ideological code" (1995, p. 115). To write this book, I began with the sexual stories of rape survivors and added those of abuse survivors as well. From them, I have extracted the language and the form of account that connects them all to this dominant ideological code, as I show how victims and their advocates use vocabularies of victimization in individual and collective identity work.

"Telling" Stories and Their Sources

The last bit of foundation I want to lay before describing how this book is organized has to do with how I chose the particular narratives whose common theme is a shared vocabulary hinging on such a pervasive and powerful cultural code. When I began this research, I was interested in what seemed at the time a rather mundane question arising out of interviews and participation in a group of women who called themselves River City (a pseudonym) Survivors of Stalking. How is it, I wondered, that women who were working so hard to claim victim identities in order to get the support they needed from the criminal justice system, nonetheless preferred to call themselves "survivors" rather than "victims"? At the time, I wrote about how the language revealed victims' understanding of the shame they felt about being victims and their need to represent themselves as strong, capable, and empowered to "move on" with their lives (Dunn 2002). But where did this language come from? It certainly was not unique to the women I knew, and I set out to find out its source.

This ultimately led me to the earliest published works on rape, battering, and incest. These works are theoretically important because they are historically the closest to the time prior to the successful construction of any of these issues as social problems and the framing of those harmed by the problems as truly victims. As I read them, it became clear to me that first-person victim stories of varying length comprised significant portions of the books, often with little commentary but standing virtually alone without interpretation. Sometimes they are the briefest of explanations in response to an interviewer's question, and other times they go on for pages. Either way, they are examples of what Loseke calls "personalizing victims," a claims-making strategy used to "encourage audience members' feelings of sympathy" (2003, p. 82). Of course, the stories were often edited for more impact. For example, stories from the first speak-out on rape in 1971 appear to have been published verbatim in an early New York Radical Feminists (NYRF) chronicle of that event and of other antirape activism (Connell and Wilson 1974) but are somewhat more dramatic in Susan Brownmiller's famous manifesto, *Against Our Will: Men, Women, and Rape* (1975). Accuracy of transcription is less important than the uses to which the stories are put, however, which is my interest here.

More important, though, is that these early stories in the antirape movement, told well before survivor language emerged, are clearly responsive to victim-blaming, in ways that are likely much more subtle now, even as victim-blaming itself is these days. Having looked first at the early stories, I found that they reveal the cultural terrain on which the survivor movements fought their first battles. Gail Sheehy's account of the first NYRF speak-out (1971), Susan Griffin's influential article in *Ramparts* (1971), the transcriptions of the speak-out and consciousness-raising groups published in Connell and Wilson (1974) and in Brownmiller (1975), and the interviews Diana Russell published in 1975 all comprise the foundation of the early collective identity work in this survivor movement, and all the stories help to construct a *blameworthy* victim in the process of deflecting blame (I will say more about types of victims shortly).

I have long been interested in social scientists as claims-makers, and when I realized that many of the foundational stories in the battered women's movement had been written by scholars (Straus 1992), I began a systematic review of this vast literature. And it is in the response I chronicled to movement images of battered women—later constructions of battered women as survivors (e.g., Gondolf 1988; Hoff 1990)—that the seeds of my concerns with the implications of taking agency away from victims were sown (Dunn 2004, 2005). Of these many stories, I have chosen the most widely cited early books as sources of exemplars of *blameless* victim construction, in addition to the earliest books by other kinds of activists. Thus, I draw from Pizzey (1974), Martin (1976), Dobash and Dobash's research (1979), Walker's research (1979), Davidson's journalistic account in 1978, and Pagelow's 1981 research, all of which explain why battered women who "stay" are trapped rather than freely choosing to do so.

Here, it is very important to note that just as the rape activists above use the speak-out stories (or pieces of them) that individual women told to tell a story about rape victims more generally, the social scientists and other "experts" (Loseke and Cahill 1984) do the same for battered women. Thus, despite their scientific credentials, I treat them as story-tellers as well, constructing a reality that may have been more widely credible than that of the early antirape activists but is nonetheless constructed, and according to the same blueprint. For this reason, through-out the book, I treat the first-order victim narratives (Davis 2005b) and the second-order expert and other narratives about the latter as occupying the same ontological and epistemological realm. In some cases, I begin with the first-order stories, and in others, I set the stage with the stories *about* the stories.

On the topic of stories about stories, the decision to examine coun-terimages, those of *pathetic* victims, was a product of my exposure to the "victim feminism" versus "power feminism" debates in graduate school. *The Morning After: Sex, Fear, and Feminism* (Roiphe 1993) generated considerable controversy just as I was interviewing under-graduate women about unwanted sex for my seminar in field methods. Roiphe and others—the popular books of Naomi Wolf in 1993, Christina Hoff Sommers in 1994, and Camille Paglia in 1992 and 1994—became quite well known in my academic setting but also achieved considerable notoriety in wider circles, as evidenced in part by critiques of their arguments in *The New Yorker* (Pollitt 1993) and *The Nation* (Stark 1994) among other venues. To these I have added the ear-lier critiques of Elshtain (1982), Rieff (1991), and Sykes (1992). To this group, more authors could certainly be added (e.g., Kaminer 1993; Tavris 1993), and of course the same is also true of each of the survivor movements only partially represented here. My hope is that the excerpts I have chosen are compelling; my argument is that they reveal what is *ubiquitous* in stories about victims and thus the choice of storyteller may not matter so much.

From this beginning, I started to research other victim-related con-troversies and came upon a more recent (1994) book, *Rocking the Cradle of Sexual Politics: What Happened When Women Said Incest,* by Louise Armstrong, one of the first people to use victims' stories to bring the problem of incest into the public realm (Armstrong 1978). This in turn introduced me to the "memory debates" taking place in academic psychology and popular talk shows, where issues of recovered and false memory were hotly contested in the early and mid-1990s. When I read *Confabulations,* written in 1992 by Eleanor Goldstein, a parent and founder of the False Memory Syndrome Foundation, I found additional stories to supplement pathetic victim constructions. If the first books and articles countering images of blameworthy victims and constructing alternate, sympathetic versions of victims represent an early phase in changing accounts over time, the work of the self-described "power feminists" and other critics provide access to images that are far less appealing (albeit they conform to the same code, use the same vocabularies, and are foreshadowed in some of the stories that precede them).

These latter piteous and even contemptible images reminded me of the young women and stalking victims who disavowed victim identities in favor of being and presenting themselves as survivors. Having written about the emergence of survivors in the battered women's movement (Dunn 2004, 2005), I decided to choose for an exemplar of *admirable* victims the images narrated by a new and dramatically successful social movement, the Survivors Network of those Abused by Priests (SNAP). In keeping with changing times and new kinds of venues for storytelling, my data for Chapter 6 are drawn from the pages of SNAP's website. In 2007 and again in 2008, SNAP held a contest "asking survivors to write a short story about the good things that have happened to them on their journey of healing" (Survivors Network of those Abused by Priests 2007–2009). Called "Stories for Living," the fifty-four stories submitted in 2007 and the twenty sent to SNAP in 2008 are archived on the website and available for inspiration (and quotation). Both years, SNAP members voted for the ten stories they considered "most inspiring." These stories work quite well for my purpose, as they have been selected by the SNAP "community" as representative of images that presumably embody an ideal, the person who transcends mere survival to truly live.

More survivor rhetoric comes from a book titled *Victim to Survivor: Women Recovering from Clergy Sexual Abuse* (Poling 1999), a collection of six victims' stories published by United Church Press as a resource for survivors and their advocates as well as to educate others in the church. A third source is a 1995 book titled *When Ministers Sin: Sexual Abuse in the Churches,* by Australians Neil Ormerod (a theologian) and Thea Ormerod (a social worker and domestic violence advocate), that includes a chapter called "From Victim to Survivor" (pp. 33–52). I chose these last two books because they specifically construct clergy abuse victims as survivors; rape victims have been called survivors for quite some time now (Rutenberg 1983) as have victims of incest (*New York Times* 1982), and I have elsewhere documented the emergence of the term to describe battered women (Dunn 2004, 2005).

Vocabularies, Movements, and Archetypes: Organization of the Book

To help the reader understand why I have organized this book as I have, I now will introduce a typology of sorts, which provides a scaffolding for the analyses I take up in subsequent chapters. In previous work, I used the term *political empathy* to describe social movements' evoking of emotions that leads to their growth, the engagement of their audiences, and, ultimately, social change in the form of public policy (Dunn 2004). This book relies upon a slightly modified version of the model I developed. In the history of the survivor movements I chronicle, various types of victims have played varied roles at differing times. My conceptual framework develops four ideal typical possibilities for the social construction of victims. Each type has different degrees of agency (choice, free will, responsibility, accountability) associated with it and, because of this, different feeling rules and different emotional responses. Ultimately, this suggests likely consequences: how victims are interpreted influences how we respond emotionally and, via this, politically. The images created by social movements are implicated in their success, and success is a factor in how we subsequently judge the victims we meet (Loseke 2003).

Chapter 2 is an introduction to the survivor movements from which I take the stories that use vocabularies of victimization and that rely upon the cultural code of agency. After considering the historical backdrop and cultural milieu of the movements, I talk about each in turn and about a few of the founders of each movement. For each survivor movement, I have sought to briefly describe its origins and emergence, some of the key storytellers in the early stages of the movements, some of the actions taken by movement participants, and some of the important social changes that the movements have engendered. My portraits of the movements are necessarily succinct and partial; I intend them to serve as scenery and setting for the dramas that unfold. As I have indicated, I treat the movement actors, the feminists from the women's movement, the polemicists, the sociologists, the therapists, the critics, and the journalists, *all* as narrators. In many cases, I have tried to provide a bit of detail about the movement actors I am citing; the victims are mostly nameless or were given pseudonyms. Many of the activists have gone on to become famous (or infamous), and fuller accounts of their lives, as well as of the movements in which they played such an integral part, are available elsewhere (see Brownmiller 1999 for a personal recollection; see Schechter 1982; Matthews 1994; Davis 2005a; and Lytton 2008 for excellent historical discussion).

The next four chapters are the heart of the book, each illustrating victim construction in the vocabularies of survivor movements and of individuals and showing the inextricable links between claims-making and the cultural code of agency. I begin with rhetoric from the rape survivor movement, followed by the battered women's movement. Because of their significance for understanding the countermovement of the "cultural critics" and the clergy abuse survivor movement, I then talk briefly about incest survivor images, the rise of "therapeutic culture," and false memory syndrome before moving on to the emergence of survivor identity work and the movement represented by SNAP.

If I am right about the cultural code of agency and the feeling rules derived from it, victims who have been framed as agents will be portrayed as responsible in some way for their victimization, and thus they are unlikely to elicit sympathy or help. This is the image of the *blameworthy* victim, the focus of Chapter 3. In this chapter, I show how the antirape movement in particular drew on this image as a springboard for bringing public attention to the problem of rape even as they redefined victimization as *never* the victim's fault. I use rape victim vocabularies in stories from the first speak-out on rape to illustrate how victims (and their advocates) respond to the implicit cultural code questions: "What did you do to cause this?" and "Why didn't you resist?" I also show a little of how the blameworthy victim theme has been echoed in the other survivor movements and similarly has worked as a foil for the identities other claims-makers were then constructing in opposition.

In contrast to the blameworthy victim, individuals and survivor movements have sought to typify victims in ways that deflect responsibility and through this create *blameless* victims whom audiences will feel inclined to help. These victims are not the source of their own troubles. Instead, they are powerless in the face of the sociological and psychological forces arrayed against them. In Chapter 4, I draw primarily upon rhetoric that early activists in the battered women's movement used (especially in the social scientific literature), to provide exemplars of this kind of collective victim identity work. Images of battered women also reflect the cultural code of agency; they and their advocates must and do answer the question, "Why did she stay?" In addition, as in Chapter 3, I consider blameless victim typifications in other survivor movements. When looking at these, I examine how we might be sympathetic toward this kind of victim but also point out a potential for problems that I see as inherent in blameless constructions. This "identity dilemma" (Charmaz 1994) has to do with how we feel about people who are powerless and whom we can therefore label "victims." Sometimes, the blameless victim might evoke pity as well as sympathy, an emotion we tend to direct downward, toward those we feel are beneath us (Hochschild 1979).

Having illustrated blameworthy and blameless victims, and the ways in which agency and lack of agency work to foster or deflect blame, I move on in Chapter 5 to the stories and imagery generated by an incipient countermovement that has made use of the fact that victims may be negatively evaluated because they are lacking agency. Here, I examine the *pathetic* victim as she is represented in the "backlash" literature of the early 1990s, particularly in response to putative acquaintance rape victims but also to the so-called victim feminists. I cite the use of what I call "vocabularies of victimism" in popular media, especially in mass market publications and cultural criticism, to show disparaging constructions of victimization and the emergence of some very public victim contests. These images depend for their resonance on the cultural code of agency, which not only assumes choice but *privileges* it. Thus, cultural critics portray victims as naive and gullible, creating images that evoke pity and, in extreme cases, contempt. These victims are hard for audiences to identify with and undermine support for survivor movements. Included in this chapter are some of the concerns about images of rape victims and battered women raised by people within these social movements as well as by outsiders. These images, intended or not, are more likely to evoke our disdain, and they may dissuade us from offering our help.

In Chapter 6, the final substantive chapter, I look at victims who are cast as agents but who are *not* blamed. These are the "survivors," whom I call *admirable* victims. New media representations of clergy abuse survivors, including victims' stories on survivor movements' websites and support groups on the Internet, use a new vocabulary of victimization, a vocabulary of surviving, that alludes to the courage and heroism characterizing contemporary images, many of which now include adult male survivors in addition to women and children. I preface this examination with early stories from Louise Armstrong's (1978) "speak-out in print" on incest, to show how even children's victimization confronts the cultural code of agency. I also examine typifications of "vulnerable adults," who appear to be agents as individuals but whose stories present them as structurally powerless. In the end, it is the vocabulary of surviving that helps produce collective identities that oppose *and* affirm the cultural code, thus mitigating the tensions described above and appealing to movement participants as well as to broader publics.

In Chapter 7, I collect my thoughts on the vocabularies of victimization, victimism, and surviving illuminated in the book and consider the implications of studying the social construction of victims and survivors. Have I added anything of interest to ongoing discussions of the uses and consequences of using the term *survivor?* How does the research contribute to a sociological understanding of victimization as a meaning-laden social process and to what we know of the collective identity work in which survivor movements engage? And further, what can these vocabularies tell us about deviance, social problems, and social movements more generally? How can this study contribute to victimology? Finally, what issues for public policy and social change can be extracted from the analysis?

First though, I turn to the stories' milieu, and to the historical processes of "collective definition" in which survivor movements "arise, . . . become legitimated, . . . are shaped in discussion, . . . come to be addressed in official policy, and . . . are reconstituted in putting planned action into effect" (Blumer 1971, p. 298). To understand the cultural context shared by survivor movements over time, it is helpful to know a little about their beginnings, the people involved, what they did, and what has happened as a result.

2

Survivor Movements
Then and Now

When thinking about the survivor movements I discuss in this chapter, it is helpful to conceptualize them as related and to briefly situate them in their larger cultural and historical context. The stories of victims, advocates, and survivors all were told in the United States (and other Western nations) in the years between 1970 and the present, a time of rapid social change in a country famous for the overarching individualism of its political economy and moralities. In *Telling Sexual Stories: Power, Change, and Social Worlds*, Ken Plummer asks:

> What are the links between stories and the wider social world—the contextual conditions for stories to be told and for stories to be received? What brings people to give voice to a story at a particular historical moment? What are the different social worlds' interpretive communities that enable stories to be told and heard in different ways? And as the historical moment shifts, perhaps into a late modern world, what stories may lose their significance, and what stories may gain in tellability? (Plummer 1995, p. 25)

Plummer refers to "the tale and its time . . . when an audience is ripened up and ready to hear" (1995, p. 35). How did we become ready to hear the stories from which I take my ideas?

We could arguably begin with the Constitution or the Bill of Rights (and of course these emblems of a cultural narrative of individualism and individual rights did not emerge full-blown from a historical vacuum). Gwyneth Williams and Rhys Williams, however, characterize what they refer to as the "master frame of equal rights" as an "innovation" that is simultaneously "recognized and resonant" and thus can be used by a variety of social movements (1995, pp. 191–192). Albeit somewhat arbitrary, the emergence of this frame is a good starting point. Because it can be linked back to independence and because it is founded on the notion of social relationships as "the products of persons entering into equal, voluntary exchange relationships" (Williams and Williams 1995, p. 194)—that is, the notion of persons as agents—the master frame of equal rights qualifies as a historically and culturally situated backdrop for the processes of victim image making I will be describing.

According to Williams and Williams, this master frame is a particularly flexible and useful way of understanding and framing the need for a social movement, and became widely used beginning with the civil rights movement in the United States in the 1950s and 1960s. Certainly, there is abundant evidence that it caught on. Joel Best has used the term *piggybacking* (1990) to capture how social movements can build on the successful claims-making of earlier collective efforts. He cites the example of the ways in which the civil rights movement laid the groundwork (and developed the vocabulary of victimization) for successive "rights" movements, including those "demanding equal rights for women, homosexuals, the disabled, the elderly, children, and others" (Best 1997, p. 9). Of these, the women's movement is primary for understanding survivor movements, both because it came first following the struggle for civil rights, and because it is most significant.

A history of the women's movement is beyond the scope of this book, and even the histories of the survivor movements have been covered in much greater detail elsewhere (e.g., Schechter 1982; Matthews 1994; Davis 2005a; Lytton 2008). But the survivor movements I discuss below began with the consciousness-raising groups of the second "wave" of the women's liberation movement, in which "women . . . particularly radical feminists, were the first to address violence against women through sharing experience" (Matthews 1994, p. 9). This sharing has been used strategically by the antirape movement, followed by the battered women's movement, the incest survivor movement, and the clergy abuse survivor movement.

What made this sharing possible and, later, ubiquitous (Plummer 1995) was in part a cultural milieu proclaiming the need for women's rights. Among them was the right for women (and children) to give voice to their victimization and claim themselves as victims. Violence against women and children became a focus of the women's movement early on, and feminists argued that such violence was yet another way in which men dominated and controlled their lives and kept them in the thrall of patriarchy (Brownmiller 1975 on rape; Martin 1976 on battering; Rush 1974 on incest; Bonavoglia 2008 on clergy abuse).

Thus, each of the survivor movements, as well as its critics, has told stories against the backdrop of a culture in a time in which individualism, agency, and individual rights have been salient features of the political landscape (Williams and Williams 1995) and in which women's rights (as well as those of other disadvantaged groups) have been continually claimed, argued, and contested (Whittier 1995). It has also been a milieu increasingly favorable to self-disclosure and the telling of secrets. In her work on twelve-step recovery groups, Leslie Irvine writes usefully of what she calls the "therapeutic ethos," a "collection of discourses about self-fulfillment that has developed over the past thirty years or so" (1999, p. 5). Plummer, discussing stories of "sexual danger," similarly notes the "acceleration of the individualistic 'therapeutic/expressive culture' which fosters the telling of self-narratives." He says this shift helps to enable "social worlds waiting to hear" and communities that have been "fattened up, rendered ripe and willing" (1995, pp. 121, 124–125). Finally, as the survivor movements established organizations to aid victims, political and economic pressures led to an increasingly therapeutic and individualistic model of recovery from trauma within them (Loseke and Cahill 1984; Matthews 1994; Schechter 1982; Armstrong 1994).

I turn now to those movements. In 1971, at the same time my chronicle begins, the symbolic interactionist Herbert Blumer published an article called "Social Problems as Collective Behavior" in *Social Problems*. In it, he argues that sociologists should turn their attention to the ways in which groups of people define social problems in social interaction, from the early stages of coming to believe and assert that a problem exists to the point where something is done about the problem. It is a process of collective definition, Blumer argues, adding that it is through this process that social problems have "their being, their career, and their fate" (1971, p. 305).

Blumer identifies stages of social interaction and collective definition: "emergence," "legitimation," "mobilization of action," "formation of an official plan of action," and "implementation" of policy (1971, p. 301). For each of the survivor movements, I say a little about these processes and about some of the individuals who engaged in them. Although the processes have become more salient than the people who instigated them, I trace some of the linkages between activists and their biographies, in part as evidence that all social movements begin and continue with activists who share values and who come to know, and know of, one another as they interact and create meaning together. It goes without saying that there are many who go unnamed, like the victims and survivors who are then and now anonymous. For the sake of brevity, I tell stories about only the storytellers in this book.

The Antirape Movement

In the beginning, there was the NYRF, a group that emerged out of women's liberation consciousness-raising groups in the late 1960s. The NYRF kicked off the antirape movement with the first speak-out on rape in 1971, with the slogan Rape Is a Political Crime Against Women. A speak-out is an event in which victims are encouraged to stand up and tell their stories to the audience assembled before them. At this first one, held at St. Clement's Episcopal Church on West Forty-sixth Street in New York, there were ten panelists and about 300 women in attendance, and a few men who were admitted (only if accompanied by women). The speak-out was followed by a two-day conference later that year at Washington Irving High School, at which some of the original panelists appeared as well as others (Brownmiller 1999, pp. 199–203).

Gail Sheehy, then one of the original contributors to *New York* magazine, attended the speak-out and wrote an article for the magazine in which she retold some of the stories she heard that day (1971). That same year, Susan Griffin, who was to become a founding member of Bay Area Women Against Rape (BAWAR), published her article, "Rape: The All-American Crime," in *Ramparts*. Susan Brownmiller, herself a founding member of NYRF who also had been at the speak-out, refers to this piece as a "trailblazing article, the first in a national publication to put rape in an historical context" and says that it "was passed from hand to hand inside the movement" (1999, p. 205).

That same year, a San Francisco jeweler named Jerry Plotkin was acquitted of rape after a highly publicized trial where a scholar and activist named Diana Russell was among the protesters at the courthouse. Women Against Rape (WAR) groups began to form in several cities. Then, according to Brownmiller:

> A fresh concept was born in the nation's capital early in 1972 when eight women in consciousness-raising groups loosely attached to D.C. Women's Liberation formed a special support group for rape victims [inspired by] taking part in a Women's Liberation Conference on Rape held at George Washington University in April . . . with genius, they named their service a Rape Crisis Center. (1999, pp. 205–206)

At the same time, BAWAR was formed in Berkeley, California, and their organization and the D.C. Rape Crisis Center became "national network hubs for the growing movement" (Matthews 1994, p. 10). The D.C. Center was a prototype, and centers soon followed in Ann Arbor, Michigan; Boston, Massachusetts; Philadelphia, Pennsylvania; and Hartford, Connecticut (Weed 1995).

In 1973, feminist groups organized and sponsored a National Rape Prevention Month, in part to gain support for rape law reforms under consideration in New York. In the following year, two more highly publicized trials, one of Inez Garcia, accused of murdering the man who raped her, and Joan Little, tried for killing a prison guard while resisting rape, "attracted more support" (Rose 1977). Elizabeth Montgomery appeared in the made-for-television movie *A Case of Rape,* a drama about a housewife who experiences not only rape but unsympathetic treatment from the people to whom she reports it (Brownmiller 1999). New York ended the requirement for corroboration (physical damage or witnesses) in order to charge rape (Tobias 1997). At the height of the rape movement in the mid-1970s, there were 400 feminist rape crisis centers among "approximately 1500 separate projects" (Schechter 1982, p. 39). By 1976, when the National Center for the Prevention and Control of Rape was formed, there were crisis lines in almost all major cities in the United States and 300 rape task forces. As of the mid-1990s, there were thousands of rape crisis centers nationwide (Weed 1995).

In 1974, the NYRF published *Rape: The First Sourcebook for Women by New York Radical Feminists,* drawing on transcriptions of the "rape testimonies" of women at the original speak-out, a rape consciousness-raising workshop, and a videotaped conversation among four victims of rape held at an NYRF conference organized shortly after the speak-outs (Connell and Wilson 1974). Thus, that book is a source of the earliest public first-person stories about rape, including some of the stories Sheehy (1971) had written about. The next feminist book on rape to be published by a mainstream publisher was *Against Rape,* by Andra Medea and Kathleen Thompson (Medea and Thompson 1974). Medea was a self-defense instructor and Thompson a member of WAR in Chicago (Brownmiller 1999).

In 1975, Brownmiller retold many of stories from the speak-outs and *Rape: The First Sourcebook for Women* in *Against Our Will: Men, Women, and Rape,* a book that became as famous as it was controversial and eventually was published in sixteen languages. That same year, Diana Russell, a Harvard-educated professor at Mills College in Oakland, published *The Politics of Rape: The Victim's Perspective,* based on her interviews of rape victims. Russell's book is perhaps less well known outside of feminist scholarship on rape and the antirape movement, but it launched her long career of writing and activism on violence against women. Together, the work of Sheehy (1971); Griffin (1971); the NYRF *Rape: The First Sourcebook,* edited by Noreen Connell and Cassandra Wilson (1974); Medea and Thompson (1974); Brownmiller (1975); and Russell (1975) provide the best-known and most influential early victim narratives (Davis 2005b) from the antirape movement, which in 1975 was at its zenith (Schechter 1982).

In the years since, rape crisis centers have continued to provide services for rape victims across the United States, often forming statewide coalitions and working toward legislative change. They have been helped by federal funding provided after passage of the Violence Against Women Act (VAWA) of 1994, and since then have become collaborators with community-coordinated Sexual Assault Response Teams (SARTs) and help provide education for Sexual Assault Nurse Examiner (SANE) programs (Office for Victims of Crime 2009). There have been significant changes in rape laws in many states: in addition to dropping the corroboration requirement, some have also ended requirements that victims report assaults immediately to law enforcement, and most have passed "rape shield" laws that limit the kinds of questions that can be asked of survivors in court. By 1993, the spousal exemption for marital rape had been removed in all fifty states (Konradi 2007).

Although some observers express concern about the ability of rape crisis centers (and battered women's shelters) to continue feminist survivor movement work while relying on federal and other funding sources (Johnson 1981; Matthews 1994; Martin 1990), and others suggest that rape law reforms have limits (e.g., Konradi 2007), it is clear that the antirape movement has helped to accomplish significant social change in response to rape. Although the vocabularies of victimization I examine in Chapter 3 are from the early days of the movement rather than the present day, if I am right about the power of the cultural code of agency, there may still be significant blaming of victims and more to accomplish in the changing of public perceptions.

Wife Abuse and the Battered Women's Movement

In the mid-1970s, some of the same women involved in the antirape movement, as well as other activists, began working to raise public consciousness of what they then called "wife beating" (Schechter 1982). The National Organization for Women (NOW) formed a National Task

Force on Battered Women/Household Violence at their annual conference in 1975, and the following year, Del Martin, a member of NOW in San Francisco and a coordinator of the task force, published *Battered Wives*. This book, like much of the scholarship on battered women that followed, relies upon the stories of victims to illuminate previously hidden and, for some, shameful victimization. How shameful is indicated by the title of the first book on battered women, Erin Pizzey's *Scream Quietly or the Neighbours Will Hear* (published in Great Britain in 1974).

Pizzey had founded a London shelter for battered women called Chiswick Women's Aid, and in 1976 the Parliament passed a law giving more protection to battered women. According to Kathleen Tierney, in the United States, the emphasis of the battered women's movement has been on providing shelters and crisis services, and "early programs became prototypes for later efforts" (1982, p. 207). Local and national chapters of NOW organized task forces in the mid-1970s, and in 1982, Tierney estimated there were more than 170 shelters (p. 208). In the early 1970s, the National Institute of Mental Health began funding research on family violence. After a national conference held by the US Commission on Civil Rights in 1978, the National Coalition Against Domestic Violence was formed (Tierney 1982, pp. 208–209). The year before, *Reader's Digest* called battering "one of this country's least recognized and most appalling social problems" (cited in Loseke 1989, p. 191).

Antirape and battered women's activists shared their strategies and knew of one another: Elizabeth Pleck observes that the antirape movement "provided the ideology, methods, and public acceptance" the battered women's movement needed (1987, p. 185). Not only did many of the same people work to publicize and seek help for battered women, but they often did so in close affiliation with the rape crisis centers (Schechter 1982). Brownmiller, in her chronicle of the women's liberation movement (1999), notes that even though Pizzey's book was never published in the United States, "many of us managed to acquire copies at feminist bookstores or conferences." Brownmiller also asserts that Del Martin's 1976 book was "highly regarded" in the women's movement (1999, pp. 259, 266). In less than a decade, activists were able to "start 500 shelters, win legal and social services reforms in hundreds of localities, form almost 50 state coalitions, and capture the imagination of a nation" (Schechter 1982, p. 320).

Tierney (1982) cites "substantial headway" in legislation, government policy and programs, and research and public information: by

1980 most states had passed laws increasing penalties for batterers and broadening protections for victims, and in 1984 the federal government specified funding for domestic violence in the National Victims of Crime Act (Weed 1995). The Violence Against Women Act of 1994 created federal domestic violence penalties (United States Department of Justice 2009). Government agencies such as the Law Enforcement Assistance Administration (LEAA) in the late 1970s and, later, the Office of Domestic Violence provided funds for shelters, and more than $1,000,000 in grants went to research in 1976 on the prevalence of family violence (Pleck 1987).

The VAWA legislation passed in 1994 provided for assistance to battered women as well as to rape victims; it was reauthorized in 2000 and 2005. Today, what is called "intimate partner violence and stalking" falls under the purview of the Centers for Disease Control (CDC), partnered with the National Institute of Justice (NIJ), which jointly sponsored the National Violence Against Women Survey in 1996. Since 1993, and continuing through the present, the NIJ has sponsored research under its Violence Against Women and Family Violence Program (National Institute of Justice 2009).

The battered women's movement, like the antirape movement, is rooted in the broader women's movement, from which it draws much of its ideological and practical inspiration. From its inception, the claims-making of the movement has been infused with scholarly research undertaken by researchers who considered themselves feminists. Some of these studies use excerpts from first-person victim narratives (Davis 2005b) to illustrate the harms of victimization, and so "speak-out" in their own way. In turn, many early activists drew on this work to dramatize this violence and to typify its victims. As mentioned earlier, in 1976 Del Martin wrote *Battered Wives,* the first book published in the United States on this emerging social problem. She drew on the early published work on "family violence," acknowledging Richard Gelles, Suzanne Steinmetz, Murray Straus, and Rebecca Dobash, "another sociologist who understands the role of research as an agent for social change" (Martin 1976, p. xvi).

Also in 1976 Murray Straus published an article titled "Sexual Inequality, Cultural Norms, and Wife-beating" in the first issue of *Victimology,* in which he framed wife beating as a consequence of sexism that perpetuates the oppression of women. Straus (1992) has argued that researchers in this field "are almost always ideologically aligned with social movements seeking to aid victims" (p. 232) and described himself as a pioneer feminist researcher on wife beating. In 1978, Terry

Davidson, an investigative reporter for the *New York Times,* published *Conjugal Crime,* in which she cited scholarly research, including that of Straus, to explain why men batter and why women cannot easily leave violent relationships.

Books for the general public on the topic of family violence peaked in the late 1970s and early 1980s, and sociological articles on the same subject grew exponentially between 1974 and 1988. Increasing numbers of women, influenced by the women's movement, were entering graduate school in sociology to further their research and political aims, including addressing violence against women (Straus 1992). In 1979, activist Jennifer Fleming, working with a group called the Women's Resource Network and the National Coalition Against Domestic Violence, published the manual *Stopping Wife Abuse.* Fleming's book was one of the first books to cite Lenore Walker's early work, an article published in the second volume of *Victimology,* and Walker's first book, *The Battered Woman* (1979), which appeared earlier that year.

Fleming also cited other influential feminist scholarly works such as R. Emerson Dobash and Russell Dobash's *Violence Against Wives* (1979) and Kathleen Barry's *Female Sexual Slavery* (1979). Walker had a Ph.D. in psychology, Dobash and Dobash were on the faculty of the University of Sterling in Scotland, and Barry was a young professor of sociology at Brandeis. All were explicitly feminist, and all defined and explained the problem of violence against women and advocated solutions to it. These authors could all be considered advocates as well as scholars, and support Straus's (1992) argument that researchers and activists had mutual influence.

By the early 1980s, the battered women's movement itself had become the subject of scholarly research on its origins, transformations, and outcomes. In that decade, it is important to note, the images of battered women constructed by activists began to be examined and questioned and countered with alternate representations (Johnson 1981; Loseke and Cahill 1984). As early as 1979, the construction of battered women as "pure victims" had been criticized by Barry. Typifications of battered women increasingly began to emphasize their agency instead of, or in addition to, their victimization (Gondolf 1988)—a topic I will take up more fully in Chapter 6. In Chapter 4 I will examine how the battered women's movement constructed "sympathetic" victims through emphasizing their *lack* of agency, whether it be due to social structures, social forces, or psychological effects of victimization. To do so, I will draw upon arguments made by Walker (1979), Dobash and Dobash (1979), Pagelow (1981), Martin (1976), and Davidson (1978).

Following this, I will use excerpts from the first-person narratives pre-
sented in these works to show how battered women account for staying.
To these, I add the stories of women who wrote to and spoke with Erin
Pizzey (1974).

Child Sexual Abuse and
the Incest Survivor's Movement

Florence Rush, whom Brownmiller (1999) describes as a member of the
NYRF's Westchester "brigade" and of Older Women's Liberation
(OWL), attended the 1971 speak-out on rape. Rush then took the podi-
um at the two-day conference to talk about "The Sexual Abuse of
Children: A Feminist Point of View"—an event that launched the "new
story" of child sexual abuse, what Davis calls an "account of innocence"
(2005a). Transcripts of Rush's talk, as well as of the speak-out stories
and a consciousness-raising group on rape held in conjunction with the
conference, appear in Connell and Wilson's *Rape: The First Sourcebook
for Women* (1974) that chronicled these events.

In 1977, an article on incest appeared in *Ms.* magazine, followed by
what Joseph Davis has called a "tide" (2005a) and Armstrong a
"cacophony" (1994). The *Ms.* article, titled "Incest: Sexual Abuse
Begins at Home," by Ellen Weber, refers readers to the Santa Clara
Child Sexual Abuse Treatment Program (CSATP) in San Jose,
California. At that time, CSATP was "the only comprehensive program
designed to meet the needs of both victims and offenders" (Weber 1977,
p. 66). With the Weber article was the story of "Mary C."—"I tried to
fantasize that all fathers had intercourse with their daughters" (Stucker
1977, p. 66). This may be one of the earliest uses of an incest victim
narrative (Davis 2005b) in print form.

In 1978, several books on incest appeared, including works by
Louise Armstrong, Sandra Butler, Susan Forward and Craig Buck, and
Karin Meiselman. Of these, Armstrong's book, *Kiss Daddy Goodnight,*
is by far the most well known; after its publication she wrote an article
for *Cosmopolitan* (1979) and received so much media attention that
years later she described herself as "the World's First Walking, Talking
Incest Victim" (1994, p. 2). Armstrong, herself a survivor of incest, was
a free-lance writer, living with her husband and twin sons in Greenwich
Village and soliciting letters from other survivors for a "first-person
documentary book." Its publication put her on the *Today Show* and
Donahue, and Armstrong describes how "more and more women spoke

up" and how when she was interviewed "on call-in shows around the country, the stories poured in" (1994, p. 33). It is not surprising that the 1978 book is subtitled *A Speak-Out on Incest.*

In the early 1980s, Rush wrote *The Best-Kept Secret: Sexual Abuse of Children* (1980), and activist and psychiatrist Judith Herman published *Father-Daughter Incest* (1981). Armstrong cites 1984 as a watershed year for media on incest: stories appeared in *Life* and *Newsweek,* ABC broadcast a made-for-television drama ("Something About Amelia"), and PBS did a five-and-a-half-hour program (1994, p. 99). Activists in the antirape movement worked to establish sexual abuse prevention programs in schools, and feminist mental health professionals "began to formulate a therapeutic rationale to guide treatment of adults" (Davis 2005a, p. 96). In 1988, Laura Davis and Ellen Bass, an incest survivor and a survivor workshop leader, produced the first edition of the best-selling self-help book *The Courage to Heal: A Guide for Women Survivors of Child Sexual Abuse.*

Although rooted in the antirape movement, it is arguable whether the collectivity of incest and child sexual abuse victims has been a social movement in the tradition of the earlier survivor movements or more of a self-help movement. Social movements scholar Verta Taylor makes a strong argument that women's self-help support groups are a kind of "new social movement":

> To the extent that self-help groups call attention to problems not being met by existing institutions, propose alternative conceptions of problems, support changes in the self-concepts and social identities of their members, and exert pressure on professional and public agencies to allocate resources for new solutions to problems, there can be little doubt that self-help promotes not only personal but *societal change.* (1996, p. 20; emphasis in original)

On the other hand, the thesis of Armstrong's (1994) reflection on "what happened when women said incest" is very different. "By the late 1980s," Armstrong says, "you could not tell that which the survivors were calling the *survivor movement* from what everyone else was calling the *recovery movement*" (p. 205; emphasis in the original). She decries what she sees as a result of the commodification of incest by the "talk show hosts" along with its medicalization, concluding that

> you could not, any longer, always tell the feminists from the survivors: all seemed to be suffering some disorder within, and to be in therapy and, as victims, were willing guests on the media. . . . Somewhere along the way, rather than feminism politicizing the issue of incest,

incest-as-illness had overwhelmed and swallowed feminism. (Armstrong 1994, p. 207)

In either case, I will show that both early and contemporary child sexual abuse vocabularies of victimization are patterned after the rhetoric and accounts that emerged from the antirape and battered women's movements, and for much the same reasons.

Lashing Back at the Survivor Movements

If there are doubts about whether activism and claims-making for victims of incest and child sexual abuse constitute a social movement, then the "backlash" (Faludi 1991) I describe below is probably even more ambiguous. Because of this, and because this rhetoric has been accompanied by none of the collective action or social change the survivor movements have accomplished, I characterize what I am calling a "countermovement" more in terms of the kinds of things that people were saying rather than what they did.

I begin by noting that the social critics whose language and images of victims I will examine in Chapter 5 were not the first to raise concerns about the successes of the women's movement in bringing attention to victims of rape and battering. In 1979, the same year Dobash and Dobash published *Violence Against Wives* and Walker wrote *The Battered Woman*, Kathleen Barry used the term *victimism* to characterize some unintended consequences of social constructions of victims of sexual violence (1979, p. 37). Noting that the new awareness of rape "has been a mixed blessing," Barry argued the following:

> The status of "victim" creates a mind set eliciting pity and sorrow. Victimism denies the woman the integrity of her humanity through the whole experience, and it creates a framework for others to know her not as a person but as a victim, someone to whom violence was done. . . . The assigned label of "victim," which initially was meant to call awareness to the experience of sexual violence, becomes a term that expresses that person's identity. Once one has been raped, one is not ever again a nonvictim. Victimism is an objectification which establishes new standards for defining experience; those standards dismiss any question of will, and deny that the woman even while enduring sexual violence is a living, changing, growing, interactive person. (1979, pp. 37–38)

Here Barry's argument is similar to mine. She uses "pity and sorrow" in a way that implies that they are emotions directed downward, toward people who are lessened in our estimation by virtue of their lack of "will." She both sees that victim as an identity robs women of their agency and hints at how that diminishes them. Barry adds that even "those who are supportive will often shackle a woman with the judgments of victimism," one of which is to "identify passivity as a criteria for victimism" (1979, p. 39). Thus, she alerts us early on to a hazard inherent in victim construction, related inextricably to the necessary association of victimization with lack of choice, when to lack choice means to lack will rather than to be constrained by insurmountable forces or circumstances.

As it happens, Barry presciently made reference to a liberal "cult of the victim" when talking about well-meaning but misguided attempts to respond sympathetically to various oppressed peoples in addition to sexual violence survivors (1979, p. 38). In the early stages of the criticism countering victim constructions, people expressed unease at the widespread emergence and privileging in contemporary society of victims and victimization. In 1982, the (in some ways) conservative political scientist Jean Bethke Elshtain wrote an article for *The Progressive* called "The Victim Syndrome: A Troubling Turn in Feminism." Her use of the term *syndrome* suggests both pattern and illness; in the article itself she frets about how fearful women had become, "startlingly out of proportion to the actual threat[s]" they face (1982, p. 42). She references "victim ideology" and a "victim orientation," that is, a state of mind that predisposes women to have "susceptibility to distorted perceptions of oneself and one's 'group'" (Elshtain 1982, p. 43).

Elshtain's article laid the groundwork for several general and related attacks that were to be taken up in the early 1990s: this idea of a victim "culture" as suggested above, the characterization of women as fearful and overreacting as a result, the conflation of minor offenses with real violations, and the placing of responsibility for this on feminist antiviolence activism (and later, therapeutic models developed to deal with the trauma of victimization). Taking the antipornography movement of the time as her starting point, Elshtain framed feminist arguments as "the rhetorical equivalent of nuclear war" and "rising hysteria" and as characterized by "consistent overstatement of the problem" (1982, pp. 43–44). Their definition of pornography, Elshtain asserts, "blurs the distinction between violent and non-violent sexual material," and to make this point, she informs us that "in its extreme form" (referring here to Andrea Dworkin as exemplary), "sex between a man and a woman is acceptable so long as his penis is not erect" (1982, pp. 45–46).

Although Elshtain claims that it is the feminists who "cast [women] as unfortunate victims or manipulated dupes," her overarching argument of syndrome and her statement that "there is no doubt that women are afraid" places her own constructions in much the same category (1982, pp. 42, 44).

A few years earlier, a clinical psychologist named Mary Koss had published results of a nationwide survey of college students, in which she and her colleagues reported finding that almost one-third of women respondents described assaults that met the legal definition of rape or attempted rape at the time (Koss, Gidycz, and Wisniewski 1987). In 1988, Robin Warshaw wrote *I Never Called It Rape,* a book about acquaintance rape for popular consumption that drew on Koss's *Ms.*-sponsored research. The research, published in scholarly journals as well as in *Ms.*, and Warshaw's best-selling book, generated a great deal of commentary and significantly influenced rape education efforts on college campuses.

It was not long before people were countering Koss's characterization of the scope and prevalence of rape. On a scholarly front, one of the best-known critics was Neil Gilbert, a professor of social welfare at the University of California in Berkeley. In a 1991 article in the conservative politics and culture journal *The Public Interest*, titled "The Phantom Epidemic of Sexual Assault," Gilbert argued that rape victims' advocates had vastly overstated the incidence and prevalence of rape, primarily through defining it overbroadly. Gilbert specifically attacked Mary Koss's research findings and debated her on this topic in the first edition of *Current Controversies in Family Violence* (Gelles and Loseke 1993).

Although Gilbert's primary antagonists are feminists who "present the kind of figures that incite moral panic" (1991, p. 54) rather than rape victims, he does paint a subtle portrait of women who may be led to falsely cry rape. In his attempt to show that "circumstances matter" (that ambiguities abound and that the feminist construction is too rigid), Gilbert says that

> it makes a difference . . . how much alcohol the woman had ingested, and whether and how she expressed her lack of consent. . . . Did the man order a beer or a bottle of wine during dinner? Did she select the brand and split the bill? Was she too intoxicated to reason with the man? Did she physically resist his advances or run away? (1991, p. 59)

Here Gilbert is implying, I think, that there is a distinction between real rape and the domain being carved out by the feminists, that sex in the context of dating is ambiguous but real rape is not.

Gilbert also argues that real women are characterized by the "modesty, emotional confusion, ambivalence, and vacillation that inexperienced young people may feel during the initial stages of sexual intimacy," a statement he immediately follows parenthetically with "(Remember that 41 percent of the women defined as victims of rape were virgins at the time of the incident)" (1991, p. 60). Citing the numbers of women that feminists claim did not see themselves as victims, Gilbert says "if reasonable people feel confusion rather than outrage, perhaps there is something to be confused about" and that in the feminist view "there is no place for qualification, uncertainty, and confusion, except perhaps when a woman says 'yes'" (1991, pp. 59–60). In this quote, dating is again ambiguous but rape is not (dating causes "confusion" but rape "outrage"), and you get the sense that Gilbert believes there is a population of young women who simply do not know the difference.

Contrast this with the woman Gilbert sardonically portrays in the "typical guidelines" provided by the "experts," a woman who is advised to

> tell her date the precise limits of sexual activity in which she wishes to engage; to be assertive; to stay sober; to investigate her date and his plans for the evening; to remain in control by paying her own way and taking her own car or arranging to have a friend available to pick her up if necessary; and to be prepared to protect herself by taking a course in self-defense. (Gilbert 1991, p. 63)

That Gilbert presents this image as absurd—Gilbert says this advice may "convey" that "a sure way to prevent date rape is not to date men at all" (1991, p. 63)—suggests that real women are not nearly so rational, which suggests again their susceptibility to the feminists' sway. He suggests this another way in his conclusion, when he talks about women in the low-paid workforce who "feel socially and economically oppressed" and for whom the feminists' claims "may resonate with their feelings of being, not literally raped, but figuratively 'screwed over' by men" (Gilbert 1991, p. 65). As Gilbert has, in the preceding paragraph, castigated the feminists for advocacy that "trivializes ruthless cases of abuse and feeds off the suffering of real victims," once again the distinction is implicit, but clear.

That same year, in a venue somewhat less academic (the *New York Times*), Katie Roiphe published an opinion editorial called "Date Rape Hysteria" (1991). Roiphe is the daughter of the well-known feminist novelist and essayist Anne Roiphe, and at that time, she was a graduate student in the English Department at Princeton. In her commentary, she

derided feminist activism against date rape on college campuses, calling it a "neo-Puritan preoccupation" that diverts attention from the
"real women [who] are getting battered" (Roiphe 1991, p. A27). After
claiming that "this so-called feminist movement peddles an image of
gender relations that denies female desire and infantilizes women,"
Roiphe concludes: "Let's not reinforce the images that oppress us, that
label us victims, and deny our own agency and intelligence, as strong
and sensual, as autonomous, pleasure-seeking, sexual beings" (1991, p.
A27). Here, Roiphe contrasts victimization with agency, clearly privileging the latter, and directly addressing victim imagery in the antirape
movement.

The following year (1992), Camille Paglia would chime in on this
issue in *Sex, Art, and American Culture* (followed by *Vamps and Tramps*
in 1994, in which she expands her arguments and comments on both
Roiphe and Wolf). In 1993, Roiphe published a controversial book
extending the argument she had made in 1991: *The Morning After: Sex,
Fear, and Feminism on Campus*, and Naomi Wolf wrote *Fire with Fire:
The New Female Power and How It Will Change the 21st Century*
(1993b). Each of these books ignited a firestorm of sorts, because each
argued that feminists had exaggerated the dangers and effects of male
violence and in doing so, they were exploiting the youthful naïveté of
pampered middle-class college students. As a consequence, young
women could no longer tell the difference between real violations and
minor offenses and, in some cases, were encouraged to lie as well as to
overreact. In addition, these authors asserted, the feminists had created
an image of women as victims entirely incongruent with the aims of
"true" feminism and the reality of women's lives, that of the pathetic
victim. In Chapter 5, after examining these counterclaims, I will show
how *their* constructors themselves created pathos.

Clergy Abuse Survivors and the
Survivors Network of those Abused by Priests

The final survivor movement covered in this book (in Chapter 6) is the
most recent to emerge, the collectivity of activists engaged in claims-
making about clergy abuse. The prevalence of "accounts of innocence"
(Davis 2005a) initiated in the antirape, battered women, and especially
the incest/child sexual abuse survivor movements likely created a hos-
pitable climate in which the telling of clergy abuse stories could
emerge (Plummer 1995). According to Philip Jenkins, very few cases

of clergy abuse were reported in the media prior to 1985, because "the media generally cooperated with the church in avoiding scandal" (1996, p. 33). Partly because of changing media attitudes, legal environments, and the politics of anti-Catholic interest groups, this began to change, beginning when a Catholic priest in Louisiana, Gilbert Gauthe, was charged in 1984 with "repeated attacks committed over several years" (1996, p. 106).

This began the first of three "waves" of activism (Lytton 2008), in all of which the media were very influential claims-makers. Jenkins discusses the mushrooming growth of news reports from about 40 per year in the years between 1989 and 1991 to more than 240 stories published in 1992 and 200 more in 1993. There were exposé-style stories (*60 Minutes* style) on all the major television networks, the Gauthe story was made into a movie for television, and by the end of 1993, clergy abuse "had been repeatedly discussed on all the major talk shows, including *Geraldo, Sally Jesse Rafael,* and *Donahue*" (Jenkins 1996, p. 112).

In 1993, Elinor Burkett, from the *Miami Herald,* and Frank Bruni, a reporter who was then at the *Detroit Free Press,* published *A Gospel of Shame: Children, Sexual Abuse, and the Catholic Church.* This important book begins its account with the story of how Frank Fitzpatrick and other victims of Father James Porter brought public attention to their case. Father Porter, like Gauthe, was an especially egregious offender who admitted to a television reporter that he had molested "anywhere, you know, from fifty to a hundred [children] I guess" (Burkett and Bruni 1993, p. 14). Jason Berry, an investigative journalist working free-lance, wrote *Lead Us Not into Temptation: Catholic Priests and the Sexual Abuse of Children* in 1994. Each of these books was published by a major press (Viking Press and Doubleday, respectively) and reprinted in paperback in the early 2000s. The *Boston Globe* won the Pulitzer Prize in 2003 for their coverage of the cover-up of clergy abuse in the Catholic hierarchy (The Pulitzer Prizes 2009).

Although incest victims formed self-help groups and sought therapy, as well as the "courage to heal" (Davis and Bass 1988), clergy abuse victims have been more organized in the form of a social movement. SNAP is among the most influential claims-makers. SNAP was founded in 1992 by Barbara Blaine, who was abused by a priest as a young girl but told no one until 1985, when she was twenty-nine. That is when, Blaine says, "I first came to some level of awareness that what had happened to me was abuse" (quoted in Adams 2002). She had read Jason Berry's 1985 article about Gauthe in *The Catholic Reporter* (Bonavoglia 2008), and after a long period of frustrating attempts to get her abuser removed from a position where he could continue to abuse, in 1988 Blaine formed SNAP.

> By 1988 I realized [the bishops] were not going to help, although I was still hurting and needed healing. I thought that if I could get together with other survivors, we could help each other heal. That's why I started SNAP. Anytime I found a newspaper article, I would call the reporter who wrote it. I would ask the journalist to pass along my number to the victims of sexual abuse. . . . After talking to a lot of different people, I suggested that we all meet. I booked a hotel room at the Holiday Inn as a meeting room. I invited everyone to come, but most ended up not coming. I put an ad in the National Sunday Reporter, which is a weekly that comes out on Friday. Maybe twelve or fourteen people came to the event. . . . We ended up having events all over the country. Each time we advertised that we were having an event, we let the media know so they could publicize it. Little by little our group kept growing, and then we started local chapters. Now we have over four thousand members and about twenty chapters, and we're still growing. (Blaine, quoted in Adams 2002)

At the events Blaine describes, clergy abuse survivors shared their stories of abuse. Blaine started appearing on national television talk shows, and in 1992, on *Oprah,* she named Father Chet Warren as her abuser. In 2002, the *Boston Globe* revealed a massive clergy cover-up of abuse and the moving of abusive priests from parish to parish without informing parishioners of the danger (Hidalgo 2007). This attention was the beginning of the third wave (Lytton 2008) of public awareness and survivor movement activism. Cardinal Bernard Law of the Archdiocese of Boston was forced to resign as a result of the *Boston Globe* scandal, and a lay Catholic group that called itself Voice of the Faithful (VOTF) formed in response, to "keep the faith, change the church" (Voice of the Faithful 2009).

Also in 2002, Blaine was one of *Ms.* magazine's Women of the Year (*Ms.* 2002), and SNAP's membership increased to more than 5,000 people, as more cases of clergy abuse came to light and lawsuits began to be settled (BishopAccountability.Org 2004). SNAP's website refers to the organization as "the nation's largest, oldest and most active support group for women and men wounded by religious authority figures (priests, ministers, bishops, deacons, nuns, brothers, monks, and others)" (Survivors Network of those Abused by Priests 2007–2009). It is perceived as important by media: "Nationally, SNAP's become the most influential advocacy group for victims of clerical sexual abuse. SNAP's membership has exploded in conjunction with the unprecedented publicity surrounding the Catholic abuse scandals" (BishopAccountability.Org 2004).

In 2002, the *Chicago Tribune* did a story on Blaine, in which the reporter wrote that "although SNAP is the largest organization of its kind, with 4,000 members, two other groups—the Linkup and Survivors Connections, which maintains a database of perpetrators—also are being swamped with new attention" (Rubin 2002). The Linkup began as a local group of survivors who started meeting in Chicago in 1992, initially calling themselves Victims of Clergy Abuse Linkup (VOCAL). They were active in the early 1990s much like SNAP, raising awareness of clergy abuse and supporting survivors; in 1993, the group actually had 4,500 members, compared to SNAP's 1,200 (Plante 1999). In 2005, Linkup shifted its emphasis to recovery issues and changed its name to the Healing Alliance. Healing Alliance purchased property it called The Farm in rural Kentucky and used it to provide group workshops and "alternative" thirty-day treatment programs (Nevens-Pederson 2006). In October 2009, I was unable to locate the group or The Farm on the Internet; the domain to which other sites link (such as the BishopAccountability.Org site) is for sale. Survivors Connections was formed by Frank Fitzpatrick and other victims of Father Frank Porter in 1993, when they began maintaining a database of perpetrators and publishing a newsletter called *The Survivor Activist* (Fitzpatrick 2009). Today, SNAP is by far the most visible activist/support group, claiming a registered membership of 9,000 survivors and 48,000 hits on their website daily in their 2008 Annual Report (Survivors Network of those Abused by Priests 2007–2009).

In response to the "sex abuse crisis of 2002" (and in part almost certainly due to the efforts of activists beginning much earlier), in 2002 the Catholic Church set up a National Lay Review Board and an Office of Child and Youth Protection, with compliance audits, as well as conducting surveys in 2003 of Catholic clergy on the incidence, causes, and context of abuse. By 2004, "some seven hundred priests had been removed from the ministry" (Bonavoglia 2008, p. 83). Also in 2004, the results of a survey of clergy, conducted by the John Jay College of Criminal Justice, were released to the public (Lytton 2008).

Other important claims-makers advocating for clergy abuse victims have been in the legal profession, after "charitable immunity" ceased to excuse churches from liability. Numerous lawsuits began to be filed, especially after the Gauthe settlement (more than a million dollars to one family in 1986) (Jenkins 1996). Timothy Lytton argues that litigation (strongly supported by SNAP and other survivor groups) has had a "significant impact on church and government policy making. . . . [Benefits] include victim compensation, church policies designed to prevent future abuse, greater willingness among law enforcement officials to investigate allegations and prosecute where appropriate, and the therapeutic value of public disclosure" (Lytton 2008, pp. 163–164). In addition to these examples of social change, SNAP's annual report for 2008 lists the removal of 5,000 "child molesters" from religious institutions, the use of criminal background checks for employees (including clergy) in some of them, and the assignment to clergy of the status of being mandated reporters of child sexual abuse and states that "at least 31 states eliminated, extended or temporarily lifted statutes of limitations" on pressing criminal charges (Survivors Network of those Abused by Priests 2007–2009).

The report also notes that, with the help of SNAP, "at least 11,000 victims have courageously come forward for help" (Survivors Network of those Abused by Priests 2007–2009). This rhetorical conjoining of the admirable ("courage") with victimization is a hint of what we will see in the victim and survivor vocabularies associated with SNAP as well as in earlier movements. All of the survivor movements in this book tell stories about victims and talk about them in ways that create images such as this, and the rhetoric they use to do so is my focus. As SNAP members' and others' stories show, being a survivor is a way of reconciling victimization with the cultural code of agency, of cleaning (and redeeming) what Davis (2005a) calls "tarnished."

On History, Culture, Hierarchy, and Accounts

Each of the survivor movements whose members tell the stories from which I glean vocabularies of victimization and surviving has a social location. Like individuals, the movements have a placement in the structures of our society that profoundly shaped and continues to shape images of victims and victimization. C. Wright Mills saw the importance of what he called "a typal vocabulary of motive" for understanding how a culture enables action, but he argued that

> motives are of no value apart from the delimited social situations for which they are the appropriate vocabularies. They must be situated. At best, socially unlocated terminologies of motives represent unfinished attempts to block out social areas of motive imputation and avowal. Motives vary in content and character with historical epochs and societal structure. . . . The research task is the locating of particular types of action within typal frames of normative actions and socially situated clusters of motives. . . . The language of situations as given must be

considered a valuable portion of the data to be interpreted and related to their conditions. (1940, p. 913)

This chapter represents a modest effort to delineate the historical situation within which the language I analyze is situated. Survivor movements blossomed and flourished during a time in which successive social movements, beginning with the civil rights movement (which itself had nurturing historical precedents), prepared the way. Donileen Loseke argues for a "cumulative effect of social problems," citing the example of the "countless 'victim' claims we've heard in the past thirty years." She interprets the phenomenon of people claiming to be victims as meaning that "our moral climate surrounding the morality of individualism has changed" (1999, p. 141); my argument is that the stigmatization of victims reveals the ways in which it has *yet* to change.

This "moral climate" is part of a larger cultural climate: what Loseke calls the "morality of individualism" is an integral component of the cultural code of agency. What can the stories in this book help us to infer about the "societal structures" Mills refers to, the pervasive social arrangements dictated by culture and producing systems of stratification such as gender? And how might these arrangements influence vocabularies of victimization, victimism, and surviving? To answer this, we need to consider the effects of at least two additional factors related to the rise of survivor movements: the much-maligned "therapeutic ethos" and the gender system of the times.

Therapeutic Culture

I take the term *therapeutic ethos* from Leslie Irvine, who calls it a "collection of discourses about self-fulfillment that has developed over the past thirty years or so" (1999, p. 5). Irvine describes this as the idea that the self is "innately good, with 'needs' that deserve priority over conforming to society's norms" and argues that "large numbers" of Americans have come to think in these terms. While disagreeing that people are overly self-absorbed, she notes that "therapists and treatment professionals may have created the vocabulary with which people come to describe their problems" (p. 42). Phillip Rieff expressed concern about a culture of self-fulfillment in *The Triumph of the Therapeutic* in 1966, at a time that Lichterman refers to as being "on the eve of countercultural upheaval in the United States" (1995, p. 275).

Christopher Lasch called ours a "culture of narcissism" (1979), and others called our individualism an "American sickness" (Bellah et al. 1985). Lichterman calls it a culture of "personalism," the notion that "one's own individuality has inherent value, apart from one's material or social achievements, no matter what connections to specific institutions or communities the individual maintains" (1995, pp. 276–277). To support his claim for the centrality of personalism, he cites research (Kulka, Veroff, and Douvan 1979) showing that the number of people seeking therapy tripled between the mid-1950s and mid-1970s, when survivor movements began to emerge. He also refers to Wuthnow's (1994) finding that by the early 1990s, 75 million people were participating in some kind of support group (Lichterman 1995, p. 277).

Recently, Joseph Davis has called child abuse survivors' "accounts of innocence" themselves a product of the interplay between social movements, trauma therapy, and culture. When the stories victims told at speak-outs became a "collective story," the themes of victim innocence, victim harm, and the hidden nature of victimization became part of a new psychology "and a new treatment rationale that institutionalized and reproduced it. These interpretive structures, in turn, became the basis for identifying, labeling, and treating new survivor cases" (2005a, p. 108).

Davis details how the collective story of child sexual abuse formed the basis of the psychological trauma model, beginning with the publication of Judith Herman's book *Trauma and Recovery* in 1992. Clinicians were able to use the category of posttraumatic stress disorder (PTSD) to encompass the effects of child sexual abuse, and by the late 1980s, Davis argues, the model had taken hold as the framework for understanding the effects of child sexual abuse, as a coping mechanism with pathogenic consequences.

Davis argues that the trauma model "reconciles" psychiatry and clinical practice with the collective story of the innocent and injured victim.

> As formulated, the trauma model supported the coherence of the condition-category of sexual abuse and the innocence of victims by locating harm in the conditions of the sexual experience itself . . . encompass[ing] a very wide range of distresses, disabilities, somatic symptoms, and life problems as trauma aftereffects. It helped to depathologize and destigmatize the adult survivor's symptoms and experiences by explaining them as necessary coping responses . . . in the trauma model, no aspect of the harm could be construed as self-inflicted. (2005a, p. 134)

Davis's central argument is that "disorder was conceptualized to reflect the collective story already worked out by movement activists" (p. 135), working in ways that others did not to "preserve and encode" victim innocence. Why this is so necessary, this preserving and encoding, is a central theme I will highlight in my own analysis.

Davis also discusses how therapists make use of the collective story with their individual clients through the inculcation of a "therapeutic rationale." In this rationale, "the 'healing' or 'recovery' process is conceptualized as an identity change, a transition from being a victim to being a survivor and beyond" (2005a, p. 145). Clients come to recognize their "survivor strength" and to understand that they are not responsible for their symptoms (p. 148). Davis says "the standard of health is drawn from a therapeutic ethic of personal liberation" whose assumptions are taken for granted (p. 149). Integral to this process is participation in the self-help "movement," through books and groups in addition to therapy, all of which are intertwined. Together, they provide a "pathway" to the survivor identity (p. 154).

Even though the rape crisis centers, battered women's shelters, and organizations formed by incest survivors did not set out to inculcate a "therapeutic rationale," many critics have observed that they ultimately, and perhaps inevitably, did so. Nancy Matthews argues that rape crisis centers have moved from their collectivist beginnings and grassroots countercultural staffing to mainstream organizational forms and professional staff in addition to, and sometimes replacing, peer counseling. "While rape crisis work originated as an expression of the new feminist politics, today it is also a manifestation of a therapeutic society" (Matthews 1994, p. xiii). Matthews connects this directly with state funding, which has shifted the emphasis to "therapeutically managing the aftermath of rape rather than to changing social relations to prevent rape" (p. xiv).

As early as 1982, Susan Schechter discussed the cooptation of the battered women's movement related to funding needs and the resulting programs based on "individualized and professional counseling and advocacy" (1982, p. 245). More recently, Kendrick has said that the "psychological theories" of the mental health professionals the shelters were forced to hire have led to "shifting the focus of a domestic violence discourse toward therapeutic concerns," adding that "the contemporary dominant discourse on domestic violence relies on therapeutic vocabularies to both deflect challenges to the shelter and to construct battered women as the proper and deserving clients of shelter work" (1998, p. 170). And as I noted earlier in this chapter, Louise Armstrong decries the medicalization of incest in her 1994 retrospective examination of the incest survivor movement, *Rocking the Cradle of Sexual*

Politics. In it, she concludes that its founders "could not have anticipat-
ed the degree of dominance of the therapeutic ideology. Nor the way in
which a concept like speaking out would be transformed from a political
one into a clinical or therapeutic one" (Armstrong 1994, p. 270).

Gender Culture

As the discussion immediately preceding might suggest, the feminists
involved in the women's movement who went on to engage in survivor
movement collective action were concerned about therapeutic ideology for a reason—it diverted attention away from the patriarchal roots
of violence against women and children and toward individual
pathologies. The broader women's movement has inarguably and
increasingly become a salient aspect of US culture and a relatively
potent force for social change these days. Like the cultural code of
agency, however, we possess a cultural code of gender (Bem 1993;
Lorber 1993) with its own logic and rules for assigning agency,
accounting for victimization, and feeling sympathy. In the period of
time I cover, this cultural code was probably at its most uncontested
and taken-for-granted when "victim precipitation" theories (Amir
1971) came to the fore, and certainly the efforts of survivor movements have made problematic some of our tendencies to blame women
in particular for their victimization. Nonetheless, it is still a cultural
code and therefore still powerful.

A compelling illustration is that made by Edwin Schur in *Labeling
Women Deviant: Gender, Stigma, and Social Control,* written in 1984
when the antirape movement and battered women's movement had
already become well entrenched. Schur's central thesis is that "to be
female has itself amounted to occupancy of a 'deviant' status" (1984, p.
18). For Schur, women's deviant status is a master status that colors
every interpretation, such that women perpetually face the identity
dilemma he calls being a "deviant-either-way" or "stigma-either-way"
quality (1984). Schur explains: "Women are often subjected to norms
that contradict one another. As a consequence their efforts to conform to
one standard may be treated as deviance when viewed from the standpoint of the opposing one" (Schur 1984, p. 55).

Schur gives the example of emotional display:

> If a woman does not openly demonstrate stereotypically "feminine"
> qualities—warmth, nurturance, supportiveness, and so on—she is like-
> ly to be defined as "cold," "calculating," "manipulative," and "mascu-

line." Correspondingly, her direct display of emotions that are prized or accepted in men—such as coolness, assertiveness, aggressiveness, and anger—will usually be disapproved. (1984, p. 55)

This is similar to the situation of victims, who also are damned-either-way. If a victim does not act helpless, passive, and overwhelmed by her attacker, she is likely to be defined as a "participant" or "precipitant." She is too much the agent, and so we "disapprove." But if she does help-lessly and passively submit, she is too much the victim, of whom we also disapprove. Women who both fail and succeed in meeting the expectations for victims can be discredited. "Thus," Schur says, "women are in a double bind as regards the dominant gender prescrip-tions: they are vulnerable to labeling if they violate them but also if they conform" (1984, p. 205).

Schur's assessment is a nice exemplar of the power of a gender cul-ture that sometimes blatantly and sometimes more subtly holds women constrained by sets of expectations, feeling and acting rules that they cannot avoid nor successfully negotiate. Despite the gains made by the second wave of the women's movement, which by then may have been in abeyance (Taylor 1989), women still faced (face) a cultural logic that defines them as inherently deviant. Schur's characterization also has significance for the cultural code in which I am most interested, that of agency. It is not a coincidence that the survivor movements are the cre-ation of women and of people victimized as children, because in a sys-tem of stratification along the dimension of gender, women and children are at risk of being abused with relative impunity.

In addition, they are more susceptible to being held to account, despite their greater risk. Schur points out that women who are victims are treated as deviant, or blamed for their victimization, if they have violated gender norms (even as men "conform" to them by victimizing). Schur notes that the concept of victim precipitation "has had an unfortu-nate effect in reinforcing the already-existing tendency to hold the woman responsible in rape cases" (1984, p. 153). This "already-existing tendency" is the result of enculturation into a society in which women rank lower than men, a hierarchical social arrangement that surrounds and permeates the condition of victimization and the "activities of indi-viduals and groups making assertions of grievances and claims" (Spector and Kitsuse 2001 [1977], p. 75) about victimization.

Each of the survivor movements whose members contribute to this book sprang from the same culture, then, an individualistic, rights-ori-ented, therapeutic, and gendered culture. They emerged during a time when some have argued that individualism was conquering communalism (Lichterman 1995) and when others feared that the gains made by the women's movement were succumbing to the depoliticizing side-effects of "therapeutic ideology" (Armstrong 1994). This is the context for what has happened since the consciousness-raising groups of the early 1970s, when women met together to consider and construct their collective identity. When we look at how they and their critics used the vocabularies of which I write to construct blameworthy, blameless, and pathetic victims, and now, admirable survivors, we do well to keep these things in mind. Certainly, they must have influenced the rhetoric of the antirape movement, the subject of the next chapter.

3

The Antirape Movement and Blameworthy Victims

This chapter is about the social construction of rape victims in the early 1970s, processes that are characterized by what Ken Plummer has called the "debunking of myths" in which "stories are not formulated in isolation, but through antagonisms" (1995, pp. 66, 68). This notion succinctly captures a cornerstone of this project. The feminists who launched the first of what would be many social movements against sexual violence began their insurgency with "subversive stories" (Ewick and Silbey 1995) that drew their power through first articulating the dominant cultural narrative, the cultural code of agency. They realized that the victim in the then dominant account of rape was a *blameworthy* victim, because people assumed that she had made choices that ultimately brought her victimization on herself. In the victimology of the time, there was even a category of the crime called "victim precipitated rape" (Amir 1971). In order to refute this conception, activists strategically foregrounded it, specifying it in ways that allowed them to argue against it.

Early activists believed that the culture they organized themselves to change was one in which most people believed that women could not be raped against their will. Or bystanders thought that a victim's actions encouraged the rapist, or even just that the victim should have known better than to make herself vulnerable. If this was how people thought about women who reported being raped, they would not have been very sympathetic or helpful toward them. They thought of them not as victims, but as the agents of their own sexual downfall. To change this, activists set out to establish victim precipitation as a myth and redefine the rape victim as a true victim, not the instigator of her own undoing.

In what follows, I focus on the typification of rape victims in the early antirape movement through the articulation of myths and the "truths" with which activists countered them (Pleck 1987; Plummer 1995). This myth debunking is identity work (Snow and Anderson 1987) on many levels. It manages the deviant identity of victims who violate expectations (Goffman 1963) that they not be agents, it accomplishes victimization through the social problems work (Holstein and Miller 1997) of establishing innocence and enabling audiences to match up individual victims with their typifications, and it frames the collective identity of rape victim in a way that is consonant rather than dissonant with the cultural code of agency (Williams 1995; Benford and Snow 2000).

I will use texts to illustrate several themes. I begin with the accounts of the victims themselves, as they describe what happened to them and how they defined and responded to the situations in which they found themselves. I do this to show the ways in which their words reflect their own understanding of the cultural code of agency and to show the ways in which they are reflexively aware that their actions before, during, or after the rape may cast doubt upon their victimhood. It is clear that they feel the need to explain; they are conscious that there will always be a "valuative inquiry" (Scott and Lyman 1968) because no matter what they do, it will violate some normative expectation (Goffman 1963). Some of these accounts are accompanied by the commentary of the activists who first presented them and who collaborate in the accomplishment of victimization (Holstein and Miller 1997).

Next, I shift my focus to the activists as storytellers; I examine their characterization of cultural narratives as myths, imagery that the movement used as the basis for its "subversive stories" (Ewick and Silbey 1995). Then, I attend to the vocabularies of victimization in their claims-making, first in excerpts from the victim narratives (Davis 2005b) that activists used to redefine rape victims as true victims (again with the commentary of the activists when possible). I finish with vocabularies of victimization I found in another kind of narrative. In addition to dramatizing "victim-blaming" in the larger culture, activists built on the research of social scientists such as Amir (1971) to further establish the ideology from which they wanted to distinguish their own typifications. Here, I include examples from other survivor movements as a segue into Chapter 4 on battered women and the construction of *blameless* victims.

Accounting for Victimization: Rape Victims and the Cultural Code of Agency

We will see that antirape activists create images of victims, especially through the process of describing myths and then telling stories that refute them. Here, my aim is to show that the activists have recognized and tapped into a potent force for understanding and reconfiguring victims in emotionally and culturally resonant ways. I do this by first showing how the stories of victims account for their presumed agency, or "choice," even when there seems to be no explicit doubt or questioning. In the testimonies from *Rape: The First Sourcebook for Women* (Connell and Wilson 1974), and from Brownmiller (1975), and in the interviews in Russell (1975), the victims repeatedly appear to be fending off potential discrediting of their claims with explanations of why they were unable to fend off their attackers. Some of these accounts appear to recognize that victims, not rapists, will be on trial, and others allude to myths the activists who have collected and published the victims' stories make explicit.

Thus, in the excerpts I have chosen, victims talk about blaming themselves for provoking the rape and about their understandings that people believe that women cannot be raped against their will. In addition, appearing throughout the stories of the rapes are women's explanations of why they stopped resisting or did not resist—because only resisting attests that the act was against their will. In some cases, they were asked directly by an interviewer whether they resisted, and women who had told family or friends or reported their rapes to police probably had been asked about this prior to telling their stories in the speak-outs (Sheehy 1971; Connell and Wilson 1974; Brownmiller 1975) and in interviews (Russell 1975). In some of the excerpts, however, the accounts seem spontaneous, and all the more suggestive of the ways in which the women *expect* to be asked "Why didn't you know better?" and "Why didn't you scream?" and "Why did you stop struggling?" and, dominating, "Why didn't you resist?" After showing how women refer to the cultural code of agency, I will illustrate responses to each of these potentially discrediting questions in turn. These are what I call "vocabularies of victimization."

"They Would Think I Had Consented":
Articulating Adherence to Cultural Codes

In these examples, most of which come from the first speak-out on rape (Connell and Wilson 1974), the women show a clear belief in two things. First, they acknowledge that their relative or presumed lack of resistance to the rape will cause people to question whether what occurred was really rape rather than consensual sexual intercourse. Second, they then conclude that if their experience is judged as something other than rape, they will be judged as something other than victims. Merged with the attitudes they faced or imagine are descriptions of their failure to struggle and, almost always, the reasons why not.

Here is one woman matter-of-factly describing first her reaction to waking up one night gagged, her hands pinned, and a razor held to her throat and then what the doctor who examined her said to her. At first, she thought she was having a bad dream:

> And then I did get my wrist cut slightly and realized that I was risking my life and that I'd better hold still and let the man have intercourse with me. . . . [The doctor] then explained to me that it was impossible for me to have been raped as I wasn't *ripped* around the vaginal area. I had long since ceased to be a virgin and intercourse does not normally rip the vagina open, but men hold it is true that a woman cannot be raped against her will. (Quoted in Connell and Wilson 1974, p. 39; emphasis in original)

Although this woman's restriction of mythical thinking to men suggests that she did not herself believe this, nonetheless she provides an explanation for why her genitals do not reveal the injuries associated with resistance and, therefore, that she *was* in fact raped.

Here is another example, this one from the Rape Tape made by the New York Radical Feminists, in which they videotaped four rape victims who were sharing their stories with one another (Connell and Wilson 1974). This woman, who is identified as "Jane" in the transcript (the use of quotation marks in these accounts indicates a pseudonym), was raped by a man she had just met. She had gone to his apartment to evade police officers threatening to arrest her for violating curfew. Afterwards, Jane faced less-than-sympathetic relatives, including her mother:

> It was just so awful that [my mother] didn't believe that I had gotten raped. She was sure I had asked for it. . . . They so totally brainwashed me that I wasn't raped that I actually began to doubt it. Or maybe I really wanted it. People said a woman can't get raped if she doesn't want to. I thought maybe I should have fought harder, maybe I should have kicked him in the balls, maybe. (Jane, quoted in Connell and Wilson 1974, p. 51)

Jane refers to the notions that "women provoke rape" (held by her mother) and that "women cannot be raped against their will" (what "people said"—presumably, others whom she told, but also reflective of more general attitudes). Taken together, these ideas are powerful enough to cause her to question her own victim status and whether she had sufficiently resisted enough to demonstrate the falsity of the accusations directed against her.

Here are the words of another woman on the tape, "Sandra," who was raped by a man showing her an apartment. She had her "very young" daughter with her at the time, who had fallen asleep on one of the beds, and Sandra submitted to the rape in part because she was afraid to wake the little girl—in which case, she might be injured as well. Afterwards, she said,

> the thing that made me the most upset, I think, was the feeling I got from the others whom I had talked to that the one thing I didn't have the right to do was try to save myself by submitting to the rape, that really, you know, a virtuous woman fights back and screams. That was the time I really did get angry at the cops. I said, "God damn it, he threatened me with a weapon." (Sandra, quoted in Connell and Wilson 1974, p. 52)

The "others" Sandra refers to are "your friends and your doctors and your policemen and the district attorney" (quoted in Connell and Wilson 1974, p. 51), and the maxim she describes brings together the beliefs that (1) "good girls do not get raped" and (2) "women cannot be raped against their will." And as in the first example, Sandra provides her audience with an explanation, one in which the implication of choice is refuted by the circumstances, the use of a weapon.

Also as in the first example, Sandra makes it clear that she herself does not subscribe to these ideas. But because the cultural code of agency is so pervasive, it is common for victims to find reasons to doubt their own victimization, through attributions of choice to themselves, linked directly to the code. Here is a woman who at the time of her interview insisted on anonymity, and who is called "Ms. X" by Russell (1975). Of her experience, in which she was held prisoner in her home for forty-eight hours by a gun-wielding stranger, Ms. X had this to say:

> Up until this time, I had believed that rape was impossible if a woman didn't want to be raped, that it could only happen to a woman who submits. But I found out how a woman could be totally immobilized. . . . I don't want anyone to know what happened to me. . . . I thought that other people thought the way I had thought, that this couldn't happen to a woman who didn't want it, or allow it. . . . I assumed that if I told people, they would think I had consented, because they would think as I had thought. (Ms. X, quoted in Russell 1975, p. 19)

Of this story, Russell concludes that it "illustrates the impossible position in which the myth that women cannot be raped places rape victims. . . . When even a highly respectable 'privileged woman' like Ms. X chooses [not to tell anyone] rather than face people's reactions to her experience, something is terribly amiss in our society" (1975, p. 24). By saying "up until this time," Ms. X indicates that she no longer believes all women, even rape victims, have the choice whether to "submit," even as she discloses her understanding of others' acceptance of the myth.

Finally, in a perhaps more subtle example, Sandra says:

> The experience itself was—I felt it had this awful quality to it because I did want more than anything else just to haul off and just punch him in the teeth. I really wanted that. I was furious at him. I don't see how anybody could possibly relax and enjoy rape when it's actually happening. (Sandra, quoted in Connell and Wilson 1974, p. 46)

Brownmiller has a list of "deadly male myths" and includes this one: "if you're going to be raped, you might as well relax and enjoy it" (1975, p. 346)—the myth, of course, being that such a thing is possible. That Sandra makes the comment without explanation or qualification further evidences its taken-for-granted character at the time she told her story.

Also, as in the previous testimonies, Sandra includes an account for her decision not to physically resist: in her situation, it would have been "stupid." This leads me to the next theme in victims' accounts, which is related to their understanding that they must explain why they did not scream, continue struggling if they had begun to, or decide not to struggle at all. Why must they explain? The need for an account resides in the cultural code of agency, which gives sustenance to the idea, once again, that women cannot be raped against their will. In the excerpts that follow, victims show their awareness that if people believe in women's "will," they will assume that a compliant victim is instead a willing participant. If so, a rape did not occur.

"The Reason I Didn't Scream":
Seeking Help and Lack of Agency

In stories from all the sources I have been citing, rape victims provide accounts for why they did not scream. Screaming is an action that presumably signifies an effort to get help. The cultural code of agency implies that if a potential rape victim does not actively seek help, she must not really want or need assistance. That is, she is not really afraid—and what is happening to her is not really rape. Consider the following comment from Jane, raped as a young woman by the person from whom she sought refuge. After noting that "we must have fought for a very long time . . . [until] my muscles sort of just gave out," she adds: "I was very afraid of screaming because he seemed sort of scared anyway. I was very afraid that he would have a knife and that he would stab me. So he raped me" (Jane, quoted in Connell and Wilson 1974, p. 50). Like so many of these stories, there is more than one explanation embedded in just a few lines, each addressing the issue of "consent," what I call choice or agency. Jane *did* resist until she was no longer physically capable of doing so, and she interpreted screaming as an act that might escalate the violence. These constraints (exhaustion and danger) cause her to be assaulted ("So he raped me"), but the content of her story and its phrasing tell us that she was not at fault.

Similarly, in her testimony at the 1971 speak-out, a woman who was followed off the train and taken at gunpoint behind a building in her "poor, ghetto neighborhood" where it was "very dark, no lighting and you never see any police," reports that

> while he was taking me there—with this gun on me—a car passed and there were people around the block and nobody noticed anything. With this excitable man with a gun I didn't appeal to anybody in the cars or the people I saw down the block because I had no confidence that anybody would help me anyway and that people would just mind their own business. I would end up getting shot and nobody would help me if I tried to call out to anybody. (Quoted in Connell and Wilson 1974, p. 42)

Like Jane, whose assailant "seemed sort of scared," this woman refers to the emotional state of the rapist and the danger of escalation it represents. She also describes a context in which asking for help would have been futile. And even so, she feels it necessary to remind the listeners that she had a gun pointed at her at the time. Another woman, "Ms. Fujimoto," was asked directly by Russell's interviewer, "Did you scream at all?" Ms. Fujimoto replied in the negative, adding that "his reaction was so extreme, I thought he was crazy enough to kill me after he raped me" (Russell 1975, pp. 38–39).

Here is a testimony reported in both Connell and Wilson (1974) and Brownmiller (1975):

> I knew there was no getting out of this since there were three of them and one of me, and it was about 1 A.M. and no people were around. . . . I was told to be quiet or I'd be buried here and no one would know. Since I chose to save my life, I decided to cooperate. (Quoted in Connell and Wilson 1974, p. 33; see also Brownmiller 1975, p. 401)

This woman provides a number of reasons for being "quiet": she was outnumbered, no help was available, and her attackers threatened her with murder. Her last sentence captures the way in which the cultural code of agency interpenetrates even the direst of situations. In her own words, she "chooses" and "decides," but at the same time, she articulates the overwhelming constraints within which she does so. From this, we can infer that she, as did (and still do) other victims, believes that it is better to be raped than killed and that reasonable fear of the latter excuses submitting to the former.

Here is one more victim, "Helen Rawson," explaining her failure to scream, which I am arguing is an *expected* response to the threat of rape. Helen was raped by her date. He accosted her suddenly in her apartment after she let him in to retrieve a package he had left in her refrigerator. With no warning, he knocked her to the floor and quickly overpowered her while she was still in shock at being assaulted. After describing how he "very rapidly" penetrated her, Helen says, without pausing,

> I had the feeling that I could get seriously hurt if I screamed. . . . I couldn't remember ever being knocked down by anybody. I was really stunned, and my arm was hurting. So when he said, "I don't want to do anything to you. Don't scream," I took his advice. Also, I had been listening to my mother talk to women, and eavesdropping on all those women's conversations, and the wisdom that I had gleaned from them was that if you see no way out, relax, and hopefully you get away with your life. (Helen Rawson, quoted in Russell 1975, p. 90)

In addition to the fear of escalation reported by the other victims I have quoted, Helen, like them, also suggests that her compliance is strategic in a confrontation with the highest possible stakes. And that she provides this kind of account further emphasizes its necessity, in a culture in which we expect that "real victims" scream and otherwise resist. What is even more important, we presume that women are free to *make* this choice. It is interesting, too, that Helen refers to women's "wisdom" rather than myth when she uses the term *relax* but links it directly to saving her life rather than "enjoying" what transpired.

"I Said, I'm Going to Fight My Way out of This": Claiming Resistance and Its Futility

Some victims assert that they resisted but to no avail, an interesting kind of account because it acknowledges the necessity of including "fighting against the rapist"—a crucial element of a believable rape story. At the same time, this kind of vocabulary of victimization explains that the rape occurred anyway, so it is a direct refutation of the idea that "women cannot be raped against their will" (Connell and Wilson 1974; Brownmiller 1975).

In this first example, a bar waitress went on what she thought would be a "couples" date with a man she had previously dated and two of his friends. The other women never materialized and she found herself out in the country with the three men. At the 1971 speak-out, she told this story and said,

> I kept struggling with my date and finally when he said, "If you don't let me, I'll put it in your mouth," I gave in. Then the other fellows took their turn. I wasn't screaming or fighting anymore. I just wanted to get it over with and not have anything worse happen to me. (Quoted in Brownmiller 1975, p. 394)

This woman uses the words *kept struggling* and *finally* to suggest the length of her efforts to resist, as well as providing her rationale for eventually submitting; something "worse," in this case, oral rape, would happen. Here is a similar account, from "Ms. Gomez," who was raped by a friend's acquaintance after meeting him at a nightclub. Afraid to leave her friend alone, she ended up alone with the rapist in a motel room. Here is an exchange between her and one of the interviewers in Diana Russell's book:

> *Ms. Gomez:* Then he started hitting me. He knocked me across the room. I tried to fight. I said, I'm going to fight my way out of this, which I tried to do. I tried to push him away, and I tried to pick up something to hit him with.
> *Interviewer:* Did you scream?
> *Ms. Gomez:* I did. But he was a lot stronger than me. I realized this when he hit me across the room. There wasn't any way I was going to be able to fight my way out of it. I'd just get beat up more. So I said, "Oh, yeah, OK." (Quoted in Russell 1975, p. 60)

Like the previous victim, Ms. Gomez tells her story in a way that first establishes the fact of her resistance. Although the question from the interviewer could be simply a request for more detail, Ms. Gomez responds as if she were required to explain why her resistance and her seeking for help were insufficient. Fighting would be futile and escalate the violence, and her "Oh yeah, OK" vividly evokes her resignation.

"Susan Gage" was raped by her lover after he verbally abused her for much of a day while the two of them had "dropped acid." When he told her he "wanted to fuck," she said she didn't want to,

> but he started shoving and knocking me down and pulling my clothes off. And every time I said no, he shoved me down and hit me. He'd never been violent with me before. I was already so psychologically destroyed that I didn't know what to do. I was in a strange place, and he was all I had, and he was my only way of getting back to my home. I tried to resist, but he was getting more and more violent. Then he just turned me over on my stomach and fucked me in the ass. (Susan Gage, quoted in Russell 1975, p. 83)

While it is unclear in this excerpt that when Susan says "resist" she means physically as well as verbally, the excerpt has many elements of a vocabulary of victimization. Susan tells the interviewer about the violence and suggests that it was shocking because it was the first time her lover had been violent. She was also emotionally vulnerable, "psychologically destroyed" by the verbal abuse he'd inflicted on her (she also reported that earlier in the day he spat on her when she started having a bad reaction to the drug and was asking him for help). Moreover, she reports, she was stuck there, dependent on him for transportation, and she implies that the violence was escalating the more she resisted. The last sentence, spare and graphic both, creates a sense of inevitability; "he just" signifies the pointlessness of resistance.

A final illustration comes from Susan Griffin's *Ramparts* article, a story she refers to as a "classic tale of rape" (1971, p. 35). For my purposes, it is equally quintessential, revealing yet again how a woman accounts for being raped despite fighting back. In this case, the rapist was an acquaintance who knew the victim was alone that night. In her story, the unnamed woman describes how she had "locked all the doors," but the man entered anyway. She says that "I thought I would try to talk my way out of it," but this strategy did not work. "I did fight him—he was slightly drunk and I was able to keep him away," she says, as if in answer to an unspoken question. She adds, "I had taken judo a few years back, but I was afraid to throw a chop for fear that he'd kill me," a statement that also suggests the "valuative inquiry" (Scott and Lyman 1968) as well as its counter. When the man threatened to kill her, she says, "Then I started saying my prayers. I knew there was nothing I could do." Ultimately, she was strangled into unconsciousness and raped. "I *did* scream, though my screams sounded like whispers to me," she says (Griffin 1971, p. 35; emphasis in original). Again, she uses the interesting "I did" turn of phrase, once more as if she were being asked, "Why *didn't* you?"

"It's Much Better to Get It Over and Done With": Accounting for "Extraordinary" Compliance

The previous examples of how rape victims describe their victimization and the reasons they were unable to defend themselves against the rapist are strongly suggestive of victims' understandings of what society expects from them. Rape victims know that many, if not most, people will assume that they had consented to the rape. They appear to be acutely aware of the victim-blaming attitudes the antirape movement was working so hard at the time to make salient. Thus, they explain why they did not seek help, and why they stopped struggling or were raped anyway, accounts that demonstrate their unwillingness to have sexual intercourse with their rapists and their right to claim "victim" identities despite what "others think."

This phenomenon, of aligning their responses to rape with societal expectations of innocent, nonprecipitating, nonconsenting victims, appears even more vividly when victims do not fight back at all or act in ways that might be less explicable. Sometimes there is no physical resistance, or the victim may seem overly rational, or she may act afterwards in ways that could call her victim status into question. In the case below, cited in both Connell and Wilson (1974) and in Brownmiller (1975), the victim ironically defines her eventual acquiescence as meeting the expectation to be properly feminine.

> Testimony: I was raped when I was 17 by my fiancé the night before he was due to ship out with the Navy. Up to then I had tried to be everything he wanted according to the religious, social and moral codes by which both of us had been raised. I played the expected role throughout our engagement, deferring to him in judgment, in conversation, even in the way I dressed. I was sedate, demure, humble, submissive—and a virgin. He kept begging me to have intercourse and I kept saying, "No, not yet. It's not right." On our last date he pushed me in the back of the car and held me. I just gave up. After all, wasn't I supposed to defer to him in everything? (Quoted in Brownmiller 1975, p. 393)

Brownmiller uses this testimony to illustrate a case that is unlikely to be taken seriously, because of police "assumptions that a woman who has been raped by a man she knows is a woman who 'changed her mind afterward'" (Brownmiller 1975, p. 393). I have chosen it because it is a story that reveals the coercive power of cultural codes as well as their ability to be drawn upon as explanation for a victim's lack of resistance. Here, the woman frames herself as lacking agency mainly because she is acting appropriately according to her assigned gender role and thus implies that she is just as trapped by what she is "supposed to" do as by being "pushed" and "held." Note, too, that she indicates lengthy verbal resistance ("he kept begging me" and "I kept saying") prior to her surrender, a feature of her story that reinforces the inevitability of what happened.

Below are examples of rape victims describing the feelings and thought processes that, as they delineate them, seem calculated to show that their lack of resistance was a result of paralyzing fear or a rational choice under the circumstances. Here is an excerpt Brownmiller specifically uses to illustrate the "theme" of women's not fighting back because "they were convinced they were going to die": "Testimony: Did you ever see a rabbit stuck in the glare of your headlights when you were going down a road at night? Transfixed—like it knew it was going to get it—that's what happened" (quoted in Brownmiller 1975, p. 400). Brownmiller makes the argument that "rape in exchange for life, or rape in exchange for a good-faith guarantee against hurtful or disfiguring physical damage . . . dominates the female mentality in rape" and that "most women believe that they are confronting the realistic possibility of death" (1975, p. 401). I am not claiming that she is wrong about this; I am suggesting in addition that (1) "most women" are cognizant of the need to provide an account for their paralysis or passivity given the cultural code of agency, and (2) for them, it appears that they believe that their explanations should draw from the appropriate cultural "toolkit" (Swidler 1986).

Here is more of Sandra's story (the woman I quoted earlier raped by a man showing her an apartment, who was angry that the people she told about the rape expected that "a virtuous woman fights back and screams"). Of her decision to submit, she says:

> He was over six feet and I think even if I'd had any kind of weapon I wouldn't have put up a struggle because I was really stuck in there. I was afraid of getting beat up myself. I was afraid of the baby waking up. I was afraid of her being beaten up too. So I did allow him to rape me. . . . I was terrified because he just did seem like a real sicky. And so I didn't—I was like lying low. I was not going to shake him up any more. . . . The only degrading thing that I can recall about it is simply not being able to hit the guy. I just really wanted to sock him in the teeth. But there are circumstances in which it would be stupid to struggle because it would make things worse. (Sandra, quoted in Connell and Wilson 1974, pp. 45–46)

Sandra provides a multitude of reasons for "allowing" the rape, an interesting phrasing that again belies the compelling case she is making for a situation in which she believed she was "stuck," that is, essentially with no other options available. Yet again, a rape victim confronts the assumptions of choice, with the victim-blaming implications that follow.

Here is more of Ms. Fujimoto's narrative, from which I quoted earlier regarding her account for not screaming. I have included several excerpts, because her story so powerfully captures Brownmiller's "fair exchange of rape" as an emotional process, a rational process, and an account. Ms. Fujimoto was raped by a classmate when she was a college student, after a picnic at the beach. When she helped him carry the picnic supplies back to his apartment, he closed the door, tried to kiss her, and then quickly picked her up, "swung" her on a couch, and removed her pants.

> And then he got on top of me and said that he wanted to make love with me. I said I didn't want to. He said that if I would just let him do it once, he would get up and let me go. I kept saying no, no, no, no, no, no. But he took his pants off and said that he wouldn't hurt me. I thought he was going to hurt me. I thought he was going to kill me or something. I guess I was really hysterical then in a rational sort of way, because I wasn't screaming or anything. The reason I didn't scream was that I thought that he would beat me up or really hurt me if I did. So I submitted. (Ms. Fujimoto, quoted in Russell 1975, p. 37)

It is significant that as Ms. Fujimoto describes the rape, she discusses her submission; it is a critical component of her story. A little later, the interviewer asks her to "describe the degree to which [she] resisted," and Ms. Fujimoto replies:

> When he approached me, trying to force kisses on me, I tried to push him away. . . . When he was on top of me, I tried to push him off, but he was so heavy I couldn't move him. The main resistance I offered was verbal. I pleaded with him for ten minutes. I said, "Please, Joe, don't. Please, please, don't!" I was pleading with him, almost crying, but he'd just wait until I would stop, and then he would try again. And I would plead and plead and plead with him. I wasn't screaming. I was not yelling. But he was dead set on what he was going to do. (Ms. Fujimoto, quoted in Russell 1975, p. 38)

Clearly, this is a description not only of verbal resistance but also of the futility of physical resistance.

Then, when the interviewer asks Ms. Fujimoto to "describe the amount of force he used," she answers in terms of her perceptions of her lack of "a chance" (which can be read as "a choice") and her pondering of a strategy that would "get her out of the situation" (implicitly, alive).

I tried to push him away, but when I realized that I couldn't push him away if he didn't want to be pushed, I got very frightened. When he threw me on the couch, I knew I didn't have a chance, and I just wondered how I was going to get out of the situation. The look in his eyes, that's what scared me! It was very menacing, and he looked so moody, like some sort of maniac. It convinced me that I shouldn't do anything more to try to get away. (Ms. Fujimoto, quoted in Russell 1975, pp. 37–39)

She emphasizes her fear of force based on the rapist's actions *prior* to the rape, because once on the couch, she did not resist him further, and suggests that "the look in his eyes" alone was "force" enough to compel her. Then, when asked what advice she would give other women on handling a rape situation, Ms. Fujimoto elaborates:

I would tell them not to resist, if they don't think they can overcome the person physically, and if they know they'll get physically hurt if they do resist . . . the reason it's not traumatic for me now is that I didn't get beat up. I wasn't subjected to any physical violence per se. I didn't get hit in the face, I didn't get slapped around, and I didn't get thrown around that much. I think that's what I wanted to avoid more than anything. I wasn't concerned about losing my virginity, because I wasn't a virgin. The thing I was most interested in at that time was my own personal security, physical and mental. I figured that if I got pregnant, I could always get an abortion. So what I did was resist as much as I could verbally. People have told me that I should have resisted more physically. Some people have said that if I had, he wouldn't have thought it worth the trouble. . . . I think that everyone's got their own opinions. I think it's much better to be physically raped than mentally raped. It's much better to get it over and done with, and not be traumatized for the rest of your life. (Quoted in Russell 1975, pp. 42–43)

In this excerpt, Ms. Fujimoto justifies her own submission by saying that she would advise others to do the same and links her decision not to resist directly to what she got in exchange—she "didn't get beat up" and thus was less "traumatized" by her experience than she could have been. She also brings in the evaluative audience, the people who questioned her, which allows her to further rationalize the *"quid pro quo,"* as Brownmiller puts it (1975).

The last of the rape victim excerpts I include here explain behaviors that are potentially even more problematic for victims than "not resisting." First, there is Helen Rawson, whom I quoted earlier regarding the first time she was raped by an acquaintance, explaining why she did not scream. In this example, she is telling the story of the *second* time she was raped, by another fellow college student. She had initially planned on "going to bed with him" after their first date but begged off because she felt ill. "Graham" then pushed her against a wall:

> And I've got a losing battle against the wall. I'm pushing him, but obviously I'm not going to overcome him. I realized I was losing the battle, my pants were coming down. I imagine I could have screamed and hollered. I didn't, because of an inhibition about scenes. I'm slowly overcoming it with age, but it was there. Also, I'm not convinced screaming and hollering is protection. I also recall having the feeling that I'm not going to give this jerk the satisfaction of beating me in a fight, damn it. I could see that my struggling was exciting to him. . . . So I said, "Okay, Graham, look, let me get my diaphragm on, because I don't want to get pregnant from something like this." He let me do that, and then I just lay there, and he came in. If you look at it from a time point of view, I got rid of him faster than had we struggled more. (Helen Rawson, quoted in Russell 1975, p. 93)

Of this story, Russell says:

> Many would not regard Ms. Rawson's experience with Graham as rape. Her relative lack of resistance, combined with her being able to insert a diaphragm to protect herself from pregnancy, doesn't fit the "classic" definition. However, the classic definition of rape would seem to apply only to a minority of cases. (1975, p. 95)

The "classic definition" that Russell refers to is the cultural narrative depicting only women who resist until the end as true victims, the women in what Brownmiller calls "the legend of virgin martyr whose inspirational value rests on being beautiful, chaste, and dead" (1975, p. 370). It depends for its meaning upon the cultural code of agency, which requires Helen to justify her "choices," and thus her story takes the form, yet again, of an account. Like the other stories I have recounted, she begins with a description of resistance, followed by her realization that it was futile. She mentions screaming and provides two reasons why she did not, as well as another reason for truncating her struggle. She explains to Graham, but at the same time to the reader, why she needed to use birth control.

Finally, she concludes this section of her story with one more reason for her "relative lack of resistance": her ordeal is over with sooner. And all this comes in response to the question, "How old were you at this point?' (Russell 1975, p. 92)—not, as in some cases, to a direct prompting. Women do not need the "valuative inquiry" (Scott and Lyman 1968) to be *explicit* to respond to it. The inquiry is inextricable from the story of rape, where women's "consent" is always the salient issue.

In the following testimony, the victim reports that after being "pushed to the roof" and being told to take off her clothes, "I didn't fight because I was too scared." She tells about her clothing being ripped from her body and of being shoved and falling to the concrete. She "kept telling him" that she was a virgin, but he raped her anyway. "Finally," she states,

> he stopped, and said that he believed me when I said I was a virgin. I said, "But that's what I've been telling you all along." He said, "Women lie, but I believe you." I thanked him because I was scared and didn't want him to get angry. He brought me to the door leading to the top floor, opened the door for me, and said, "Maybe we should try later? May I call you tomorrow?" I wanted to kill him, but I had to say, "Please do." (Quoted in Connell and Wilson 1974, p. 34)

She concludes her discussion with: "I felt guilty and ashamed and didn't report it" (Connell and Wilson 1974, p. 34). She does not explain this last; perhaps it is because she was introduced to the man at a bar and had been "high and kissing" him before attempting to leave. But it is within her relating of her interactions *afterwards* that she interjects another "because" and then "but I had to"—that is, the reasons behind her politeness toward the man who raped her.

The last illustration here is similar; I excerpted part of this victim's testimony as an example of accounting for not screaming (the man had a gun; it was a neighborhood where no one would help anyway). As in the previous example, before the rape, the victim "was trying frantically to talk him out of it." During and after the rape, the rapist was "solicitous," which the victim characterizes as a "contradiction," a term that foreshadows and could well describe the following:

> And after the rape it was as though he was doing two contradictory things at the same time. He was asking me did I want a cigarette, was I all right and he didn't hurt me, did he? . . . I don't know (pauses), I was trying all kinds of stuff. I was acting as though I was concerned for him because he had this gun, right? . . . And okay, we were having this discussion and the chummy thing about the cigarettes afterward, but every once in a while he would say, "Are you going to tell anybody?" and he still had the gun. "You're not going to tell anybody, are you?" and like these threats in between this friendly conversation. And so I said, "No, I'm not going to tell anybody. No, I'll certainly not." I still continued not to be angry and to be concerned for him and his welfare, I mean to ward off his killing, which he easily could have. I said I was married and I said no, I couldn't tell anybody. (Quoted in Connell and Wilson 1974, p. 43)

As in the previous testimony, this excerpt reveals the more subtle dimensions of the cultural code of agency, through broadening the behaviors that it calls into question. Not only does the victim feel the need to tell the audience about the gun when she describes her lack of resistance prior to the rape, but she reminds them of the gun when she relates her lack of resistance afterwards, her "chummy" interactions before it was finally over. The implication is that true victims fight back even after the rape has ended and that if they choose not to do so at *any* point, they must give us once again the reasons why they did not.

In sum, when we look closely at what rape victims say about being raped, we see that for almost any action they take or do not take, they provide an explanation. I take this to be evidence of the power of culture to shape storytelling and of the utility of examining accounts to understand more about the cultural frameworks within which the stories are told. Scott and Lyman argue that accounts are the "manifestations of the underlying negotiation of identities within speech communities," which means that that they are "situated" in the way Mills (1940) describes. That is, they are "standardized within cultures so that certain accounts are terminologically stabilized and routinely expected" (Scott and Lyman 1968, p. 46). Because accounts have to be "appropriate," their form sheds light on the "background expectations" (Garfinkel 1964) that undergird a particular social order. It is when a norm is violated that it becomes salient; when victims account for their victimization, we come to a sociological awareness of the cultural code of agency. As members of a victim-blaming society, activists possess this awareness and have been able to make use of their familiarity with the "rules," as I show below. First, I will show how claims-makers in the antirape movement framed the code as myth, followed by how they illustrated this.

Ideology and Mythology:
It's Not Her Fault No Matter What

The accounts above allude to myths about rape; activists make these explicit. Gail Sheehy's 1971 *New York* article describing the NYRF speak-out was the first publication to come directly from early antirape activism. Although she does not use the term *myth,* she attributes women's failure to make citizen's arrests or police reports of rape to "our public rape psychology, which emerged as the real villain at the speak-out" (Sheehy 1971, p. 26). This is clearly a cultural reference, and Sheehy adds: "The reason is simple. The woman feels, or is made to feel, like the criminal. . . . The conditioning is there long before a rape victim—one who dares to report it—is confronted by police attitudes" (1971, p. 28). Then Sheehy further emphasizes her point:

> Even the Radical Feminists faced terrible resistance from the ten women asked to be official speakers. "My rape wasn't important enough," protested one. "We'll really infuriate men with this issue," said another woman, pleading against the speak-out. "If you think it was bad before, they'll really be out to rape us now!" Every one of the women suffered from the private conviction that in some way it must have been her fault. (1971, p. 28)

By using the language of psychology and conditioning, Sheehy suggests that victim-blaming "attitudes" are so pervasive that victims are afraid that others will judge them as they judge themselves.

The very title of Susan Griffin's *Ramparts* article that same year alludes to culture: she calls it "Rape: The All-American Crime" (1971). In the article itself, she refers to "belief [that] has no basis in fact" (that rapists are insane), "another canon in the apologetics of rape" (that rape is natural), and "this culture's concept of rape" (that rape is universal). Then she discusses the "myth that men have greater sexual needs" and the "companion myth about the nature of female sexuality . . . that all women secretly want to be raped" (Griffin 1971, p. 27). *Beliefs, canons, cultural concepts,* and *myths:* all of these terms suggest broader understandings that are both widely shared and false. Griffin directly links women's agency and lack of victim status in the following: "The theory that women like being raped extends itself by deduction into the proposition that most or much of rape is provoked by the victim. But this too is only myth" (1971, p. 28). Like Sheehy, Griffin's essential point is that the cultural image of the victim as someone who, as Griffin puts it, "has wished for her own fate" (1971, p. 27)—that is, as responsible and thereby blameworthy—is myth, and therefore untrue.

Noreen Connell and Cassandra Wilson, members of the NYRF who edited *Rape: The First Sourcebook for Women* (1974), put the theme of myth at the foreground of their introduction to the chapter presenting the "personal testimony" from the 1971 speak-out, explaining that the women who told their stories "did so to counter the myths that (1) women cannot be raped against their will, (2) women really want to be raped, and (3) women make false accusations" (Connell and Wilson 1974, p. 27). In their introduction to *Against Rape,* Andra Medea and Kathleen Thompson state forcefully:

Rape, we must remember, is a crime; women are the victims of it. Rape is *not* the just desert of any woman who dresses casually, goes out at night, or lives alone. And women do not *cause* rape by their growing freedom. . . . Rape victims have been treated as the guilty ones, the outcasts, for too long. (1974, pp. 5–6; emphasis in original)

This discussion of what rape is *not,* that is, that it is not the fault of victims, is followed first by a page with the epigraph "Nice girls don't get raped" and then the chapter "What Is Rape?" Here, after defining rape as "any sexual intimacy forced on one person by another," Medea and Thompson discuss the simultaneous lack of serious discussion of rape and the prevalence of the subject in comedy, fiction, pornography, drama, and films. They conclude:

It is the fantasies of rape, or perhaps we should say the myths, that have formed our ideas of rape because they are all we ever hear about it. . . . It is not surprising, really, that a myth should fail to match a reality. What is surprising is that, in the case of rape, myth has for so long been served up to us as reality. (Medea and Thompson 1974, pp. 16–17)

Clearly, there are common, related themes in these excerpts: that predominant cultural understandings condone rape, that these "fantasies" are myths, that they lead to blaming victims, and therefore, because they are myths, women are not to blame. To change this "rape culture" (Herman 1984), activists sought to educate women and the public and to replace myths with "facts" (Pleck 1987).

In 1975, Susan Brownmiller, in a chapter from *Against Our Will* called "Victims: The Setting," uses all capital letters for the following, the only place in the book in which she chooses this format:

"ALL WOMEN WANT TO BE RAPED"
"NO WOMAN CAN BE RAPED AGAINST HER WILL"
"SHE WAS ASKING FOR IT"
"IF YOU'RE GOING TO BE RAPED, YOU MIGHT AS WELL RELAX AND ENJOY IT" (1975, p. 346)

Brownmiller refers to these as the "deadly male myths of rape," puts them "at the heart of our discussion," and then analyzes the uses to which men put them, especially to shift blame from rapists to victims:

The popularity of the belief that a woman seduces or "cock-teases" a man into rape, or precipitates a rape by incautious behavior, is part of the smoke screen that men throw up to obscure their actions. The inse-

curity of women runs so deep that many, possibly most, rape victims
agonize afterward in an effort to uncover what it was in their behavior,
their manner, their dress that triggered this awful act against them.
(1975, p. 347)

Even though the myths are "preposterous," Brownmiller argues they
must be "dealt with, because the popular culture that we inhabit, absorb,
and even contribute to, has so decreed" (1975, p. 348). In the wide-rang-
ing discussion that follows, she sets out to document the mythology in
books, psychiatry, movies, poetry, religion, popular songs, television,
and tabloid journalism.

Finally, Diana Russell's book, *The Politics of Rape*, was published
the same year as Brownmiller's (1975). In her introduction, Russell tells
of her changing understandings of rape following her attendance and
protest of the highly publicized rape trial of Jerry Plotkin in San
Francisco in 1971. Russell reports that this "began the destruction of
some myths about rape that I shared with most other people" and that
"the idea of collecting women's accounts of their rape experiences
occurred to me during the trial as the most obvious way of correcting
my own and others' ignorance" (1975, p. 12). She then, like each of the
other author-activists, uses a series of narratives to illustrate the "realities of rape" (Winkler 2002). This brings me to the next section, in
which I show how activists present victims' stories and frame them.

Vocabularies of Victimization:
Representations of Blameworthy Victims

Activists who write and speak about social problems can make effective
use of the personal stories of victims (Loseke 2003), and this is a common journalistic technique (Johnson 1995) for evoking emotions as
well. In the following, I will show how the authors I have been citing
use vocabularies of victimization to illustrate and refute the myths they
have articulated, all of which, these activists assert, cast women as provoking rape and therefore as not really victims. By showing that victims
are the ones facing accusations (that is, that victims are constructed as
blameworthy), and that this is based on false assumptions, activists
reconstruct victims as innocent, and worthy of sympathy, instead
(Holstein and Miller 1997; Clark 1997; Loseke 2000; Dunn 2004,
2005).

It is interesting that the activists take pains to establish that even the victims *most* likely to appear at least partially at fault are not responsible, a strategy that seems linked to the roots of the antirape movement in the women's liberation movement. Put differently, Griffin (1971) and her colleagues attempt to reconcile victims' agency with the cultural codes that dictate that victims should play no part in their victimization, in an era in which the larger movement sought to portray women's rights to choose and to be agents of their own fates. To accomplish all of this, they present stories that depict victims rather than rapists as the ones "on trial" and that show how victims are blamed for being foolish, or fallen women, or feminine, or feminist. Although I have separated these categories for analytical purposes, we will see that the images are often intertwined.

Who's on Trial?

In Griffin's groundbreaking article on rape (1971), she tells the story of the victim in the Plotkin rape case. Jerry Plotkin was a San Francisco jeweler accused of a rape and kidnapping, in which he was alleged to have used a gun and accomplices. According to Brownmiller, who has written a memoir of the times, the victim was "raked over the coals for her prior sexual activity" and Plotkin was acquitted, a verdict that Brownmiller said "had a galvanizing effect on Bay Area women" (1999, pp. 204–205).

Griffin precedes her description of the trial with a discussion of the cultural dictate that a "fallen woman" cannot be raped: "what has once been defiled cannot again be violated" and "a woman who does not respect the double standard deserves what she gets (or at the very least, 'asks for it')." Then, after a terse description of the accusations, Griffin tells how the victim was effectively discredited by Plotkin's defense attorneys, who "through skillful questioning fraught with innuendo . . . portrayed the young woman as a licentious opportunist and unfit mother" (1971, pp. 30, 32). Here is Griffin's report of the testimony:

> MacInnis [the defense attorney] began by asking the young woman (then employed as a secretary) whether or not it was true that she was "familiar with liquor" and had worked as a "cocktail waitress." The young woman replied (the Chronicle wrote "admitted") that she had worked once or twice as a cocktail waitress. The attorney then asked if she had worked as a secretary in the financial district but had "left that employment after it was discovered that you had sexual intercourse on a couch in the office." The young woman replied, "That is a lie. I left because I didn't like working in a one-girl office. It was too lonely."

Then the defense asked if, while working as an attendant at a health club, "you were accused of having a sexual affair with a man?" Again, the woman denied the story, "I was never accused of that."

Plotkin's attorney then sought to establish that his client's accuser was living with a married man. She responded that the man was separated from his wife. Finally, he told the court that she had "spent the night" with another man who lived in the same building.

At this point in the testimony the woman asked Plotkin's defense attorney, "Am I on trial? . . . It is embarrassing and personal to admit all these things to all these people. . . . I did not commit a crime. I am a human being."

At this point in her representation of the testimony, Griffin continues ironically:

The lawyer, true to the chivalry of his class, apologized and immediately resumed questioning her, turning his attention to her children. (She is divorced, and the children at the time of the trial were in a foster home.) "Isn't it true that the children have a sex game in which one gets on top of the other and they—"That is a lie!" The young woman interrupted him. She ended her testimony by explaining "They are wonderful children. They are not perverted."

The jury, divided in favor of acquittal ten to two, asked the court stenographer to read the woman's testimony back to them. After this reading, the Superior Court acquitted the defendant of both the charges of rape and kidnapping. (Griffin 1971, p. 32)

Of note is the contrast set up by the structure of the narrative, which mirrors the questioning and answering of the cross-examination, naturally, but does so in a way that highlights the inquisition of the victim and the injustice of the questioning. Having illustrated the "innuendo," Griffin argues that sexist society holds that women who are not monogamous cannot be raped and, thus, that "the courts and the police, both dominated by white males, continue to suspect the rape victim, *sui generis*, of provoking or asking for her own assault . . . the police tend to believe that a woman without a good reputation cannot be raped" (1971, p. 32).

Russell, whose observations of the trial prompted the research that culminated in *The Politics of Rape,* begins her introduction to the book with the following:

"Who's supposed to be on trial here?" Gillian Jones, exasperated and bewildered, put the question at the end of a long day of testifying at what she had previously thought was the trial of Jerry Plotkin. . . . On the day that Ms. Jones, a twenty-three-year-old secretary, complained that she appeared to be the one on trial, she had been subjected to numerous questions about her present and past sex life, the sex life of her lover, and even the sexual play of her two children.

Ms. Jones, like millions of other Americans, was not at that time having a monogamous relationship with a man. Irrelevant as this was to establishing whether or not Ms. Jones was raped by Jerry Plotkin, his attorney's chief line of attack was to try to show that she had a background of promiscuity and emotional instability. . . . Ms. Jones' multiple sexual relationships were used as damning evidence against her claim to having been raped. (1975, p. 11)

Russell, like Griffin, uses the story of Plotkin's victim as a typifying example (Loseke 2003), one in which the notion of "victim on trial" is inextricably linked to the image of the social problem of rape—and of victims' moral worth—that she is constructing. Antirape activists provide narratives and analyses of how the criminal justice system treats raped women. Again, they first establish that victims *are* blamed, in order to make the oppositional statement that victims should *not* be blamed. And as they do, they sometimes emphasize the "liberated" (agentic) characteristics and behaviors they want us to allow women, while still conceiving of them as victims.

Brownmiller's use of this strategy is most evident in her discussion of legal aspects of rape, including the infamous Hale maxim, included in instructions to juries until "as late as 1973 in California" (1975, p. 414). Hale, a seventeenth-century English judge, said: "Rape is an accusation easily to be made and hard to be proved, and harder to be defended by the party accused, tho never so innocent" (quoted in Brownmiller 1975, p. 413). Brownmiller says that this is "based on the cherished male assumption that female persons tend to lie" (1975, p. 414). Her wording ironically signifies the opposite. Then she offers "testimony" from the speak-out transcriptions:

Testimony: The suspect was arraigned but the grand jury refused to indict him. I think it was because they saw that my boyfriend was of another race. That made me a bad woman, right? (Quoted in Brownmiller 1975, p. 416)

Testimony: They trotted out my whole past life, made me go through all these changes, while he just sat at the defendant's table, mute, surrounded by his lawyers. Of course that was his right by law, but it looked like I was the one on trial. (Quoted in Brownmiller 1975, p. 417)

Testimony: I don't understand it. It was like I was the defendant and he was the plaintiff. I wasn't on trial. I don't see where I did anything

wrong. I screamed. I struggled. How could they have decided that he
was innocent, that I didn't resist? (Quoted in Brownmiller 1975, p. 418)

Each of these descriptions of victims' experiences in the courtroom
illustrates misplaced blame and through this, the victims' innocence.
Following this last testimony, Brownmiller discusses the preponderance
of jury trials in rape cases, in which juries are "allies" not of the victims,
but of the defendants. Why? According to Brownmiller, because they
are "composed of citizens who believe the many myths about rape, and
they judge the female according to these cherished myths" (1975, pp.
418–419). To further illustrate, Brownmiller cites the following characteristics of victims inappropriately taken into account by juries, citing a
study by Kalven and Zeisel (1966):

Women who went drinking with the offender prior to the act, women
who were "picked up," women who knew the offender previously and
women whose past sexual history was judged to be "promiscuous"
were assessed by juries in this national study as having taken an undue
risk and morally not worth a conviction for rape. (Quoted in
Brownmiller 1975, p. 419)

Brownmiller, then, like Griffin before her and like Russell, uses
excerpts from courtroom testimony to convey vivid images of women
on the stand, unjustly cast into the role of the accused rather than the
accuser. And also like Griffin and Russell, she shows that it is women
who do not meet the sexual (double) standards of the time who are
called to answer for their "crimes." With this, I turn now to additional
excerpts from victim narratives (Davis 2005b) that activists use specifically to emphasize the myth that certain kinds of women provoke
rape.

The Fallen Women: "Bad Girls Are Asking for It"

As Brownmiller's citation of Kalven and Zeisel (1966) suggests, by
telling us that some women are considered "as having taken an undue
risk," activists draw on the cultural code of agency to show that victims
who make choices, even "bad" choices, are nonetheless victims. The
second chapter in Russell's book is entitled "The Virgin and the Whore,"
followed by a chapter called "Good Girls Get Raped Too," a juxtaposition that further emphasizes the moral categories that overarch perceptions of victims. First, I will illustrate the ways in which activists tell
stories of discreditable women to emphasize the myth that women of

questionable character cannot be raped. Then, I will turn from the "bad girls" to the "good girls" in the stories at hand.

"The Virgin and the Whore" is the story of a young girl, "Rosalind," who had been having sex with multiple partners, sometimes on the same occasion, and was eventually violently gang-raped by more than twenty men. Russell includes Rosalind's history of what many people might call "promiscuity" because she believes that it "illustrates very dramatically what the costs of a sexual double standard can be, and how it can relate to rape" (1975, p. 26).

Here is how Russell ends the interview, with Rosalind's response to being asked how she reacts to people who think that rape is "usually provoked."

> I get very hostile and I want to kill them. In spite of the fact that I knew a lot of the people who raped me, it was rape. I did not ask for it! I did not wish it! I did not bring it on myself! So when people say that I get very, very hostile. Because no matter who you are or what you've done, that's not something that you're asking for. There may be a whole lot of psychological problems when we end up allowing ourselves to be sexually abused, but that's not what we wanted. I believe we're just truly taken advantage of. (Quoted in Russell 1975, p. 33)

Russell argues that women who are seen as "bad" can be raped with impunity, claiming that "loss of virginity, particularly at a young age, can evoke in males a 'no holds barred' approach" and that the sexual double standard "bolsters a rape mentality" (1975, pp. 25, 33). But because the interview includes the graphic and horrific details of the gang rape as well as the earlier promiscuity, the story also can be seen as an example of debunking the myths that "bad girls cannot be raped, because bad girls are asking for it."

Russell begins a chapter called "Sexual Liberation Without Sex-Role Liberation Can Get You Raped" with this epigraph from the interview that follows: "Then there's the question of can a hippie prosecute a rape? All hippies believe in free love, so, you know, who cares if someone rapes a hippie?" (1975, p. 208). Medea and Thompson had earlier attributed an increase in rape to a "meeting of the old sexual mores and the new" (1974, p. 44). Russell, who cites them in her bibliography, similarly argues that a latent consequence of the sexual revolution was increased vulnerability for women who choose "the male model of sexual liberation." This is because "in a sexist society a promiscuous woman means a 'bad' woman, hence one that a man can feel less guilty or even righteous about raping" (1975, p. 209). Or, as Medea and Thompson had put it, "rape does not apply to a woman who falls outside the limits of respectability; she is just a free lay" (1974, p. 45).

Although Griffin shows how the victim in the Plotkin case was being constructed as a "licentious opportunist and unfit mother," it is interesting that in another story she tells about a topless dancer, hired for a bachelor party.

> At the high point of the evening the bridegroom-to-be dragged the woman into a bedroom. No move was made by any of his companions to stop what was clearly going to be an attempted rape. Far from it. As the woman described, "I tried to keep him away—told him of my Herpes Genitalis, et cetera, but he couldn't face the guys if he didn't screw me." After the bridegroom had finished raping the woman and returned with her to the party, far from chastising him, his friends heckled the woman and covered her with wine. (Griffin 1971, p. 30)

Here, she makes no comment about the actual problematic characteristics of the victim, her occupation, and her sexually transmitted diseases. It is as if Griffin is saying that they are irrelevant, a subtle way of emphasizing the "bad girls" myth. And like each of the other activists quoted, Griffin's central argument is that no matter how much a rape victim deviates from our standards of "moral worth" (Loseke 2003) when we are judging her complicity, she is nonetheless an innocent.

Feminine, Foolish Women: "She Should Have Known Better"

A different type of innocence is represented in the tales of women who are morally worthy but are raped anyway. Sometimes, they are simply behaving as women have been taught. On other occasions, they are (wrongly) blamed for errors of judgment that—if they do not provoke rape—at least make it possible. Sheehy's article is titled "Nice Girls Don't Get into Trouble," the irony of which becomes clear as she makes the argument that it is women's socialization into femininity that makes them vulnerable. For example, she reports that one victim at the speak-out "didn't scream for fear of seeming rude" (Sheehy 1971, p. 28). Both Griffin and Brownmiller make similar points. Griffin says: "If being chaste does not ward off the possibility of assault, being feminine certainly increases the chances that it will succeed" (1971, p. 33). Brownmiller offers that in an encounter based on force, "[a woman] is unfit for the contest. Femininity has trained her to lose" (1975, pp. 402–403).

It is when Brownmiller borrows from criminology and introduces the "new concept in criminology" of "victim precipitation" (1975, p. 394) that the image of victims making careless or even reckless choices emerges. Like all of the images I have discussed, it is an image that serves as a foil. Activists construct the blameworthiness against which they stake their position that (contrary to myth) women do *not* provoke rape. Here is how Brownmiller introduces the topic:

> When a potential victim and a potential offender are thrown together by the forces of fate, a complete process is inexorably set in motion. Each word, act and gesture on the part of the potential victim serves to either strengthen or lessen the resolve of the potential rapist, and hinder or help him to commit his crime. (Brownmiller 1975, p. 394)

This assertion would seem to confer responsibility upon the victim. Brownmiller goes on to state, however, that the argument that "had the victim behaved in a different fashion the crime in question *might have been avoided*" is "part *a priori* guesswork and part armchair-detective fun and games." It "rests," she says, "in the final analysis on a set of arbitrary standards" (1975, p. 394; emphasis in original). Brownmiller then immediately presents the following:

> Testimony: We were living in Houston. My husband was at work and the children were at school. It must have been, oh, two o'clock in the afternoon. The doorbell rang and this young man asked if he could rake the leaves for a couple of dollars. I said, "Wonderful, how terrific." Well, he raked the leaves and then he came to the door and asked if he could have a glass of water. I was quite conscious of being alone in the house, but a glass of water did not seem like an unreasonable request. He finished the water and then asked for another glass. Of course I gave it to him. We were chatting about this and that and I wanted him out of my living room but I didn't know quite how to cut him off. I was also wondering if perhaps I was overreacting to be a little nervous. He was black and I had been very involved in the first civil rights movement, and after all, he was only asking for water. He must have had four glasses of water before he made his move. He broke my jaw in the process. (Brownmiller 1975, p. 395)

Brownmiller comments afterward that some men might think this "precipitant." More would so consider a hitchhiker, she adds, and a rapist would consider either type of action "tantamount to an open invitation." Her own opinion is that both women are "insufficiently wary" but not at all "provocative or even mildly precipitant" (1975, p. 395). Note, too, that the story Brownmiller has chosen to support this argument is one in which the victim takes care to *account* for her mistake, presenting the situation as commonplace and reasonable and explaining why she saw her own sense of danger as "overreacting." This victim is an ordinary housewife, and her thought processes as she describes them likely make sense to many readers.

Diana Russell uses a more dramatic case, that of a victim who was a hitchhiker, to argue against the idea that women's bad decisions provoke rape. In a chapter called "Females as Prey," she writes of the "vulnerable and naïve fourteen-year-old girl," "Carla," who was raped six times within two weeks while hitchhiking across the country. By framing Carla in this way (as a child and thus an innocent), Russell confers moral worth upon her before the details emerge of her continued hitchhiking despite repeatedly being raped. Russell seems to anticipate the likelihood of blame under the circumstances, asking: "Why are females prey? And is the prey really responsible for predatory behavior?" (1975, p. 44). Carla is presented as both blaming *and* excusing herself. She says:

> After each rape I felt dirty and disgusting, and I really hated myself for having allowed myself to get raped. I thought I was really dumb, really stupid to have fallen again for a man's lies. I felt like I'd brought out the worst in these men just by being an available female body on the road. I felt like if I hadn't been on the road, these men would have continued in their good upstanding ways, and that it was my fault they'd been lowered to rape me. But now I see that there was nothing I could have done in the situation, and it wasn't my fault. (Quoted in Russell 1975, p. 48)

In this last comment, Carla refers to her lack of choice regarding hitchhiking, which is her only means of transportation: "Hitchhiking alone is sometimes necessary. I feel like all the hitchhiking I've done, which is about nine thousand miles altogether, was absolutely necessary. I didn't have any friends, male or female, who could have hitchhiked with me, so that was the only way I could go" (quoted in Russell 1975, p. 50). Russell cannot help but note, it seems, that the victim's "casualness about what many would consider horrendous experiences is one of the most remarkable aspects of this case" (1975, p. 51). But Russell uses this to argue that even though all women face the choice of taking risks or not, they nonetheless should not blame themselves. She then suggests that there may be good reasons to hitchhike and compares the risks with that of driving more generally, pointing out that we "do not argue that drivers who have automobile accidents are similarly 'asking for it' or don't mind having accidents all that much, if they continue to drive afterward" (Russell 1975, p. 51).

It appears that Russell is aware of how outrageous this story might seem to some readers—"Why, after being raped once, then again and again, Ms. Stewart did not change her behavior . . . is often the only question asked in such a case" (Russell 1975, p. 44). Russell provides us with the "valuative inquiry" (Scott and Lyman 1968), which implies that the victim made choices that led to being raped and therefore she was responsible. Russell also gives the account, which provides a culturally appropriate rationale.

The "only question asked" is Russell's reference to the cultural code of agency. We assume that people can choose, so why did she choose so badly? The cultural code is also implied in the arguments she and Griffin make, that women should be free to *take* risks, sexual and otherwise, without being raped as punishment. Freedom is the valued attribute, after all. The "good reasons to hitchhike" are part of a vocabulary of victimization that *narrows* the notion of choice. Russell says that "systems of public transportation in this country are often inadequate, and hitchhiking means being mobile," and she points to the dangers of public transportation. She deflects blame, and by doing this, potentially evokes sympathy for women whose victim identities we might doubt. Says Russell:

> It is widely believed that a person's taking responsibility for what happened to her is the first step in seeing that unpleasant things stop happening to her. However, taking personal responsibility for things that are not one's responsibility, like being a rape victim, is indicative of self-hatred, and self-hatred is the biggest block to change. (1975, p. 51)

Russell takes care in her framing of Carla's story to make it clear that the blame we assign to victims is misplaced, and because it is misplaced, it is also problematic.

Thus far, my central argument has been that in order to create images of rape victims with which victims would identify and for whom audiences would feel sympathy, the antirape movement set up the "blameworthy victim" as a typification to refute, using the strategy Ken Plummer calls the "debunking of myths," in which "stories are not formulated in isolation, but through antagonisms" (1995, pp. 67–68). And activists accomplished this by drawing upon the first-person stories of victims "speaking out" and linking them explicitly to the myths they delineated. By bringing our attention to the ways in which women *are* blamed, and then arguing that they should *not* be blamed, the antirape movement sought to foster a fundamental change in the cultural attitudes toward rape victims that deny their victimization.

I began with the accounts of victims in part to show that these attitudes are *real* and not merely a useful social construction. Activists were fighting a problem at its source, and the stereotypes they castigated spring from what Plummer has called "much wider human stories that are part of our heritage and which are emotionally identifiable by listeners and tellers" (1995, p. 55). The "wider" narrative is the cultural code of agency, a way of thinking about people and their actions built on the presumption of choice in every circumstance. To reveal the pervasiveness of this shared understanding, I drew on the same first-person stories the activists did, showing how rape victims almost always offer "accounts" (Scott and Lyman 1968), using what I term (following Mills 1940) a "vocabulary of victimization" (Dunn forthcoming). Rape victims and activists are cognizant of the stereotype and the expectations linked to the cultural code, and all of their stories show their understandings of the myths and their apprehension of the logic behind them.

The Legacy of the Movement:
The Blameworthy Victim as a Foil

From here, I have one more argument, building on those already discussed. Donileen Loseke (2001) has used the phrases "stock characters" and "formula stories" to suggest that activists engaged in constructing social problems and urging social change tend to draw upon widely shared understandings. These are so widely shared, in fact, that they are formulaic as well as melodramatic. Victims people these stories, and they have stock characteristics, including innocence and lack of culpability. In the case of the blameworthy victim, activists argue that she is the chimera, but she is such a potent foil that she becomes in her own way a "stock character." That is, activists in many survivor movements, not solely the antirape movement, can draw upon her image to contrast it with the innocence and lack of agency they must construct if they are to get people to care and to act. In this, they have been helped by social science, which provides more "evidence" of how widespread victim-blaming is. Below, I show how survivor movement claims-makers have drawn on sociology, psychology, psychiatry, and the criminological subdiscipline of victimology to argue the pervasiveness of the blameworthy victim. These activists seek to show that her image is not clung to merely by the ill-informed masses but also by those who should know better.

Victimology and the Concept of "Victim Precipitation"

Social scientists generally consider victimology to be a subdiscipline of criminology (Karmen 2007; Kennedy and Sacco 1998). From its inception in the 1940s, victimologists have been interested in whether some people are more likely to be victimized than others and, most controversially, what role victims might play in their own victimization. The latter interest has not always been controversial; in fact it is only since the advent of survivor movements' focus on the implications of looking at victims' behaviors and attributes that it has become so. Below, I examine in chronological order how activists have engaged victimologists in their victim construction efforts. I begin with the antirape movement, followed by the battered women's movement, ending with the incest survivor movement.

Victim precipitation and rape. In 1967, Menachem Amir published an article in the *Journal of Criminal Law, Criminology, and Police Science* entitled "Victim Precipitated Forcible Rape," followed by a book in 1971, *Patterns in Forcible Rape.* In these publications and others, Amir used data from Philadelphia police files to show that some rapes occurred because the rapists interpreted the victims' behavior as an invitation to have sex or an excuse for rape. Amir's work has become quite well known in victimology, where it is usually presented as controversial (Kennedy and Sacco 1998) and as the "most widely cited (and most heavily criticized) study of victim precipitation in rape" (Karmen 2007, p. 246).

At the time the antirape movement was beginning to make claims and to mobilize, Amir's book was one of the few research reports available to activists; Medea and Thompson comment that the "world of academic research tells us almost nothing" and that "sociologists supply one book," citing *Patterns* (Medea and Thompson 1974, p. 14, citing Amir 1971). Brownmiller similarly refers to Amir's Philadelphia study as "the only other study of victim precipitation in rape" in addition to the National Commission on the Causes and Prevention of Violence she cites first (1975, pp. 396n–397n).

It is interesting that Medea and Thompson do not use Amir to argue the myth of victim precipitation but rather to claim that the rapist is likely to be someone known to the victim and that the majority of rapes are premeditated rather than impulsive (1974, pp. 29, 31). Nor does Brownmiller emphasize this aspect. Although she cites Amir eight times, like Medea and Thompson, she does so in all but one instance to make other arguments, for example, that rapists are ordinary men, and many victims are children or young girls (Brownmiller 1975, pp. 196, 302). Where she does mention Amir on victim precipitation, she does so in a footnote but has the following to say, including a quote from him that was to become notorious:

> Amir believed that a stunning 19 percent of the rape cases he examined had been victim precipitated and he concluded that for the women in question, "The contingencies of events may not make the woman solely responsible for what becomes an unfortunate event; at least she is a complementary partner, and victimization is not, then, a wholly and genuinely random affair." From my reading of the Philadelphia study I gather that Amir's definition of precipitation was more generous [than the Commission's study] to the rapists. (Brownmiller 1975, p. 397n)

Clearly Brownmiller does not give much credence to Amir's finding. Just prior to this footnoted comment, Brownmiller additionally makes the argument I described earlier in this chapter, that some women may be "insufficiently wary" but that no women actually provoke rape. Just after that, however, she begins her discussion of the question of whether women can "fight back successfully," again citing Amir, this time suggesting that resistance is the better choice (1975, pp. 395, 397–399). Overall, her treatment of the criminological conceptualization of victim precipitation is somewhat equivocal.

This is less true of Russell (1975), who includes three works of Amir's in her bibliography but does not cite him directly. She likely alludes to him, however, when arguing that women as well as men believe the "myth that women cannot be raped" and that "one of the consequences is that women, like men, often 'put down' raped women by disbelieving them, or by seeing them as responsible for their victimization. (The increasing popular field of victimology contributes to this view)" (Russell 1975, p. 259). Then, in her final chapter, under the heading "Research," Russell asserts that "so much of the research on rape has been done by men who subscribe to the common cultural myths about it that we need to start almost from scratch with the research" (1975, p. 293). Like Medea and Thompson (1974) and Brownmiller (1975), Russell links the ideas of social scientists to widely held beliefs and myths.

Victim precipitation and battered women. The earliest scholarly work attributed to the then new field of victimology was research on battered women. Most often cited by early activists and feminist social scientists in the battered women's movement are Schultz (1960, cited by Dobash and Dobash 1979, Pagelow 1981), Snell, Rosenwald, and Robey (1964, cited by Dobash and Dobash 1979, Pagelow 1981, Schechter 1982), and Gayford (1975a, 1975b, cited by Dobash and Dobash 1979, Pagelow 1981). The victimologists serve as the scientific antagonists against which these scholars and other claims-makers explicitly positioned themselves.

This is what the Scottish scientists R. Emerson Dobash and Russell Dobash had to say about Schultz (1960). After asserting "obvious weaknesses in the evidence presented to support [his and other victimologists'] premises," they cite his statement (1960, p. 103) that "the victims in spouse assaults can always be assumed to have played a crucial role in the offense, and may have directly brought about or precipitated their own victimization." They summarize Schultz's finding that the four men he interviewed were "submissive" and "passive," and the three surviving women "masculine, outspoken, and domineering" (Dobash and Dobash 1979, p. 195). They comment:

> At one point he actually referred to the relationship as "the husband-*wife* (victim-*offender*) relationship" and the tenor of the article certainly would support the contention that despite the murder of one woman and long histories in which women seemed to get the worst of a violent relationship, Schultz regarded the women as the offenders . . . blame is placed squarely upon the women in the violent scenario. (Dobash and Dobash 1979, p. 195; emphasis in the original)

Of Schultz's theories (and the others whom they cite), Dobash and Dobash say that they have "continued popular appeal" and refer to them as "myths" and research in which "by some magical mental twists and contortions come these extraordinary conclusions" (1979, pp. 193, 197). They conclude that

> women [are blamed as] the primary source of violence, including that which is directed at them. Although such ideas have never been adequately supported and have been severely criticized and challenged, the theory has a great deal of appeal in a patriarchal society; it is very popular, especially with the media, and underlies much of the training in the helping professions. (Dobash and Dobash 1979, p. 199)

Once more, there is reference here to ideology, myth, and culture and to the construction of the blameworthy victim as evidence and as ripe for "debunking" (Plummer 1995).

Another source cited by activists as illustrative of the concept of "victim precipitation" is Snell, Rosenwald, and Robey (1964). In an article tellingly titled "The Wifebeater's Wife," Snell and his colleagues interviewed the wives of batterers referred to their psychiatric clinic for evaluation, arguing that the beatings, "some of [which] were quite severe," fulfilled "masochistic needs of the wife" and maintained the "equilibrium" of the family "even though she protests it." Snell and his colleagues described the wives as "aggressive, efficient, masculine, and sexually frigid" and concluded by saying: "One cannot hope to understand the offender and his offense without having some understanding of the people with whom he has to deal" (1964, pp. 110, 112).

Dobash and Dobash call Snell, Rosenwald, and Robey's work "another very interesting twist on the theme of female accountability for the violence that is perpetrated upon them" and say that for the researchers, interviewing wives "may have started out as an expedient but it ended with the problem being made hers" (1979, pp. 195, 197). Soon after, Susan Schechter, historian of the battered women's movement, said of this article that it was a theory of "victim provocation" that well might "keep us scrutinizing the victim's behavior and, as a result, remove responsibility from the man, the community, and the social structures that maintain male violence" (1982, p. 24).

Although sociologist Mildred Pagelow includes both Schultz (1960) and Snell, Rosenwald, and Robey (1964) in her references, she does not cite them specifically. In a chapter called "Common Myths and Stereotypes," under the heading "Battered Women Must Somehow Be at Fault," she discusses the "propensity to search for 'reasons' women cause men to be violent" (1981, p. 64). She mentions Gayford (1975b) and his "assumption of female provocation" and includes this quote from him: "Though they flinch from violence like other people they have the ability to seek violent men or by their behavior to provoke attack from the opposite sex" (Gayford 1975b, p. 197, cited in Pagelow 1981, p. 65). Pagelow also quotes Straus, Gelles, and Steinmetz (1976), who said that "victims often precipitate their fate through verbal aggression" and Goode (1971), who makes a similar argument (1981, p. 65). In keeping with the structure of the chapter, in which Pagelow names and illustrates each "myth" and follows with the contradictory data from her research, she says that:

> Interviewed women did not agree with these ideas; they stated repeatedly that there was no apparent reason for the attacks, that there was

no pattern, nor did all batterings have identifiable precipitating factors. A number of women reported having been asleep when some attack began by spouses just arriving home. (1981, p. 65)

Then, as I will show a bit later, she uses a battered woman's first-person account to exemplify nonprecipitation.

Finally, there is Lenore Walker. Her now famous first book, *The Battered Woman* (1979), cites very few people and none of the people mentioned above. She is clearly alluding to them, however, in her introduction, where after discussing the negative consequences of victim-blaming, she says:

> What gets lost in this *victim precipitation ideology* is the fact that such violence is not acceptable behavior. Although some researchers have tried to understand the offender's behavior by studying the possible provocative behavior of the victim, this research leads up blind alleys and simply encourages continuance of such crimes through its rationalization. (Walker 1979, p. 15; emphasis added)

Then, in her chapter entitled "Myths and Reality," under the heading "Myth No. 2: Battered Women Are Masochistic," she frames as "prevailing belief" that "only women who 'liked and deserved it' were beaten," citing a "study of battered women as recently as twenty years ago" (Walker 1979, p. 20). Another heading is "Myth No. 18: Battered Women Deserve to Get Beaten," under which Walker notes: "The myth that battered women provoke their beatings by pushing their men beyond the breaking point is a popular one" (1979, p. 29). Like Pagelow (1981), Walker sets up the oppositional structure of myth and counter, using the "victim precipitation" narratives of social science as a foil for her own scientific findings.

Victim precipitation and incest. One might suppose that activists in the incest survivor movement had more difficulty finding victim precipitation theories upon which to base their arguments against victim-blaming. We usually believe that child victims are not as accountable as adults, and we take for granted their "purity" and innocence (Loseke 2003). In a far-reaching study of incest survivors' "accounts of innocence," Davis (2005a) shows how activists in the 1960s and 1970s produced a sharp break with previous images of child sexual abuse, hinging upon the discrediting of "victim-blaming" clinical opinion and findings.

Davis read and analyzed all the research on child sexual abuse written before 1977, finding that researchers and clinicians believed incest to be rare, both absolutely and relative to other forms of sexual deviance. Like other sexual offenses, it was considered minor and its effects "relatively slight and short-lived," and if children showed personality disturbances, these were not necessarily thought to be the effect of the abuse, but even in some cases contributing factors (Davis 2005a, p. 37). Victims could be "accidental" or nonparticipants, but some (the number varying by study) were "participant" or "collaborative" victims, those who were "involved in any way, passively or actively, by a provoked or mutual desire, in the initiation or maintenance of the sexual experience." Some were even perceived as seductive, trying to meet "unconscious needs" (Davis 2005a, pp. 38, 40). An "extreme" version of this was the family system theorists' emphasis on "complicit daughters," and Davis concludes that scholars argued that children's "innocence of cooperation or collaboration . . . could not be assumed. In fact, some held that the child could be the instigator or the more sophisticated participant" (2005a, p. 53).

All this changed in the 1970s, with the advent of the child protective movement and the antirape movement, which together constructed a different narrative, a "new story" that not only did not draw on the old story but also specifically made a "moral critique" of it as part of the retelling (Davis 2005a, p. 56). Moreover, Davis locates the origins of the new story in a talk Florence Rush gave at the first New York Radical Feminists Conference on Rape in 1971, not long after the first speakout. According to Susan Brownmiller, who attended both events, Rush (a friend of hers, a social worker and radical feminist who was writing a book on child sexual abuse) "calmly dissected four current academic studies and their 'psychiatric mumbo jumbo'" (1999, p. 203).

Rush's conference paper was subsequently published in Connell and Wilson's *Rape: The First Sourcebook for Women* (1974). First Rush quotes statistics from an American Humane Association study that she characterizes as the "one most sympathetic to child victims of sex crimes . . . [and] the least prejudiced and the most scholarly, most humane and most informative" (Rush 1974, p. 66). Next, she turns to the studies she has chosen to illustrate "general and professional attitudes that relentlessly forgive the adult male offender and indicate little concern for the female child victim" (1974, p. 65). From one of these, "Study Number 2," Rush quotes extensively. She excerpts several different passages back to back, in which the author writes that experts "frequently considered the possibility that the child might have been the actual seducer rather than the one innocently seduced," refers to "the myth of childhood innocence," and concludes that "some degree of participation by the victim group is accepted by all studies" (Burton 1968, cited in Rush 1974, p. 69). Of the cited work, Rush asserts:

> Isn't it strange how victims are held responsible for offenses against them! Our sexuality as women and children is not used to understand us but to psychologically trap us so that, we are told, the woman seeks to be raped and the child wants sexual abuse. . . . The myth of consent, that is, the psychiatric and popular use of ill-defined sexual motivation and acting-out to explain and condone the victimization of women and children, is unforgivable and shameful. (1974, p. 69)

Here we see that Rush, just like her peers in the antirape movement, speaks of victim-blaming myths (ironically, the "myth of innocence"), finds their source in social science and popular culture, and counters with a different image, the "myth of consent" (1974, p. 69). Later, in her book *The Best Kept Secret,* Rush used the same phrase to indict Sigmund Freud in particular and psychology more generally: "The myth of consent . . . is freely cited to explain victim participation and therefore accepts as inevitable the sexual abuse of children" (1980, p. 99).

Rush was the first to publicly tell the "new story" of child sexual abuse and encouraged feminists to include the topic in consciousness-raising groups (Davis 2005a). In 1978, the first speak-out on incest appeared in book form, when Louise Armstrong wrote *Kiss Daddy Goodnight,* a compilation of her own and other women's stories. When she turns to the "incest literature," in a chapter called "Our Brazen Poise," she writes that "everywhere I turned I ran into quotes from a paper"—referring to Bender and Blau (1937), whom Rush had also cited earlier. Like Rush, Armstrong presents several excerpts. In them, Bender and Blau comment on victims' "brazen poise, which was interpreted [by probation officers] as an especially inexcusable and deplorable attitude and one indicating their fundamental incorrigibility," and argue at one point that "the children may not resist and often play an active or even initiating role" (1937, cited in Armstrong 1978, p. 18).

Here is Armstrong's response, immediately following the excerpts cited above:

> Not only that, but we "do not deserve completely the cloak of innocence with which [we] have been endowed by moralists, social reformers, and legislators." If we say daddy threatened to break both our legs if we didn't do it, or if we told, Bender and Blau observe, "the child often rationalized with excuses of fear of physical harm or the enticement of gifts, but these were obviously secondary reasons. Even in the cases in which physical force may have been applied by the

adult, this did not wholly account for the frequent repetition of the
practice." No ma'am. The only possible accounting is that we tried it,
we liked it. (Armstrong 1978, pp. 18–19)

Armstrong's sarcasm notwithstanding, she uses the image of the "initiating" child, whom earlier she has described as "Age three. Age four. Age
five . . . little, little kids," to shock and to shift blame.

Later, Armstrong reflects on the publication of *Kiss Daddy
Goodnight* and her early efforts to find out more about the kind of victimization she had experienced. Of this, she says: "I set out in search of
what was known about child sexual abuse/incest. Remarkably little, as it
turned out, and of that little, much that seemed more perverse proclama-
tion than knowledge" (Armstrong 1994, p. 12). She again mentions the
characterization of girls as "participants" and refers again to Bender and
Blau (1937), calling their work a "classic paper, widely cited, [that]
trumpeted this theme unabashedly" (Armstrong 1994, p. 13). She goes
on to castigate Alfred Kinsey for his failure to recognize the harm and
then cites, as "echoing Bender and Blau et al.," Schultz (1960), whom
the sociologists in the battered women's movement had singled out for
much the same reasons. Armstrong's choice of words to quote? "So
great can the role of the victim be in sex offenses that many should be
considered offenders themselves" (Schultz 1960, cited in Armstrong
1994, p. 20).

In sum, activists in the incest survivor movement have used social-
scientific constructions of blameworthy victims, in this case children,
that are markedly similar and in some cases drawn from the same
sources as their predecessors in the antirape movement and in the battered women's movement. All three movements have focused their
attention on images of victims that make them responsible for their own
victimization, whether it be through intentionally or naively provoking
their dates to rape them, driving their husbands to batter them, or preco-
ciously seducing their brothers, uncles, and fathers. Each movement has
charged that "victim precipitation" is as much a myth as any of the others they have articulated and, perhaps implicitly, all the more dangerous
coming from the "factual" realm of data, research, and science.

In *Telling Sexual Stories,* Plummer writes that the antirape movement's strategy of "debunking myths" was a "major rhetorical ploy":

> It takes all the elements of the old narrative and in one sweep undoes
> them. It provides in effect the tightest, most minimal account of the
> old narrative structure, and by placing them in a frame of "myths"
> immediately discredits them. Indeed, by simply inverting each myth

the key elements of the new story are provided: thus, all women are potentially victims and they never invite rape . . . every position is constructed out of a sense of opposition. (1995, p. 68)

Thus, it makes sense that movements following the antirape movement would employ the same "ploy," if it is indeed "classic," as Plummer puts it.

There are other reasons for movements to take this tack, however, beyond the effectiveness of a form of argument. Because the cultural attitudes at hand are intrinsically victim-blaming, discrediting them is the first step toward evoking audiences' sympathy for victims. This is crucial for creating social change: social problems claims-makers *must* create images of essentially innocent victims if they are to get people to take action to help them. If people hold victims responsible, their response is more condemning than compassionate. The myths are *harmful* myths, and in each movement, activists recognized that they were consequential; friends, family, the public, and law enforcement all were judging victims to the latters' detriment. Therefore, the images had to be refuted, and new images put in their place. In the case of rape, activists delineated all of the ways in which victims were blamed and extended the "person-category" of victim to encompass every attribute and behavior and circumstance for which victims were held responsible. As we have seen, they had a lot to explain, because the prevailing image of "true" rape victims was (and remains) so narrow.

An additional harmful consequence of widespread acceptance of myths, as activists point out, is that victims who believe them blame themselves. They carry a burden of guilt, or fail to recognize their victimization, either of which may prevent them from getting help, from healing, or from empowering themselves in the ways the larger women's movement sought to realize. We see evidence of this in the victims' stories themselves, wherein women explain to invisible but stern moral arbiters their every action and reaction in the face of violence and violation. Further, women who do not identify as victims are less likely to mobilize to help themselves and others; they may not ever see the political in the personal. For all these reasons, then—fostering sympathy, alleviating shame, evoking anger, and shifting blame—activists have used images of the blameworthy, and mythical, "precipitating" victim to create a vision of her opposite.

In Chapter 4, I focus on the next step for activists: the revelation of what some have called the "ideal victim" (Christie 1986). The *blameless* victim is more sympathetic, but here again, there are hazards to negotiate. For the battered women's movement, feminist social scientists took upon themselves the task of explaining a phenomenon that inclined audiences away from sympathy: "battered women who stay." An examination of their accounts, and of battered women themselves, reveals more about the cultural code of agency and its relationship to survivor movement identity work.

4

The Battered
Women's Movement and
Blameless Victims

In the early 1970s, close on the heels of the antirape movement, activists in an emerging battered women's movement worked to increase public awareness of wife beating, change public perceptions of battered women, establish crisis hotlines and shelters for battered women, and change the structural inequalities that activists believed contributed to abuse and constrained women from leaving violent relationships (Schechter 1982; Tierney 1982; Davies, Lyon, and Monti-Catania 1998). In the process, they found themselves butting up against the cultural code of agency, forced by its logic to justify and account for an aspect of victimization that is so closely linked to the phenomenon of battering, as claims-makers defined it, that it can be seen as part and parcel of battered women typifications.

As shown in Chapter 3, activists and victims involved in speak-outs had revealed the experiences of rape victims and dramatized the widespread cultural practice of blaming women for their rapes (Schechter 1982; Brownmiller 1999). Thus, from the beginning, battered women's movement activists believed that audiences had a tendency to blame victims, especially women who were the victims of male violence. Thus, they were already sensitive to the need to manage the deviant identities attributed to the victims they were constructing. They had also defined battering as an *ongoing* process, however, meaning that all battered women could be said to remain in or return to violent relationships. Finally, activists had constructed "wife abuse" as constituted by violence that was extreme and harmful and perpetuated by an abuser who was irredeemable (Loseke 1992). Given this, they were faced with the problem of explaining why battered women might "stay" under such conditions.

In her study of scholarly research and popular media constructions of battered women, Donileen Loseke found that most of the claims-makers she reviewed attempted to explain the "unexpectable behavior of staying in a relationship containing wife abuse" (1992, p. 27), writing journal articles, chapters in books, and magazine articles on this topic. More recently, Nancy Berns reviewed articles in women's magazines from 1970 to 1997 and found that with the exception of battered women's autobiographical narratives, they "generally discuss . . . why women stay in abusive relationships" (1999, p. 89). My own review of scholarly work cited by Loseke (1992), Okun (1986), Davies, Lyon, and Monti-Catania (1998), and Peled et al. (2000), in addition to the other research and activism I discuss, confirms the continuing pervasiveness of this theme (Dunn 2005).

Like their antirape predecessors, activists in the battered women's movement recognized that perceptions of battered women included ideas that could be constituted as myths (see Chapter 3). But in addition to employing myth-debunking (Plummer 1995), they also provided accounts for the behavior that cast the most doubt on battered women's "true victim" status. The identity work (Snow and Anderson 1987) in which they engaged is much like that of the antirape movement and equally reflective of the power of the cultural code of agency. Just as the antirape movement had to argue that rape victims who did not "resist" were not in fact *consenting,* the battered women's movement needed to show that battered women who "stayed" in violent relationships were not doing so by *choice.*

Unlike the antirape movement, however, the battered women's movement was able to draw upon a considerable body of research to employ scientific vocabularies of victimization as well as those in the stories victims told. These "expert constructions" (Loseke and Cahill 1984) have been tremendously influential, and the ways in which sociologists and other claims-makers employed their accounts is something I will illustrate at length. First, however, I begin with some of the stories the victims they interviewed provided, for much the same reasons I did so in the preceding chapter.

Accounting for Victimization: Battered Women's Responses to the Cultural Code of Agency

If it is true, as I will show, that social scientists and others interested and invested in the study of and advocacy for battered women have routinely asked (and answered) the question "Why do battered women stay?" (Loseke and Cahill 1984; Dunn 2004) then we can surmise that this question is rooted in broader perceptions and understandings of victims of violence at the hands of intimates. Once again, to ask this kind of question implies that victims have choices in how they respond to victimization, stemming from our beliefs about free will and individual responsibility. Thus, we require that battered women explain why they did not choose to leave, assuming that this is always an option. Otherwise, we do not count them in the "victim" category.

In Chapter 3, I argued that rape victims appeared well aware of the cultural code and that they told the stories of their rape experiences as if they needed to explain why they did not scream, or resist, or otherwise keep themselves from harm. They offered accounts even when their audience was sympathetic and there was no sign that they were being held responsible, suggesting the power of the myths and of their perceptions of how they might be judged. Because the excerpts of battered women's stories I have chosen are mostly those selected by social scientists to illustrate their research, in the excerpts the women often are responding to explicit questioning, albeit not necessarily "valuative" (Scott and Lyman 1968). Nevertheless, their accounts serve to deflect blame and responsibility (Holstein and Miller 1997) by showing that, in fact, battered women have or see no choice but to stay. In this way, women who discuss their fear, guilt, and helplessness in the face of obstacles to leaving, like rape victims, respond to the cultural code of agency.

"He Said He Would Kill Me If I Left": Trapped by Fear

In Erin Pizzey's book, *Scream Quietly or the Neighbours Will Hear* (1974), she includes letters that were sent to her after she established Chiswick Women's Aid in Great Britain and began advocating for more shelters and help for battered women. Most of these letters illustrate the desperation of victims who appear to be asking her assistance. Nonetheless, they hint at the need for explanation of their circumstances. One woman reported that her husband "smashed my big toe with a hammer one night and I didn't dare tell the hospital the truth in case he got off with a fine or conditional discharge and was free to exact retribution." Another victim tells of asking her husband for a divorce, saying, "My husband now threatens to bash the baby's brains in. He swears I will never leave him. . . . Now I dare not say I want to go or he

starts and I am afraid that either my life or my son's is in danger"
(Pizzey 1974, p. 23). In addition to these accounts for keeping the battering secret and for staying, a third victim tells about her inaction at
one point, well into the violence:

> Between 1969 and 1972 I had suffered twenty-seven brutal attacks,
> including ten which required me to be admitted to hospital for two
> days or more. Once I lost the baby I was expecting. The police came
> on all of these occasions and, while sympathetic, did nothing, except
> to tell me to take him to court. I was reluctant to do this, knowing he
> would attack me seriously, and maybe the result would be fatal.
> (Pizzey 1974, p. 29)

This excerpt comes in the middle of an extended discussion of the
inability of this woman to get help from any quarter, so in a way, it is
part of a fuller account of a marriage in which the victim stayed for
eight years, six years after her husband began beating her. That she
would feel it necessary to explain why she did not go to court at this
time suggests her awareness or experience of others' need to know why
not. Then, after recounting more incidents of violence (and no recourse)
after finally leaving, she adds: "People say that the reason so many
women suffer this sort of treatment is that women don't know their
rights. Well, I knew mine" (Pizzey 1974, p. 29). Her reference to "people" and what they say shows that she is responding to implicit questioning of her "reasons" to "suffer."

Feminist activist Del Martin, who wrote *Battered Wives* (the first
book published in the United States about battered women), quotes a letter written to "Dear Abby" in 1975, in which the writer pleads her case
and says, "I mentioned divorce once and he beat me up so bad I could
hardly get out of bed for two days" (1976, p. 84). Mildred Pagelow, a
sociologist, heard similar things from the battered women she interviewed in the early 1980s. When she asked them directly why they
stayed, she quotes them as telling her they did so because of "fear, mostly, of him and his threats." One said, "I was too afraid to tell him I was
leaving him. I tried once," a poignant suggestion of disaster; another
stated, simply, "I was afraid he would kill me if I left. Also I had no
place to go. My husband is extremely anxious to find me and will go to
any extreme to do so. I'm going to have to be very careful" (Pagelow
1981, p. 72).

Terry Davidson also asked women directly to explain themselves.
She tells the story of "Betty," for example. After the police who came
when her husband forced her into her apartment at gunpoint refused to

stay while she packed for herself and her child, Betty told Davidson: "He would not let me leave then. He made me take off my clothes. He got a .22 pistol, put one bullet in it, and said, 'We're going to play Russian Roulette.'" When asked by Davidson why she didn't leave, she replied, "It is not as easy as many people think. I was a prisoner in my own home" (1978, p. 76). Once again, there is the reference to "many people," an audience that judges and thinks that leaving is "easy."

Finally, there is "The Story of Anne," the prologue for Lenore Walker's first book (1979)—itself an extended explanation for staying that relies on the concept of "learned helplessness." Walker, who claims that the stories she includes in *The Battered Woman* are "typical examples" of what she heard in her many interviews, makes no comment on the narrative other than that she has edited it to protect the anonymity of "Anne." Here is some of what Anne has to say, much of which serves as explanation for why she did not fight back, get help, or leave her violent husband sooner than she did.

> A few times I would slug him back, but I learned that he could hit harder and it was no use because he would use it as an excuse to hurt me by saying, "Oh, you hit me first." . . . He wouldn't let me associate with any of my friends that he didn't like. He would threaten to hurt me if I did. If I'd write letters, he'd want to read them before I mailed them to make sure I wasn't blabbing that he was hurting me. He used the threat of hurting me physically more and more to get me to stay. At one point, he took his belt to me and put welts on me. . . . Anyway, the police came. There was a complaint filed. They wanted to make sure I was O.K. What could I say? I said, "Sure, I'm fine," because I knew if I didn't, he would probably hurt me again. (Walker 1979, pp. 3–4)

Clearly Anne is using the violence and threat of violence to justify her inaction. "What could I say?" invites the reader to share her perspective. She continues:

> [Leaving] was a hard decision that I had trouble making for a long time. . . . I was also afraid that if I left him and told my parents what was going on, later on . . . he would really hurt me if he knew I had told anyone what was going on. . . . Before I left, I had told him that I was going to leave if things didn't get better, and he threatened me with how easy it would be for him to hire someone to kill me and my parents. He said that he had someone following me. (Walker 1979, p. 6)

Here, Anne tells of her fears and their source, adding at one point that "I just can't tell you in words the fear that was instilled in me because of the beatings and physical abuse" (1979, p. 7). My point is that these details are not merely part of the story but are integral to the story as an *account* (Scott and Lyman 1968). When Anne concludes her narrative, she notes that "from listening back over my story, I know that it sounds unreal that anybody would put up with all the things that I did" (Walker 1979, p. 9). By "unreal," I think she means questionable, and her story is told in part to make her actions "real" and explicable.

"I Stayed for the Children's Sake":
Trapped by Tradition

Children enter into battered women's stories in a few different ways; women fear for the welfare of their children if left with their fathers, as children of divorce, and as potentially impoverished as a result. All of these can be characterized as altruistic reasons for staying, and activists appear to have employed them to elevate the moral standing of victims. When victims mention children, they emphasize them as a constraint upon leaving. For example, a woman who wrote a letter to Pizzey says: "I have left my husband in desperation five times but have had to return for my children's sake, as he didn't take care of them in my absence. . . . I need a divorce but can't get one because I don't want to leave my children with this monster as he is cruel to them" (Pizzey 1974, p. 21). Apparently, this woman is unable to take her children with her, and Pizzey asserts the difficulty of doing so; "It is impossible to get rented accommodations on the open market if you have children," she argues, adding that "landlords don't want to take on families because it is illegal to evict them" (1974, p. 30). Given this, the woman above is claiming that her only choice is unacceptable, to leave her children with a "monster."

In the story that Pizzey uses to begin "A Man's Home Is His Castle" and show the obstacles preventing women from leaving, the victim contacted social services after a particularly vicious assault. Earlier, the social worker had advised her to "give [her] marriage a chance." On this occasion:

> They told me to leave the children with my husband. He would look after them. I pointed out that three weeks before he had been placed on probation and had another assault case coming up the following week. I was told that if they felt he wouldn't care for the children (however, they had no evidence to this effect), they would be taken into care. All the children were being affected by this disturbing atmosphere, having witnessed almost every attack upon me, so I didn't think it would be wise to take the social worker's advice. (Pizzey 1974, p. 28)

Faced with this dilemma, the victim reports, "I realized I would have to stick it out" until she had the financial resources to leave and bring the children with her. The incident above is only one of many futile attempts to get assistance that she describes, which together explain why she stayed as long as she did. It is also ironic in tone, as she indicates through juxtaposition of her husband's criminal record with her own concerns for the children's psychological state, the foolishness or insensitivity of the social worker's advice. At the same time, she casts herself as an ordinary mother who must think of her children first.

Also from Pizzey is the following:

> My children scream because he shouts and hits me in front of them. He has thrown me out at night and told me to go but I can't leave the children and it is a job to get a room with children. He said if I went he would get the children in a home. He has never bought them any clothes and I have to keep on to him to buy the children a pair of shoes twice a year and I can't afford to buy clothes for them. You can see what I'm up against. (1974, p. 48)

This story paints the children as victims and as the source of entrapment; their needs will not be met if the woman leaves and this is what she is "up against." Another victim told no one of her injuries and did not allow the doctor or the police to take action. "I said to say nothing," she writes, "as I had two other children at home and it would be terrible when I went back" (Pizzey 1974, pp. 52–53).

Sometimes battered women say that they fear for others' safety as well. Pagelow writes of a woman she interviewed and whose story she uses as a "case study" for illustrating battered women's "pain, fear, frustration, and help-seeking efforts that were largely unsuccessful" (1981, p. 179). "Anne" tried to leave her husband, only to be discovered by unsympathetic relatives who convinced her to return:

> They told me I had to come back, that he was driving everyone crazy. They were all scared of him; he had been going around like a mad man, threatening all of them. He told them he'd kill them, or set fire to their homes, anything, if I didn't come back. They told me it wasn't fair—that he was my problem—that it was up to me to come back and straighten things out with him so he'd leave them alone . . . one day my stepmother called me to tell me that my father was in the hospital—he had been hurt, she said. . . . She said, "You better get home—he needs you." I felt so guilty—they had been working on my guilt for a month. . . . I packed up the children and went back. . . . He [her husband] gave me the worst beating of my whole life the very night I returned. I never tried to leave again; I knew it was hopeless. (Pagelow 1981, pp. 186–187)

This story combines the elements of fear and of concern for others, and Anne uses them in conjunction with the violent consequences she faced for leaving to show that her situation was "hopeless." She explains that she feels guilty, presumably for putting family members in danger—"I figured it was my fault that something bad happened to Dad" (Pagelow 1981, p. 186). Another woman Pagelow interviewed spoke of her husband as "sick" and explained that she stayed because "I loved him and felt I could help him. At one time I really believed he would never hit me again. Then I was afraid he would hurt someone else if I left" (1981, p. 72).

Others described how they felt about the sanctity of marriage and the obligations that follow. One woman, who "suffered her beatings in silence," told Del Martin, "I didn't think I had the right to talk about it. You just didn't let anyone else know about anything like that. There had never been a divorce in our family. No one ever admitted that there was anything wrong in their marriage" (Martin 1976, p. 81). R. Emerson Dobash and Russell Dobash, the Scottish sociologists who wrote *Violence Against Wives: A Case Against the Patriarchy* in 1979, quote a woman who said she stayed "because I was quite sure there was something in me that could make the marriage work. I was quite positive about that." Another woman the Dobashes interviewed explained, "I wanted to try and make a go of it and find the things that were going wrong. . . . I mean, you [cannot] just walk out at the first thing" (1979, p. 145).

This argument is perhaps even more compelling when women consider the effects of divorce on their children. "I thought my child should have a father," said one (Pagelow 1981, p. 72), and another commented, "I thought they should have a daddy, you know, so I always went back" (Dobash and Dobash 1979, p. 148). To illustrate "staying for the children's sake," Dobash and Dobash provide this interview passage:

> I would have liked my marriage to work for my kids' sake. I don't like the idea of them growing up and just with me, you know. I mean, you hear of kids in trouble and they say, "Oh, well, their mother and father's divorced." "She's a widow." Things like that, you know. And it worries me, really. (1979, p. 148)

And Davidson says the following are "typical 'reasons' given by middle-class battered wives for why they haven't left their husbands, or why it took them so long to leave":

> "I have to keep a home going for the children. What sort of home could I manage on my own?"

"Children need a father."

"He loves the children; I can't separate them." (1978, p. 114)

Davidson puts "reasons" in quotes because, as the child of a batterer, she suffered from her mother's inability to leave and later characterizes her as "vanquished in mind as well as body." Yet it is clear from all of the above that these are common accounts that women tell themselves and others, whether or not this constitutes the "denial" or "tragic nonsense" of Davidson's experience (1978, p. 153). In fact, it is not nonsense but its opposite, an attempt to make the violence, the relationship, and the staying "sensible" and thus, comprehensible. Moreover, it is storytelling that draws upon the cultural narrative of what constitutes a woman's obligations to her husband and children to counter the cultural code insisting she can simply leave.

"I Had No Place to Go": Trapped by Circumstance

The women whose voices Pizzey draws upon to argue for more shelters and assistance for battered women tell how little help they find when they do try to leave. They speak of going to "welfare," "family advice," "solicitors," "prison welfare officers," the "Samaritans," the police, and "council." They say things like "no one helps me or wants to know," "I can find no hope or help anywhere," and "it seems that society is forcing me to stay with him" (Pizzey 1974, pp. 21–23, 35).

The following is from the story Pizzey uses to illustrate how the "agents of society" ignore battered women:

> I tried to leave my husband. I contacted the Catholic Housing Aid Society, the Samaritans, the NSPCC, the housing department of the local authority. No one wanted to know. It was always the same. "We can't give you somewhere to live because your husband can come back on us." "Obtain a separation and then we will help you." There's only one problem here. The courts will not grant separation orders if the woman doesn't get out. They say: "If the situation is as intolerable as you describe, how have you managed to stick it for this length of time?" It's one vicious circle of very large perimeter, with the woman in the middle and the husband and the bureaucracy hitting out from all points. On one occasion, after strapping my dislocated wrist, a sympathetic doctor advised me to contact social services . . . [there] I was told I must give my marriage a chance. I had been married for five and a half years at the time, so I thought the advice rather irrelevant. (Pizzey 1974, p. 28)

When this woman says "I tried to leave my husband" and then follows with a litany of unsympathy, she is drawing upon a vocabulary of victimization that counters constructions of her *choosing* to stay "for this length of time."

In *Battered Wives,* the very first chapter begins with a letter written to a friend of the author's after a "public discussion of wife beating" (Martin 1976, p. 1). In the letter, after a graphic description of the beatings she has endured, the letter writer says: "Now, the first response to this story, which I myself think of, will be 'Why didn't you seek help?'" (Martin 1976, p. 2). This is a clear reference to common beliefs, so common in fact that the victim attributes them to herself as well as others. She then goes on to detail the unhelpful responses of all the people she had asked to aid her:

> Everyone I have gone to for help has somehow wanted to blame me and vindicate my husband. I can see it lying there between their words and at the end of their sentences. The clergyman, the doctor, the counselor, my friend's husband, the police—all of them have found a way to vindicate my husband. . . . As a married woman I have no recourse but to remain in the situation which is causing me to be painfully abused. I have suffered physical and emotional battering and spiritual rape because the social structure of my world says I cannot do anything about a man who wants to beat me. . . . I know that I have to get out. But when you have nowhere to go, you know that you must go on your own and expect no support. . . . I have learned that no one believes me and that I cannot depend upon any outside help. (Martin 1976, pp. 3–4).

Here, this victim specifies the victim-blaming culture and the "social structure"—including her marriage—that hold her in bondage to her abusive husband. She adds, once more bringing in the perceptions of others, that "my situation is so untenable that I would guess that anyone who has not experienced one like it would find it incomprehensible. I find it difficult to believe myself" (Martin 1976, p. 4).

Dobash and Dobash, three years later, asked the battered women they interviewed why they stayed "as long as [they] did" and argued that finding a place to live is "fraught with difficulties, delays, and barriers, and is sometimes made impossible or so intolerable that the woman leaves the refuge and goes back to the violent home in despair" (1979, p. 158). These are the excerpts from the interviews they used to illustrate this constraint on victims' agency, after asking the following: *"Probably quite a lot of people would wonder why you stayed with him as long as you did. Why did you?"* (Dobash and Dobash 1979, p. 158; emphasis in original).

I had to go back, I mean, where can you stay with three children?

Well, as I said before, you leave them and you go and stay with some-body. Even if it's your parents, you've got small children and they've got their family, so therefore it does tell. A strain shows on everybody concerned. You go to the welfare for help and you get told you can't get help. There's nobody can help you.

You can't get a house of your own. The only way that any battered wife, or a person in my position, could help themselves is if they had money. That's the only way and that's the one thing that very few of us have.

Even if you do get a house, I mean, let's face it, you just get the bare essentials. You don't get anything. If you would like to take your kids out or go with your kids anywhere, you would need to sit down and work out a right tight budget because everything's that expensive. (Dobash and Dobash 1979, pp. 157–158)

Each of these examples, like the story that begins Martin's 1976 book, attributes the deviant act of staying to circumstances beyond the woman's control, and thus not a matter of her will. Once again, this time in response to direct questioning, victims provide explanations that shift responsibility and blame away from themselves.

Pagelow, who also interviewed battered women for her research, includes the question "Why Did She Stay?" as a subheading in the chapter "Common Myths and Stereotypes." She then reports: "Actually, most of the interviewed women revealed that they were well aware of popular ideas about them and their relationships. When they were asked directly, 'Why did you stay?' they usually stated that they felt they had few or undesirable or no alternatives" (Pagelow 1981, p. 72). To illustrate, she quotes from her interviews, including women who said they had "no place to go," that they "did not know where to go or who to turn to," and the following:

I have no money, no car—but I can't drive anyway—and no friends left. My parents kicked me out before. They sure as hell don't want me now. What chance is there for me, with three kids under three? I ran away once . . . and he found me, came after me and took me back. I never could get far enough away from him. (Pagelow 1981, pp. 72–73)

According to Pagelow, this particular woman had come to the shelter, but after a month there, "she had not been able to find a job, a place to live, or child care for her two young sons. She did not feel that there was any way she could live independently of her husband, so she returned home" (1981, p. 73). Like the other activists, Pagelow explains and allows her interviewees to tell us why they return in addition to why they stay.

In stories that are achingly similar to those of victims of rape, battered women reveal what they know of the expectations of others even as they explain why they cannot meet them. Battered women's accounts echo those of rape victims who tell of their fear and of being trapped by men who overpower them, in places where no help is to be found. Fear is rational, they explain, and moreover, they have no place to go and no help is to be found. Reading the excerpts, we discern the same vocabularies of motive (Mills 1940), their vocabularies of victimization. Their similarity derives from their source; it is their social location in a society wherein people assume choice. And again, like the antirape activists who drew on their shared understandings of the cultural code of agency to dramatize the "injury and innocence" of rape victims (Holstein and Miller 1997), activists made use of their own cultural competencies to do the same for battered women. Below, I show some of the ways in which they did so.

Vocabularies of Victimization: Representations of Blameless Victims

One means of addressing the problem of victim-blaming is to create images of "ideal victims" that absolve them of responsibility for their victimization (Christie 1986). For this reason, much of the activist and scholarly literature on battered women has focused on explaining why battered women stay with their abusers (a behavior that implies agency) and has attempted to show that battered women are, in fact, constrained rather than free agents. Einat Peled et al. argue that there are three "main explanatory themes" in the now vast battered women's literature: those that focus on the increased danger women face on separation and how fear of escalating the violence entraps them, those that focus on psychological and situational factors, and those that are more sociological, emphasizing "social values, policies, opportunity structures, and service provision" (2000, p. 11).

In the early writings that inspired the battered women's movement, images of women facing each of these kinds of obstacles are abundant. Indeed, I have illustrated these vocabularies of victimization above, in battered women's responses to the cultural code of agency. Because activists and battered women share the same cultural understandings, they use the same kinds of language. In addition, most of the images activists create seem intended to evoke emotion or use emotion accounts to elicit this. This is important because in order to engender sympathy, it is helpful to put audience members in victims' "shoes," and vivid descriptions of what they are feeling help to foster this identification as well as serving to explain the psychology of entrapment. Thus, the excerpts below "personalize the condition" (Loseke 2003) and help victims adhere, in audiences' minds, to the feeling rules (Hochschild 1979) that tell us who to care about (Clark 1997). They do this by describing the fear, guilt, and despair the battered women above associated with threats, concerns for their children, and lack of other options.

The Dangers of Leaving and the Emotion of Fear

In the first category Peled et al. (2000) cite are the battered women whom activists construct as endangering themselves by leaving and who thus are understandably fearful. In *Scream Quietly,* Pizzey makes an explicit claim that justifiable fear prevents women from getting help. She says:

> People who are being ill-treated don't usually talk about it. Some are scared of what might happen to them if they speak. They know well that if they tell how they are treated they will again be threatened and most probably beaten. Many of the women who write to us ask for the reply to be sent care of friends or at their parents', because they are afraid they'll get another beating if their husbands find out that they've contacted us. (Pizzey 1974, pp. 30–31)

Later, she offers the following example to counter the argument that "battered women are the sort of women who go out and subconsciously choose men who will batter them." After explaining that victims are "just ordinary people with nowhere to go and no one to turn to," Pizzey describes "Lucy," who married very young and did not find out that her husband was violent until after the wedding. After a graphic description of Lucy being beaten in front of her children, Pizzey relates:

> Lucy did go to social workers for help and they put her into temporary welfare accommodation, but when the social workers went home there was no one to protect her. Her husband often got into the huge unlit block of flats, broke into her room and threatened her. She explained that it was better to be at home where she knew where he was than sitting night after night not knowing if the footstep passing her door was

him, or the car idling on the street was him waiting to catch her. (Pizzey 1974, p. 39)

Here Pizzey is articulating a lack of effective protection for battered women with the real threats posed by their husbands and a rationale for returning; it was "better to be at home." Also, by using the "Lucy did go" phrasing, it appears that Pizzey is implicitly arguing against those who claim that battered women "enjoy it" and thus do not go for help; on the contrary, this victim did, but it was futile (1974, p. 37). Then Pizzey uses the emotion of fear itself as an account:

> Very few people understand this kind of fear. It is the fear of knowing that someone is searching for you and will beat you when he finds you. In the mind of someone who has been badly beaten, this fear blots out all reason. The man seems to be omnipotent. . . . So many times well-meaning social workers have said, "I found her a nice flat and the next day she was back with him." I don't think it takes much imagination to understand what goes on in the mind of someone who has been badly beaten. (Pizzey 1974, p. 39)

This excerpt also provides the "well-meaning" but "valuative" (Scott and Lyman 1968) inquiry that forces Pizzey to explain and to ask readers to put themselves, through "imagination," in the battered woman's place. Because fear "blots out all reason," the unreasonable actions of the returning victim make more sense.

Martin cites the "pioneering efforts" of Pizzey and explains, in a section called "Trapped by Fear," that this emotion is the "common denominator" in relationships in which battered women stay (Martin 1976, p. 6). "Fear immobilizes them, ruling their actions, their decisions, their very lives." It prevents victims from getting help, or escaping, and it induces them to return if they have left (1976, pp. 76–79). Martin cites women who say things like "Your belly's full of it" and describes them "cower[ing] in terror" of a "husband who often stalks her like a hunted animal." If she *should* leave, "she lives in constant dread that he will find her. With every car idling on the street, every noise outside her door, she freezes in sheer terror" (1976, p. 77). Like Brownmiller's rape victim who compares herself to a rabbit "stuck in the glare of your headlights" (Brownmiller 1975, p. 400), the language of immobility and being frozen conveys the inability to take self-protective action.

In one of the first anthologies, a 1979 publication of papers given at a Battered Women's Conference at the University of California at Davis that brought together Del Martin and Lenore Walker, Donna M. Moore, the editor, first discusses "dependency" and then writes:

> A second major reason for a woman staying in an abusive home is fear—fear of death if she stays, and fear of the unknown if she leaves. Although she knows only too well that her current battering is endangering her life, and perhaps the lives of her children, she also is afraid to leave and experience the loneliness, financial devastation, failure, possible loss of friends and family, and fear of the unknown. . . . Another fear she has is that her husband will follow her if she leaves home to hunt her down and beat her again. These fears are not unfounded. Up to 50% of these husbands have sought out and continued to beat or terrorize their wives. . . . If the battered wife decides to stay in the home and report her beatings to police departments or other agencies, she must also fear . . . the arrest which may result which often makes the man so angry that his beatings increase—a risk she is often not willing to take. (Moore 1979, p. 22)

In addition to citing fear and claiming that it is justified to account for "staying," Moore adds that it explains why battered women do not always want their husbands to be arrested. Similarly, Dobash and Dobash quote a woman who stays because of "fear, I think. Fear of going, fear of staying" (1979, p. 156).

In Davidson's discussion of "What Happens If His Wife Tries to Leave," she first talks about the batterer begging his wife to stay and promising to reform. After noting that the reforming "rarely happens," she goes on:

> A more frequent consequence of a wife's plans to leave, however, is the husband's swearing to kill or maim her or the children should she dare to try to escape or expose him. When she has no place to go, or her determination is shaky, or she has no strong support system, and he knows it, she invariably will suffer more for threatening to leave. (Davidson 1978, p. 39)

Then, when Davidson talks about "what kind" of woman a battered wife is, she starts by listing the ways in which a victim could respond, noting that she may "fight back in an effective way" or "make sure it never happens again," but then asking rhetorically:

> Or will her reaction take the form of walking on tiptoe? . . . Or will she be so overwhelmed with humiliation, shock, and fear that she will find it more comfortable to pretend—to herself, to him, and to others—that it never happened? The middle-class battered wife's response to her fear tends to be withdrawal, silence, and denial. . . . They are the ones

> whose marriages are lived out in fear, trying to please and appease, ter-
> rified of inadvertently making the wrong move. (1978, pp. 50–51)

Later, she adds that:

> Their world is limited by their cocoon of fear. They become accom-
> plices in their own downfall, as they lie about the causes of their obvi-
> ous injuries, returning to the injurer as if they loved him and were
> loved in return, defending him when anyone begins to suspect the
> truth. (Davidson 1978, p. 52)

In these excerpts, Davidson shows how battered women who try to leave are threatened and "suffer" as a consequence and goes on to paint a picture of victims who have become so immobilized that they are essentially "complicit" in their own victimization. Lest we think that we should blame women for this, however, Davidson says that "the very act of seeking help may be dangerous; if her husband-assailant finds out, he may harm her further" (1978, p. 58). She also argues that when battered women leave, they "have a terrible time getting another job," because they "hesitate to give references for fear the ex-husband, hot on their trail, will trace them and harass or harm them." This latter assertion appears in the chapter "How Society Keeps Her There" and thus con-tributes to the overall account for why battered women stay (Davidson 1978, pp. 58, 77).

Like her predecessors, Walker calls upon fear as partially responsi-ble for women's actions. Walker reports that the battered women she interviewed "lived under constant stress and fear" (1979, p. 34) and begins her book with a description of "Anne," whom I quoted above, who lived "in constant fear that [her] husband would fly off the handle." Pagelow too includes fear among the "reasons for staying" cited by her respondents (1981, p. 72). In response to the "myth" that "battered women must somehow be at fault," Pagelow describes women who attempted self-defense but asserts that "many added a statement similar to the following: 'I tried to once and he really flipped out and beat me worse than ever. He told me if I ever tried that again he'd kill me. I never tried again. I believed he would'" (1981, p. 67).

Thus, we can see that fear and true danger combine in the arguments of all these writers as a pervasive explanation for why battered women might stay in relationships when it seems obvious to others that they can simply choose to leave. Each version provides a kind of "emotion account" for behavior that could be interpreted as belying their victim-ization. At the same time, through the use of emotionality and invitations to take the role of the victim, the stories encourage audiences to identify with battered women even (Loseke 2003) as they repair their "spoiled identity" (Goffman 1963).

Being a Good Wife and Mother and the Psychology of Guilt

Another set of arguments that all of the authors made for why battered women stay in or return to violent relationships is that they do so because of their traditional beliefs about marriage and divorce. In addition, activists argue that such victims hope to protect their children from the stigma of divorce or, worse, from being in the care of their fathers.

After talking about "cold fear" as one reason for staying, Del Martin says that women "give other, more subtle reasons to explain why they stay with a violent man. These reasons are related to the social and cultural expectations we acquire concerning marriage." Because of this sex-role conditioning, these victims want to preserve their marriages at all costs and feel "ashamed" if the marriage fails—"she will try above all else to save face" (1976, pp. 79, 81). Martin says "the key factor [inducing women to stay] is guilt," concluding that battered women's doomed-to-fail efforts to please their husbands and conform to social norms ultimately lead to "despair and misery" (1976, p. 81). These emotional attributions not only encourage readers to empathize, but they remind them that the victim has a social conscience (she is capable of feeling shame and guilt).

Terry Davidson, whose own mother never left Davidson's battering father, has quite a bit to say about this explanation. When writing about "The Woman from a 'Good' Family," Davidson describes a person who is, in many ways, the antithesis of the women's movement image of "liberated." Of the former, she says:

> For these women wifebeating comes as a stupefying shock. The victims may exemplify society's old image of ideal womanhood—submissive, religious, nonassertive, accepting of whatever the husband's life brings. They may exercise no independence of income, ideas, or movement, be anxious about housekeeping, and develop devotion to home and family to the exclusion of outside friends and interests. The husband comes first for these women, who perceive themselves as having little control over many areas of their own lives. They are meek. Their reaction to their predicament—often mistaken by others for masochism—is cowering and submission, not retaliation or action. . . . Marriage is important to them. Outward appearances are important, too . . . they feel an unspecified guilt. . . . For such women, keeping the image of a socially

> and religiously acceptable marriage takes priority over the possible consequences of exposure. . . . She grew up to believe that marriage and husband were what life was about, and that it was up to her to make her marriage work. (Davidson 1978, pp. 51–52)

Davidson also argues that divorce "may be against their religion" (1978, p. 59).

Like Martin, Davidson describes a victim who feels shame and who is concerned about how her marriage is seen by others. This victim, however, has been so inculcated with traditional gender beliefs and role expectations that she has become incapable of taking action as well as unwilling. Like the battered woman immobilized by fear, she is "stupefied" as well as "meek" and "submissive." Nevertheless, Davidson works to refute the "stereotype of masochism," arguing that "many women grow up *conditioned* to accept, as part of wifely duty, whatever a husband manifests" (1978, p. 65; emphasis in original).

Lenore Walker too emphasizes and prioritizes emotions in addition to fear as rationales for victims' staying. The typical battered woman "suffers from guilt, yet denies the terror and anger she feels." Why does she feel guilt? In part, it is because she is a "traditionalist about the home, [who] strongly believes in family unity and the prescribed sex role stereotype" (1979, p. 31). Here is Walker's description of this unliberated woman:

> First, she readily accepts the notion that "a woman's proper place is in the home." No matter how important her career might be to her, she is ready to give it up if it will make the batterer happy. Often she does just that, resulting in economic hardship to the family. . . . Those women who cannot give up working feel guilty. . . . Battered women who work often turn their money over to their husbands. Even those women who provide the family's financial stability feel their income belongs to their husband. Ultimately, she gives the man the right to make the final decisions as to how the family income is spent. The battered woman views the man as the head of the family, even though she is the one actually keeping the family together; she makes the decisions concerning financial matters and the children's welfare and she maintains the house and often a job as well. She goes out of her way to make sure that her man feels he is the head of the home. (1979, pp. 33–34)

While today we might feel condescending toward such a woman, many if not most of Walker's readers would have been socialized to believe the quote about women's "proper place" with which she starts her description.

Here is how R. Emerson Dobash and Russell Dobash make much the same argument, bringing in women's role as mothers as well as the beliefs they hold about marriage:

> In our society the status of wife is deemed to be so necessary to a woman's identity that she may have considerable difficulty thinking of herself in any other way. In order for a woman to leave her husband permanently she must overcome not only personal fears, the loss of status, and ambivalent feelings about her husband but also the deeply ingrained ideas that marriages should be held together at any cost, that the split-up of a marriage is mostly the fault of the woman, and that a broken home is worse for children than a whole, though violent one. (1979, pp. 147–148)

Dobash and Dobash argue that it is these "cultural notions" that "entrap a woman in a violent marriage." They emphasize victims' maternal concerns:

> Women stay for the "sake of the children"—in the belief that children must live with their father, come from a good, stable home, and not be stigmatized by coming from a broken home. They also stay in order not to disrupt the children's schooling or friendships. (Dobash and Dobash 1979, p. 148)

In the same section, Dobash and Dobash say "a woman who has been dominated, controlled, and frightened for years has lost a great deal of confidence and self-esteem. The prospect of living on her own may be frightening" (1979, pp. 147–148). Thus, like Martin and Davidson, they bring attention to the potential shame of a broken marriage for women with traditional values and, like Davidson, construct a woman whose upbringing has ultimately made her afraid to leave. Many readers would likely empathize with such a woman; that she cares so for her children aligns the deviant behavior of staying with the normative expectation that mothers put their children's needs ahead of their own and should increase sympathy for her predicament.

Martin also indicates pro-social aspects in her earlier discussion of fear: women may not tell their neighbors about the violence because "out of fear of endangering others, her children as well, the woman may choose to sacrifice herself" (1976, p. 77). This typification of battered women clearly raises their social value, even as it accounts for deviance, thus meeting what Loseke calls the "cultural feeling rules surrounding sympathy" that require victims to be "people in *higher moral categories*" as well as "not responsible" (Loseke 1999, p. 76; emphasis in original).

In addition to evoking images of good wives and caring mothers, explanations positing victims' role-related constraints remediate their responsibility—they are only doing as they have been taught is appropriate and the right thing to do. These explanations also draw directly on emotion accounts when, as we have seen above, gender socialization and patriarchal cultural expectations are said to shape women's feelings relative to their abusive relationships. In sum, these authors are describing battered women in ways that use traditional gender role socialization and its concomitant emotionality to emphasize their entrapment and thereby their essential "victim" identities.

"How Society Keeps Her There" and the Psychology of Despair

Another prevalent image springs from a more sociological, structural approach (Peled et al. 2000). As a journalist and radical activist, Del Martin is the most explicitly feminist. In addition to arguing that women are held "captive" in battering relationships by the "social imperatives" of sex role socialization into subordination and the "feudal system of marriage," she cites a patriarchal criminal justice system including historical laws that privilege men and condone wife beating; insensitive police, district attorneys, judges, and social service agencies; and economic constraints (Martin 1979, p. 45). In the realm of social science, Richard Gelles argued early on that the attitudes of police and the courts serve as constraints, in that they offer "little benefit" to battered women who do seek help (Gelles 1976, p. 667). Terry Davidson, a journalist and the daughter of a batterer, reserves particular condemnation for "How Society Keeps Her There" (Davidson 1978, p. 71). In the remainder of this section, I illustrate these kinds of explanations and how they function as vocabularies of victimization.

Erin Pizzey begins her chapter, "A Man's Home Is His Castle," with this statement:

> Violence in the streets—straight thuggery and mugging—is treated as a serious crime. . . . If the same act is committed behind the front door it is ignored. The following account will give some idea of the way the agents of society—doctors, social workers, housing department, solicitors, police and courts—can treat a woman who is viciously assaulted by her husband. (Pizzey 1974, p. 26)

By referring to "the agents of society" and to their failure to treat battering seriously, Pizzey sets the stage for later explanations that will make this argument more extensively. The account she refers to is that of a woman who unsuccessfully tried to get help from the social services available to her, only to be told to "give [her marriage] a chance." In addition, Pizzey says, "A woman usually has children and no money and nowhere to go," which helps to show the forces arrayed against battered women and is another argument activists and scholars repeatedly put forward (1974, pp. 28, 30).

Echoing Pizzey, Martin says in her first chapter:

> These women bear the brutality of their husbands in silence because they have no one to turn to and no place to go . . . when the battered woman becomes desperate enough to reach out for help, she often meets with subtle, and sometimes even hostile, rejection. Her problem may seem insolvable to her. At least with regard to the help and support she can expect from society, she may be right. (Martin 1976, p. 5)

Martin develops this argument in a later chapter, on the "runaround" that social services make women endure. After describing an unresponsive system, she explains why this might be "understandably, enough to drive a battered woman back to the quasi security of a violent but familiar home that provides food and shelter":

> Many women stay with their violent husbands for the simple reason that they have nowhere else to go and no means of supporting themselves, even for a night, if they did leave . . . a woman who has left home in the middle of the night probably has no idea how long she will need to intrude or accept a friend's hospitality, nor when her outraged husband might show up. . . . Imagine her wondering how she will support herself and her children, especially if she has no work experience. Imagine her trying to make decisions—whether to stay away, whether to give up and go home—in a situation where she has neither time, nor space, nor quiet to consider what has happened to her and what she must do now. (Martin 1976, pp. 119–120)

Once again, Martin puts the reader in the role of the battered woman via her evocative description of the latter's "anxiety and discomfort" in the face of no shelter from the storm and an uncertain future. By saying that the victim makes her choice "understandably," Martin emphasizes that if readers can imagine being in this situation, we would accept this explanation. Martin concludes: "Even if a battered woman can overcome her sense of isolation and shame to actually ask for help, so far as the criminal justice and social service systems are concerned, her efforts may be wasted" (Martin 1976, p. 147).

As I noted, Terry Davidson devotes a whole chapter to society as a constraint, or a reason battered women stay. She begins by saying that the battered woman's belief that "she has no allies, no champions" is not "paranoid, but starkly realistic" (1978, p. 74). Then, under the heading "Guilty Until Proven Innocent," she writes:

> The battered wife lives in a Kafkaesque world. The constitutional right of being considered innocent until proven guilty doesn't seem to apply to her. The mere fact of her being so incredibly "punished" by her husband is interpreted too often by police, the courts, and the community as, "she must have done something terrible to provoke such a response." The most common reaction by others to the plight of the battered wife has been contempt, criticism, or utter disbelief. (Davidson 1978, p. 74)

Like the antirape activists framing societal responses to victims in terms of myths that lead to victim-blaming, Davidson depicts a cultural ethos where there is no sympathy despite the "plight" of the victims for whom she is advocating. After separate discussions of judges and courts, onlookers, the "policy of equal blame," social agencies, doctors, the community, the police, the law, and economics as all "against the battered wife," Davidson comments:

> It seems almost as if the professional world conspires against the battered wife and deliberately or unwittingly prevents her from leaving her tormentor while aiding him to continue his behavior. Where can the woman go when it seems as if nothing can stop her powerful husband, immune from all reasonably expected restraints and consequences? (Davidson 1978, p. 90)

She then goes on to review ways in which parents, church, and psychotherapy are similarly arrayed in opposition to battered women's attempts to leave, concluding that:

> It is disturbing to ponder these responses from professionals in social work, medicine, law, organized religion, and psychiatry—professionals whose deepest beliefs [that women are at fault] encourage the wifebeater by barring the way to relief for the battered wife. (1978, p. 92)

Then, using the example of a city councilman who had asked her, after her testimony before a Public Safety Commission, "Do we break up a marriage *merely* because a man beats his wife?" and other questions implying "tacit toleration," Davidson says:

> He was no monster; he was Everyman. To my way of thinking, he became the unofficial spokesperson of the attitudes of society and of

certain husbands, even those who are not violent themselves. The councilman's few innocent questions clearly show why the battered wife puts up with her horrendous situation, why she does not leave, why she does not report it, why she does not retaliate, why she is pressured into returning when she does manage to escape. (1978, p. 93)

By phrasing her argument in this way, it takes the form of an account, for *all* of the valuative inquiries (Scott and Lyman 1968) to which battered women are subjected. Further, it reinforces my contention that the cultural code of agency requires explanations, not only from the individual battered woman but also from those advocating on her behalf. Davidson then goes on to show how tolerance for wifebeating is rooted in "tradition," much like Brownmiller (1975) and others did for rape.

Of course, tradition is the very source of the cultural code. I have shown that the stories of rape victims, as well as their advocates, reveal the insistent presence of this prevailing set of assumptions. In what preceded, I use excerpts from the first-person accounts of the battered women cited in the early activist literature we have been examining to make the same case for what we expect of them. Taken together, the stories of activists, journalists, and social scientists concerned with establishing the problem of battered women, along with those of the women they talked to or heard from, have much in common with the rape accounts I discussed in Chapter 3. In addition to calling attention to and refuting myths, both kinds of stories draw upon a vocabulary of victimization that offers reasons for the otherwise unreasonable: for rape victims, lack of resistance, and for battered women, failure to leave (also a lack of resistance). Both social movements called for changes in attitudes linked to the cultural code of agency, that is, for an end to victim-blaming.

The legacy of the battered women's movement is a little different than that of the antirape movement, however. Activists in the former movement were less concerned with the notion of victim precipitation (and the legal consequences of blaming victims in criminal cases) than with solving the problem women's "staying" revealed—no place to go. Thus, they called for funds to establish shelters and help women to become financially independent and able to care for their children. They also advocated for treating battering as a criminal rather than civil matter and a public rather than private problem. This would help remediate the real dangers linked to the fear victims felt and used as an emotion account for staying. But if we look closely at the psychological accounts for why battered women stay in or return to violent relationships, we find a social construction of victimization that has latent consequences and that leads to new ways of judging victims. I conclude this chapter with an analysis of "helpless" images of battered women and some implications of their use.

The Legacy of the Movement: "Victimism" as a Concern

To cast a battered woman as an innocent victim with little or no choice may have been an effective strategy, especially in the early stages of women's activism against intimate violence, but these images themselves have been contentious from the very beginning (Barry 1979; Lamb 1999a). Deviance arguably accrues to *all* forms of victimization simply by virtue of its abnormality (Clark 1997; Loseke 1999). Thus the identity of "battered woman" may be discrepant even when the typification absolves her of responsibility for staying. Erving Goffman says that a stigmatized individual is "reduced in our minds from a whole and usual person to a tainted, discounted one," inspiring various strategies for negotiation of treatment as fully human (Goffman 1963, p. 3). If the same is true for the images social movements construct, and typifications *themselves* can be discrepant with normative expectations, we can consider early alternatives to—and present reframings of—the image of "battered woman" as collective identity management at work.

The proliferation of shelters and services for battered women since the publication of *Battered Wives* in 1976, when Del Martin was able to describe only eight existing "refuges," attests to the success of these particular processes, as does the burgeoning popular and social scientific literature on this topic. Nevertheless, there are problems adhering to "victim" constructions that may have contributed to the rise of a countermovement of sorts, a group of social critics and self-described "power feminists" (Wolf 1993b) who lamented the helplessness of victims lacking agency and fretted over the consequences of the cultural diffusion of this kind of imagery. Those countermovements, and the images of pathetic victims that activists created to argue against what they called "victimism" (Barry 1979), are the subject of Chapter 5. Here, I would like to provide some suggestive examples of what became grist for their mills.

Constructing the Captive

The foundation of the victim image that countermovement activists ultimately would reconstruct as pathetic probably began to take shape in arguments that brought together all the explanations for staying to construct complete entrapment. So, for example, Erin Pizzey tells of the following woman, who "had endured a nightmare marriage for thirty years":

> Time and time again she'd tried to break out. She often went to her mother's, but her husband had broken in there and taken her back. The police never did anything to stop him because it was a marital quarrel. Nobody else wanted to be involved. . . . He always kept her short of money. She took a job once, but she had to work twelve hours to earn overtime to make her salary equal to a man's and that meant leaving the children alone in the evenings. After six months of that she gave it up. Each time she and her children went back to her husband, he got her pregnant again. Each time they were treated worse, because he knew they could not choose but take it. He used to taunt her with, "Where can you go? What can you do?" This woman was caught in a trap. There was no way out but suicide, and she once tried that. . . . Her only mistake was marrying the man in the first place. (Pizzey 1974, p. 43)

This account combines societal apathy, economic circumstances, and concern for her children to explain that this woman stayed for so long because she was "caught in a trap" with "no way out." Del Martin's response to a doctor who suggested to her that battered women who return are masochistic and that "you don't have to have very much intelligence to know that you can leave" is much the same:

> Nor do you have to know much to realize that a woman who is injured, or has no money, or has nowhere to go will probably go home. There she will stay until by some miracle she discovers a refuge, gets a job, or works up the courage it takes to walk away from home with no money, no prospects, and the terrible fear that she is being pursued. (Martin 1976, p. 129)

Of the woman who stayed for thirty years and even attempted suicide, Pizzey asks, "Is this spinelessness? She knew well she wanted to get out, and tried often, but she was trapped inside the family" (1974, p. 43). This provides a clue to what will come, the implicit suggestion that in addition to a cultural code of agency, activists and victims respond to assumptions that people who lack agency are lacking in other regards. Martin refers to "courage" as something requiring a miracle to acquire; this construction also has unintended consequences.

Davidson makes similar arguments. Here is how she describes the genesis of staying:

> Although she may think of escaping her brutal marriage, and actually attempt to do so, the average battered wife does not get out. She sim-

ply *cannot* because of the inherent psychodynamics and societal blocks and pressures. These include her unconscious psychological patterns and those of her husband, legal and economic reasons, children, health, threats, fear and danger, and overall, a vestige of hope that her assailant will change. All these factors combine to enforce her captivity. (Davidson 1978, p. 75; emphasis in original)

Although Davidson refers to a variety of "societal blocks" and earlier says that a battered woman is "psychologically *and* societally incapable of saving herself" (Davidson 1978, p. 73; emphasis added), it is the psychological dimension that will become most problematic. When Davidson says, citing "therapists and experts in this field," that "it takes a lot to get most of the middle-class victims to make a move because they are so immobilized by terror, habit, and the excruciating double-binds of the situation" (1978, p. 20), it is battered women's psychological states that she emphasizes. The problem with this is that the picture that begins to emerge, however effectively it accounts for why women stay, is not especially positive. The images below show why.

Producing Passivity

This victim we have been listening to and hearing about in this chapter, typically, is terrified by her experience, has no support, and is thus helpless to respond on her own behalf. Pizzey describes her this way:

Anyone who has been badly knocked about loses all sense of reality and ability to cope. Battered women are almost permanently in a shocked state. The constant fear of another beating leaves them very tense and nervous. Some can't eat, others sleep little. Even the toughest find it hard to fight off the depression. (1974, p. 41)

To illustrate the above, Pizzey prints a letter from a woman who describes taking tranquilizers and says that the "power of action has gone from me." Pizzey concludes that "years and years of cruelty and vicious persecution can knock the determination out of anybody" (1974, pp. 42–43).

Here is how Del Martin characterized this victim in the influential *Battered Wives:*

Alone, in pain and fear, she wrestles with questions of what to do and where to go. Often she wonders whether she should do anything or go anywhere. If she has children she may feel particularly trapped. She might fear for her children's safety and emotional health but be unsure as how to provide for them alone. . . . Her problem may seem unsolvable to her. At least with regard to the help and support she can expect from society, she may be right. (1976, p. 5)

In this excerpt, Martin eloquently describes the emotions of the victim and draws on the theme of motherhood, creating an image of a woman for whom it would be difficult not to feel sympathy.

The now famous psychological construction of Lenore Walker in *The Battered Woman* (1979), upon which Martin and other activists came to draw heavily in later renderings, describes the victim this way:

Repeated batterings, like electrical shocks, diminish the woman's motivation to respond. She becomes passive. Secondly, her cognitive ability to perceive success is changed. She does not believe her response will result in a favorable outcome, whether or not it might. Next, having generalized her helplessness, the battered woman does not believe anything she does will alter any outcome, not just the specific situation that has occurred . . . she cannot think of alternatives. (Walker 1979, pp. 49–50)

Earlier, I discussed how Pizzey wrote about a woman "unable to cope" as a consequence of her victimization. Here is more of this woman's self-description:

[The tranquilizers] stop the tears but also deactivate me. I sit and sit and when the tablets wear off the tears come back . . . the power of action has gone from me, lethargy, depression, etc. I do not present an attractive picture. . . . I am now in a state called agoraphobia. (Pizzey 1974, p. 42)

Davidson interviewed a therapist about her battered women clients and reports that, regarding how they felt while being abused, "[their] responses show the sense of total inadequacy the woman feels, the total victimization. Not one was able to think how to save herself, or even *of* saving herself . . . the shock was so great" (1978, p. 54; emphasis in original). Davidson also writes of women like her own mother, who "because of her extreme dependence on her husband—for making decisions, for handling financial matters, for dealing with landlords or repair people or banks, for friends and social life— . . . feels about as capable of living alone as a ten-year-old" (1978, p. 59). Martin describes a type of woman, thoroughly socialized into her stereotypically feminine role:

Women in our culture are encouraged to believe that the failure of a marriage represents their failure as women. Many believe that marriage gives their lives meaning, that they have no value as individuals apart from their men. A woman who believes that she has no value will not have the will to take responsibility for herself. She will be para- lyzed when it comes to making a radical change for her own sake. . . . If things go wrong, well-trained wives feel ashamed for having failed their husbands in some way. They may even believe they deserve their beatings. . . . When such women do seek outside help and, as is usually the case, do not receive it, their circumstances begin to seem utterly hopeless. They feel trapped and regard attempts at freeing themselves as futile. (Martin 1976, pp. 81–83)

The most well known of these characterizations is that of Lenore Walker, who applied the psychological theory of "learned helplessness" (Seligman 1975) to the situation of battered women. Repeated battering leads women eventually to believe that they have no control over their lives, according to Walker, who argues that "once we believe we cannot control what happens to us, it is difficult to believe we can ever influ- ence it, even if later we experience a favorable outcome" (1979, p. 47). She goes on:

This concept is important for understanding why battered women do not attempt to free themselves from a battering relationship. Once the women are operating from a belief of helplessness, the perception becomes reality and they become passive, submissive, "helpless." They allow things that appear to them to be out of their control actual- ly to get out of their control. (Walker 1979, p. 47)

A little later on, Walker says this process leads women to become unable to think of "alternatives," and the battered woman says to herself, "I am incapable and too stupid to learn how to do things" (1979, p. 50).

Thus, even as they attempt to explain that battered women are trapped, these activists cast them, or relate the stories of victims casting themselves, in terms that are potentially stigmatizing: unattractive, inad- equate, incapable, stupid, and lacking "the will" to act as adults and free themselves. And the movement storytellers seem to recognize how these images might be perceived. Martin relates the story of a secretly bat- tered woman who fails to empathize with one who discloses being bat- tered, citing feelings of "pity" and "disgust" for her and of being prohib- ited by her own "pride" from confiding her own travails. Martin explains this as follows:

This woman evidently believed that anyone, including herself, who stuck around for such treatment was not deserving of sympathy. Therefore, instead of comforting her friend, she took the opportunity to strengthen her own resolve never to leave herself open to judgment by another. In this way a battered woman may spend more energy in keeping her secret and trying to salvage some self-respect than in trying to extricate herself from the trap. (1976, p. 80)

Martin goes on to talk about women who are in danger of "losing all self-respect" (1976, p. 81).

Martin is describing a stereotype of victims: because people characterize them as pitiable and disgusting, and this characterization is due to their presumed choice to remain victims, being a victim is a shameful identity. Here is how Pizzey put it, earlier:

The psychiatrists' form of the "they enjoy it" argument is that battered women are the sort of women who go out and subconsciously choose men who will batter them. They consider the women "victims" who can only be happy with a "victimizer." I will dispute with anyone the notion that women who marry men like these are natural victims. They aren't. They are just ordinary people with nowhere to go and no one to turn to. Just because a woman is in a "victim" situation, that doesn't mean that she should be labeled a "victim" and so given a life sentence. (Pizzey 1974, p. 37)

Here the term *victim* appears to connote something undesirable and, ironically, a matter more of choice than circumstance. But even if a woman does not choose to be a victim, being a victim carries along with it certain attributes. Davidson tells of the type of woman with a "battered personality," quoting Carol Victor, a therapist she interviewed who was then working with battered wives: "At the thought of removing herself from the violent marriage, she thinks, 'I know what I've *got;* I'm scared of what I *might* get.' Why is she comfortable with this behavior? It's part of the battered personality. It's what she's been subjected to all her life" (1978, pp. 52–53; emphasis in original). Then Davidson chooses an interesting comment from Carol Victor to quote:

And I'm not necessarily talking about women one would think of as *pathetic.* Many of my clients don't fit the stereotype at all. Many are outstandingly attractive and well dressed. Many are successful in business or professions. They are not ready to leave the marriage. They are not ready to identify themselves as "battered women." (1978, pp. 52–53; emphasis in original)

Here Davidson conjoins the "stereotype" of battered women with the term *pathetic,* suggesting that the cultural image of them is quite negative and implying that it is for this reason that attractive, successful women fail to identify with the "typification" (Best 1995). I would add that this is problematic not only for *individual* battered women but also for the social movement working to frame a collective identity (Taylor and Whittier 1992).

Pathetic Potentialities

It is for this reason, I believe, that some feminists were quick to note theoretical, practical, and political implications of the vocabularies of victimization I describe above. They argued that constructions of battered women as passive and trapped pathologized them, cast them as deviant, and failed to recognize them as active agents. In 1979, the same year that Lenore Walker published *The Battered Woman* and R. Emerson Dobash and Russell Dobash brought out *Violence Against Wives*, Kathleen Barry discussed this issue in her book, *Female Sexual Slavery*. After noting that the category of victims of sexual slavery includes battered wives and arguing that the "theories that explain . . . why battered wives don't leave their husbands" are part of a "rape paradigm" that makes "the victim responsible for her own victimization" (1979, p. 35), Barry defines the phenomenon that she calls "victimism":

> In creating new definitions we always risk incorporating the rigidity in the new that exemplified the old. . . . Creating the role and status of the victim is the practice I call *victimism* . . . [which] creates a framework for others to know her not as a person but as a victim, someone to whom violence was done. . . . Victimism is an objectification which establishes new standards for defining experience; those standards dismiss any question of will, and deny that the woman even while enduring sexual violence is a living, changing, growing, interactive person. (1979, p. 38; emphasis in original)

In this excerpt, Barry is saying that victim "objectifications" have unintended consequences, precisely because this identity denies women their agency. They are people lacking "will" and to whom things "are done." Barry adds that "in slavery women are active and doing" (1979, pp. 38–39) but that "the limitations of victimism confuse active survival with complicity, making it difficult to understand why a woman thinks and acts the way she does. She is in fact not fulfilling the assigned role and status of victim." Barry recasts the victim as "an active, striving agent in her own behalf," a rhetorical strategy that both recognizes societal attributions of deviance and accounts for battered women's behavior. This is an image that is in direct contrast to the "empty victim" represented in previous constructions (1979, pp. 41–42).

Esther Madriz, more recently, makes a very similar argument in her review of the early activists (Griffin 1971; Brownmiller 1975): "Without doubt," she argues, "these studies opened society's eyes to hidden issues of violence against women . . . [h]owever, they also contributed to the social construction of women as victims" (Madriz 1997, p. 73). In a chapter called "The Innocent and Culpable Victim," Madriz quotes Karlene Faith:

> The focus in the literature on the effects of adult male violence on women and children had the sum effect of reifying the female as lacking human agency. Women were no longer so thoroughly objectified as male property, but they were reobjectified as Victim. (Faith 1993, p. 107; quoted in Madriz 1997, p. 73)

Like Barry, both Madriz and, more explicitly, Faith, place victimization in opposition to agency and thereby emphasize the ways in which victims, who *lack* agency by definition, are devalued.

A number of feminist scholars have made "battered women as victims" typifications problematic by pointing to the ways in which they create "either/or" configurations that ultimately form double binds. Kathleen Barry, for example, describes "limited options for women in the society" and says of the victim of sexual slavery: "If she was not an empty victim, a victim who does not interact, who cannot be seen as engaging in survival, could she even be a victim at all?" (Barry 1979, p. 41). Sharon Lamb significantly extends this argument, in part to counter the claims of those whom she calls the "backlash writers" (Lamb 1996). These are the self-described "power feminists" (Wolf 1993b; Roiphe 1993; Sommers 1994; Paglia 1992, 1994) who refer to activists in the antirape and battered women's movement as *victim feminists,* a term that itself explicitly calls attention to problems with victim identities. In *The Trouble with Blame* (1996), noting that the backlash writers were correct to castigate the "overpurification of victims" and its "undermining [of] the expression of female assertiveness," Lamb argues that feminists "who have seen and fought against the absurd blaming of victims have, at times, gone too far in the other direction, thereby denying victims any responsibility for their behavior and for their reactions to their abuse. . . . We have [thereby] cost victims some modicum of respect and personhood" (1996, pp. 111, 7–8). Lamb's thesis is that the scholars and activists who created images of idealized victims who bear no responsibility for their victimization also created a situation in which real victims who cannot meet this normative expectation end up being blamed. "Victims drown in the sea of degrees of powerlessness," concludes Lamb (1996, p. 43).

Martha Mahoney similarly argues that a dichotomous construction of victimization versus agency can prevent battered women from identifying their experience as victimization, a problem "exacerbated when the definition of 'victim' is so stigmatizing that it is impossible to reconcile with perceiving agency in oneself or others" (Mahoney 1994, p. 62). More recently, Kay Picart has called social constructions of "the monolithic woman as pure victim" a "pernicious . . . binary dichotomy, which fails to address the complexities that victims live, with their divided loyalties and the chiaroscuro of agency and powerlessness they straddle from day to day" (Picart 2003, p. 97). Like Barry (1979) and Lamb (1996), Picart posits "double bind" qualities of expectations for victimhood that are impossible to meet (2003).

Davies, Lyon, and Monti-Catania describe how the very success of the battered women's movement has led to the privileging of not only the "clinical understandings" (Davies, Lyon, and Monti-Catania 1998) that have culminated in battered women's syndrome's becoming the prevailing image of victims, "part of 'what we all know' about battered women" but also of "widespread overgeneralizations." Davies, Lyon, and Monti-Catania discuss how advocates' efforts to counter "popular understandings" of battered women led them to construct stereotypical "pure victims" (1998, pp. 17–19). For Davies, Lyon, and Monti-Catania, the main problem with this has to do with the heterogeneity of actual victims and the ways in which they do not meet cultural expectations; that is, that they have no agency (see also Loseke 1992, 2001).

My focus is a little different, and in Chapter 5, I turn to another latent consequence of victim constructions that the arguments above anticipate. When thinking about the cultural code of agency and its demands that victims meet particular expectations requiring entrapment, we can include a fundamental precept of what Best (1997) has called a widespread contemporary "victim ideology." For Best, this set of now widespread cultural suppositions is constituted in part by the idea that "the term 'victim' has undesirable connotations" of being "damaged, passive, and powerless" (1997, p. 13). Whether victimization *actually* has a stigmatizing effect, the *perception* of victimization as a devalued identity appears in feminist and clinical discourses.

For example, bell hooks, in her 1984 book, *Feminist Theory from Margin to Center*, says that the "battered woman" label "appears to strip us of dignity, to deny that there has been any integrity in the relationship we are in" and frames the "hurt woman [as a] social pariah, set apart, marked forever by this experience" (hooks cited in Russo 2001, p. 27). Sharon Lamb argues that victims "are starting to avoid the label 'victim' in a culture that has grown to call victims 'whiners'" (1999b, p. 9) and comments that "it is shameful to be a victim in our culture . . . no matter what therapists tell victims, they feel that they have been weak, and weakness is shameful" (1999a, pp. 119–120). A clinical rationale for use of the term *survivor* in a guide to victim assistance programs is markedly similar:

> Activists in the social movement to stop victimization have begun to regard the term *victim* as pejorative, connoting relative weakness and powerlessness. Many people who have lived through victimizing experiences resist being called "victims." . . . People who have experienced victimization are at risk of being stigmatized by community attitudes that regard them as responsible for their own fate through their presumed helplessness. (Andrews 1992, p. 3; emphasis in original)

Here, it is the very quality that victims must possess (helplessness) that causes them to blame themselves.

In sum, the term *victim* has accrued associations from which even those who are harmed by social problems distance themselves. Although the reasons for this are complex, they have mostly to do with the lack of agency that appears, in the logic of this process, to define victimization. As James Holstein and Gale Miller argue: "To victimize someone instructs others to understand the person as a rather passive, indeed helpless, recipient of injury or injustice . . . [this] 'disables' a person to the extent that victim status appropriates one's personal identity as a competent efficacious actor" (Holstein and Miller 1997, p. 43). If this is true, we can add another kind of victim to our typology. In addition to the blameworthy and blameless victims, we can also consider a ramification, the victim who conforms to the expectation to be helpless and in so doing, becomes *pathetic*. The cultural code of agency has another implicit dimension: it presumes agency and it *privileges* agency. The latter feature creates a foundation upon which another kind of imagery is built. It is the source of arguments an emerging countermovement will make, Lamb's so-called backlash writers (Lamb 1996). Like the antirape activists who earlier constructed the blameworthy victim as a foil, an image to refute, the "power feminists" whose work I turn to in Chapter 5 created an image to tear down. As we shall see, they are profoundly different in their aims, which are not to evoke sympathy but to tip audiences' emotions over into pity and even contempt.

5

"Backlash" and Pathetic Victims

As I noted in Chapter 2, beginning in the early 1990s, a series of "social critics" began questioning activists' framing of victims and victimization, focusing primarily on rape, but later on incest as well. As they critiqued the definitions that had become prominent, they created counterimages of their own. In arguing that the incidence of rape was inflated by definitions that were too broad, they asserted that some women are not really victims but are overreacting to normal heterosexual interactions and relationships, and thus making false accusations. Some suggested that people claiming victimization were dupes of overzealous feminists and psychotherapists in a "culture of victims." Others argued that because victim claims deflect blame and deny responsibility, people are infantilized by them on the one hand, or they are villains robed in victims' clothing, on the other.

What all these critics have in common is strategies they share. The counterimages they construct are of victims who are so lacking in will, or backbone, or "street smarts," or common sense that we look down on them and distance ourselves. Or, victims *claim* to be trapped when in fact they do have options other than the ones they chose. The critics, knowingly or not, evoke entirely different emotions than do the activists, but these emotions nonetheless draw upon a shared set of cultural understanding: the cultural code of agency. In this case, however, images of helplessness and entrapment are either exaggerated or parodied, and the counterimages all presuppose that victims, like all people, have choices they may freely exercise. This, I will show, can sometimes shift responsibility and reconstruct *blameworthy* victims, the category we first examined when discussing "myths" of precipitation and consent.

More important, however, is another type of victim. Previously I said that some of the ways in which activists construct battered women have been worrisome to observers, even in the early stages of the social movements that brought battering into the public eye. The same can be said for rape victim images, inasmuch as they deviate from expectations that privilege agency—and of course, they *must* if they are to represent victimization. In this chapter, I will show how these arguments were taken up, first in response to more general, therapeutically inspired claims of victimization, and then specifically directed toward survivor movements' representations of battering, rape, and incest. After reviewing constructions of "victim culture," I show how the countermovement, like survivor movements, uses *vocabularies of victimism* to illustrate and to evoke—not sympathy, but rather pity or worse. I then turn to feminist responses to the constructions I call *pathetic victims* and consider how this part of the processes I describe has shaped matters.

Prelude: Therapy, Recovery, and Responsibility

One important dimension of the countermovement is the claim that there are too many victims (an interesting opposition to "anyone can be a victim"). David Rieff's critical piece in *Harpers* (1991) on the US "recovery movement" is an early and influential addition. Rieff is the son of Phillip Rieff, who had worried about cultural trends toward self-fulfillment in *The Triumph of the Therapeutic* (1966), and his argument is similar to his father's. In David Rieff's article, titled "Victims, All?" and subtitled "Recovery, Co-dependency, and the Art of Blaming Somebody Else," he takes on what he calls the "new narrative: from addiction, through discovery of the 'inner child,' to recovery" (Rieff 1991, p. 50). He is referring to the then burgeoning participation in Alcoholics Anonymous and its twelve-step offshoots, including those for people dealing with what he calls the "more nebulous, if satisfyingly all-encompassing, category of 'co-dependency'" (1991, p. 49). Rieff was making a cultural argument and a debilitation claim; he starts by asking us to "imagine a country" in which "nearly *everyone* is identified—is identifying himself or herself—as some sort of psychological cripple" (1991, p. 49; emphasis in original).

Rieff argues that recovery psychotherapists are engaged in the "politics of victimhood," because according to him, for them, "only a complete transformation of American society" will solve the problems of sexually abused, "wounded" children who inevitably become alcoholic, addicted, or codependent adults. Rieff states that people in the recovery movement "claim that virtually everyone is, in some essential sense, a victim—a victim, mostly, of abusive parents" (1991, pp. 50–51). To illustrate, he quotes John Bradshaw, a therapist and public speaker, who "confidently told an interviewer . . . that 'approximately 96 percent of the families in this country are dysfunctional to one degree or another'" (Rieff 1991, p. 51).

Rieff adds that "the one thing that all the recovery writers insist upon is that, whether an individual remembers it or not, *something did happen.*" Diminishing the significance of "*something,*" Rieff talks about the "infinitely expandable" list of recovery groups being formed at the time, including those for new categories of victimization "cropping up all the time" (1991, p. 54; emphasis in original). Rieff characterizes the categories as, "to put it charitably, broadly phrased" and suggests that the "endless questionnaires and checklists" provided by self-help groups and books make it difficult *not* to define oneself as a victim (1991, p. 55).

He concludes that "for people . . . to insist that we are all victims is pretty much the same thing as asserting that no one is a victim." In this way, Rieff, like Jean Elshtain (quoted in Chapter 2), makes it clear that the "politics of victimhood" he identifies conflates the concerns of people "buffered from the real harshness of the world" with those who are "more worried about what will befall their real children than what has befallen their inner children" (Rieff 1991, pp. 55–56).

Soon after, in 1992, Charles J. Sykes published *A Nation of Victims: The Decay of the American Character.* Previously, Sykes had published works critical of "political correctness" in academia (1990), and in *A Nation of Victims* he extends his earlier conservative arguments into broader cultural realms. In the preface, he sums up the argument he is making:

> Perhaps the most extraordinary phenomenon of our time has been the eagerness with which more and more groups and individuals—members of the white middle class, auto company executives and pampered academics included—have defined themselves as victims of one sort or another. This rush to declare oneself a victim cannot be accounted for solely in political terms. Rather it suggests a more fundamental transformation of American cultural values and notions of character and personal responsibility. (Sykes 1992, p. xiii)

Sykes presents the defining characteristic of victimization as the "mantra . . . *I am not responsible; it's not my fault*" (Sykes 1992, p. 11;

emphasis in original), which is, of course, entirely consistent with the cultural feeling rules for victims I have delineated, following Loseke (2003).

Sykes devotes a chapter to what he calls "The Therapeutic Culture," citing the elder Rieff's book on the pervasiveness of therapy and its effects. The "therapeutic mentality" has become "taken for granted," and Sykes gives it the status of an ideology, "the perfect ideology for the age of anxiety" (1992, pp. 33, 37). This mentality is the source of victimism, which Sykes argues had been latent in US culture until the 1960s. The civil rights movement became a victims' movement as it moved north, according to Sykes, and led the way for the rise of the victim. No longer *could* anyone judge victims: "The stigma that had once been attached to certain forms of conduct was replaced by a stigma on judging such conduct" (1992, p. 103).

It is interesting that Sykes expounds at length on William Ryan, author of the widely read 1971 book *Blaming the Victim,* in which Ryan had advocated for locating the sources of poverty, racism, sexism, and other ills in social structures and forces rather than in individual pathology. Ryan, argues Sykes, "not only gave victim politics its rhetorical theme but elaborated in great detail the doctrine that victims should not be held responsible for their conduct or their choices" (1992, p. 106). Sykes claims that this politics of victimization has led to the growth of a "compassion bureaucracy" and a societal disposition to seek "public— and professional—solutions to what had once been strictly private problems" (1992, p. 113). Here is how Sykes summarizes this phenomenon:

> In the 1960s, the political and moral stature of the victim was transformed and made attractive to an increasingly wide array of groups who rushed to grab a piece of the action for themselves. This rush was accelerated by the creation of an elaborate array of programs, privileges, and entitlements that were specifically attached to various groups' victim status. Besides its moral cachet, victimhood conferred specific economic and legal benefits. (1992, p. 118)

Sykes also sums up how problems were framed (although he talks about a "vocabulary" and "metaphors" rather than using the framing language from the sociology of social movements), saying that the civil rights movement talked about the Holocaust, new groups compared themselves to the civil rights movement, and the therapeutic culture provided the language of disease.

In a chapter called "Are We All Sick?" Sykes talks about the "power of the disease analogy to change social norms and attitudes"—most especially, to attribute victimization to "agents and forces largely beyond the control of an individual" and the ways in which this makes assignations of responsibility more difficult (1992, pp. 136–137). Here, Sykes notes that "the therapeutic culture tends to minimize the role of choice and free will," which creates "the same sort of double bind that characterizes the larger phenomenon of victimism" (1992, p. 146). In order to be relieved of responsibility, to be "absolved," one has to remain ill. Further, "the embrace of illness is also the embrace of helplessness and incompetence. Responsibility means choice, which means the possibility of human dignity and even of change and reform—all options seemingly foreclosed for the impaired" (1992, p. 147).

The consequences are dire. Sykes predicts the wholesale alteration of US society and articulates victimism's disempowering effects:

> Self-hatred is the final destination of any attempt to yoke one's sense of identity and power to one's weaknesses, deficiencies, and perceived victimization. Victimism debilitates its practitioners by trapping them in a world of oppressive demons that they cannot, by definition, control. (1992, pp. 17–18)

In addition to this "debilitation," Sykes, like Elshtain (1982) and Rieff (1991), points to the tendency to treat false victimization as real, thereby diminishing the gravity of the latter. To illustrate this, Sykes cites the battered women whose sentences for killing their abusers were commuted by the governor of Ohio in 1991. He casts doubt on the reality of the "battering" by putting the term in quotation marks and comparing the use of "battered woman syndrome" as a criminal defense to the putting of serial killer Jeffrey Dahmer on probation by a judge who was "immersed in the therapeutic mentality" (Sykes 1992, pp. 147–148).

A chapter that is particularly relevant to this book is the one Sykes calls "The Sexual Nightmare," in which he takes on the movement against violence against women, beginning by noting the proliferation of media treatment of the topic in the early 1990s. He argues that this "creates its own market and its own constituency," ultimately resulting in feminine "hypersensitivity" to sexual harassment and perceived assaults (Sykes 1992, p. 178).

Sykes then cites Katie Roiphe, who had yet to write the book I will discuss below, but who had published commentary in the *New York Times* under the title "Date Rape Hysteria" (Roiphe 1991). Sykes calls Roiphe a "dissident from the feminist mainstream" and uses her as an example of an alternate perspective. Sykes also cites Neil Gilbert, a "researcher" at the University of California–Berkeley's School of Social

Welfare, on feminists' use of questionable statistics in order to support Sykes's claim that "the genuine suffering of victims of sexual assault and harassment has proven eminently exploitable . . . distinctions between truth and fiction are obscured" (1992, pp. 184–185). The problem is in defining sexual assault too loosely, such that it encompasses "emotional pressure," "any amount of alcohol," "simply not being in the mood," and "morning-after regret" (Sykes 1992, p. 187). Sykes thinks it is ironic that this "feminist/puritan backlash" comes from the originators of the sexual revolution. In a passage that echoes Elshtain's (1982) concerns about the antipornography movement, Sykes describes these ironic consequences:

> What begins as a project to restore the dignity and respect of women— to empower them in their relations with men—ends with a doctrine that deprives them of their humanity by denying them any capacity for rational choice or free will. Woman as eternal victim cannot even decide whether and when to have sex with a man without becoming complicit in her oppression. It is a prison with no doors. (1992, p. 190)

Sykes concludes that "'No' means no; but so, perhaps, does 'yes'" (1992, p. 190). Thus, for Sykes, the women's movements have constructed victims with no choice, who are therefore, by implication, unworthy of "respect."

In sum, by the early 1990s, when survivor movements had made great strides toward establishing the extent of rape, battering, and incest and had worked very hard to deflect blame and responsibility away from victims, commentators such as Rieff, Elshtain, and Sykes countered with dismay. These critics sought to cast doubt on the extent of victimization and decried the ways in which claims of victimization "deprive" victims of their "free will," what I am calling agency. Especially problematic, according to them, are what James Holstein and Gale Miller have called the "debilitating" characteristics of successfully establishing a victim identity—weakness, overreaction, denial of adult responsibility. These themes, a harbinger of constructions of women as pathetic victims, were seized upon by the authors to whom I turn in the next section.

Accounting for Victimism: Critics' Co-optation of the Cultural Code of Agency

Before looking at stories about individual victims that cultural critics told, I want to set the stage briefly by looking at the political framework in which the self-described "power feminists" such as Camille Paglia, Katie Roiphe, and Naomi Wolf embedded a collective victim identity. The image of pathetic victims was part of an attack on the activists that Wolf called "victim feminists" and Paglia "establishment feminists." Pathetic victims were cultural dupes, young women taken in by the exaggerations of the antirape and battered women's activists, too naive to know the difference between real rape and feminist constructions or insecure enough to falsely claim rape for questionable reasons.

Duped by the Feminists

First to stir the pot was Paglia, a humanities professor at the University of the Arts in Philadelphia who had become famous (or infamous) after her book, *Sexual Personae,* hit the bestseller lists in 1990. In *Sex, Art, and American Culture* (1992), a collection of her previously published work, Paglia reprinted "Rape and Modern Sex War," originally published in *New York Newsday* in 1991. She followed it with a chapter called "The Rape Debate Continued," which has transcripts of interviews along with her editorial responses to some of her critics. It is in the latter chapter that she most clearly makes the argument that date rape activists are the dupes of therapists and feminists. She derisively characterizes the latter group thusly: "[They are] the people who criticize me, these establishment feminists, these white upper-middle-class feminists in New York, especially, who think of themselves as so literate, the kind of music they like, is, like Suzanne Vega—you know, women's music" (Paglia 1992, p. 60). She also refers to "Betty Crocker feminism—a naively optimistic Pollyannaish or Panglossian view of reality" (1994, p. 25) and says of Susan Faludi and Naomi Wolf that they "seem determined to cling to perpetual girlhood" and possess "bobbysoxer Fifties personae, a docile, good-daughter style" (1994, p. 55).

Paglia thinks of would-be victims as this type of feminist and also as convinced by such feminists into believing that they are at risk. In a July 1991 interview for the *San Francisco Examiner,* in a discussion of dating, she told David Talbot that "part of the sizzle of sex comes from the danger of sex," adding: "So it is women's personal responsibility to be aware of the dangers of the world. But these young feminists today are deluded. They come from a protected, white, middle-class world, and they expect everything to be safe" (1992, p. 57).

Then, in September, in an interview with Celia Farber at *Spin* magazine, she attributes these young women's "delusions" to the college climate: "I see where this whole date rape thing is coming from. . . . [The women claiming to be victims] have this stupid, pathetic, completely-removed-from-reality view of things that they've gotten from these academics who are totally off the wall, totally removed" (1992, p. 60).

Finally, in December 1991, Paglia puts the blame squarely on feminism (in an interview on CNN):

> There have been naive and stupid women from the beginning of recorded time—we have chronicles of this going back. This is not something new. . . . The focusing in on this date-rape thing in the last ten years, is an absolute madness. It's part of the parochialism and provincialism, naïveté, and *sex phobia* of American feminism! (Paglia 1992, p. 74; emphasis in original)

In these excerpts, Paglia sets the stage for imagery that paints date rape victims as irresponsible (blaming others for their bad experiences) and unrealistic, but more so, as "naive and stupid," attributes that, taken together, constitute the "pathetic" (Paglia even uses this term) victim. This victim is lacking in agency and through this, becomes the object of contempt.

Like Rieff (1991), Paglia criticizes the recovery movement in her conversation with Farber:

> It's disgusting, it's condescending, it's insulting, it's coddling, it keeps everyone in an infantile condition rather than in the adult condition. . . . Now, it's everyone who will help you, the group will help you. . . . It's this victim-centered view of the world, which is very pernicious. We cannot have a world where everyone is a victim. "I'm this way because my father made me this way. I'm this way because my husband made me this way." Yes, we are formed by traumas that happened to us . . . today's system is this whining thing, "Why won't you help me, Mommy and Daddy?" (Paglia 1992, pp. 61–62)

Although Paglia attributes this "victim-centered" perspective to "mushy" therapy, she quickly focuses her ire again on the anti–date rape movement. After commenting that "the whole system now is designed to make you feel that you are maimed and mutilated forever if something like [rape] happens" (Paglia 1992, p. 63), she states:

> What's happening with this date-rape thing is a crock. There is rape, which is an outrage, or there is not rape. . . . We as women cannot constantly be putting ourselves in this infantile position of, you know, this floating victim status, as if we were like these accidents waiting to happen . . . this endless prolongation of childhood in this country, this endless coddling and pampering of people who are in fact adult, is another paternalistic way of turning back the clock. (Paglia 1992, pp. 66–67)

Paglia has added additional dimensions to the portrait of the pathetic victim with this quote—because if what the date rape victim calls rape is "not rape," by implication, she is a "not victim." And, like Roiphe (1991), Paglia condemns victim imagery that "infantilizes" women.

This is important because although cultural feeling rules tell us that children are innocent, when adults act like children, they are not so much innocent as inappropriate and overall, rather unappealing. Once again, the emotion Paglia appears to be evoking is pity or disgust rather than sympathy (Clark 1997). From this, we can infer that the cultural code of agency, which assumes that people always have choices, makes an exception in the case of children. But, by using *infantile* as a derogatory term, the speaker points to a discrepancy (Goffman 1963)—these adults have choices that they are just too childish to recognize or to make use of.

Finally, Paglia argues that it is childish women who are most susceptible to the machinations of academic feminists. She says that "white middle-class girls at the elite colleges and universities seem to want the world handed to them on a platter. They have been sheltered, coddled, and flattered" and that it is they who "most spout the [feminist] party line" (1994, p. 28). She describes a "tumultuous lecture" at Brown University, where she watched some of these "girls, their smooth, plump cheeks contorted with rage, shriek at [her] about rape." Lest we miss the imagery of children throwing tantrums in this depiction, she tells us that seeing them prompts her to think that "these are infantile personalities, emotionally and intellectually undeveloped" (1994, p. 30). She also describes them this way: women who write names in bathroom stalls are "cowardly and infantile," and she sees "too many dopey, immature, self-pitying women walking around like melting sticks of butter" (1992, p. 53).

Katie Roiphe's arguments in 1993 are quite similar. She begins by making it clear that she herself cannot identify with victimization: in a date rape workshop her freshman year on campus, she remembers thinking "this is not me, this has nothing to do with me" before describing the "fifties-style" scenario (and victim) in the film they watched (Roiphe 1993, p. 5). Roiphe's first substantive chapter is about her observations of a Take Back the Night march and speak-out, and she uses it to paint portraits of victims hardly anyone would find appealing or with whom one might feel a sense of identification (I have excerpted these below). Moreover, she argues that there is a pattern to the speak-out narratives; "all their stories begin to sound the same" (1993, p. 35). Roiphe calls this an "archetype, a model, for the victim's tale" and asserts that the speakers "follow conventions as strict as any sonnet sequence or villanelle," that the stories are "formulaic" and "generic" (1993 p. 36). This is an interesting comment for her to make; in her own characterizations she draws on a different, but closely related set of conventions.

When Is Rape Not Really Rape?

Each of the authors I am citing here makes rhetorically dramatic contrasts between "real" rape and feminist constructions of "rape," arguing that the definitions of date rape activists, in particular, encompass too much. Like Neil Gilbert, Roiphe critiques the feminists (and in particular, research by Mary Koss) for overbroadening the domain of rape: "There is a gray area in which someone's rape may be another person's bad night" (1993, p. 54). Roiphe then uses a discrediting tactic we see repeatedly, in which she describes a blatantly innocuous incident—wrongly perceived by a mass hysteria–susceptible coed—to highlight the consequences of getting carried away by date rape claims-making. Her example: a "college sophomore" who allowed a male friend to give her a ride home after he told her he was "infatuated" with her and then is "scared" to think what might have happened (Roiphe 1993, p. 57). As Roiphe presents it, in the victim's own words, "nothing happened" and thus her fear is ridiculous. Naomi Wolf's strategy is much the same, when she writes:

> In a Newsweek editorial, Stacey Wilkins, a waitress, described customers' habitual rudeness to food-service workers. She wrote that when a group of men came late to the restaurant and, after closing time, ordered dessert, she felt like it was "emotional rape." In a college newspaper, a student described finding a computer exchange in which men had talked obscenely about her body; she remarked, "I guess that's how it feels to be raped." (Wolf 1993b, p. 194)

Obviously, neither of these incidents meets commonly shared definitions of rape. By showing that they are put in the same category, Wolf, like Roiphe, not only makes the specific claims incredible but also uses them to cast doubt on the antirape movement more generally.

Paglia is much more blunt on the topics of sexual harassment and rape. Her argument is captured in the following: "What began as a useful sensitization of police officers, prosecutors, and judges to the claims of authentic rape victims turned into a hallucinatory overextension of the definition of rape to cover every unpleasant or embarrassing sexual encounter" (1994, p. 24).

Calling this "feminist obsession . . . irrational and delusional," Paglia writes, for example, of people being forced to remove family pictures, calendars, and even famous artwork from public view. She worries that "feminist discourse is unable to discriminate the drunken fraternity brother from the homicidal maniac." Referring to sexual harassment claimants as "paranoid" and "dowdy," she asks, "Why are snippy neurotics running our lives?" (1994, pp. 24, 33, 50).

Earlier, in "Rape and Modern Sex War," she had jeered: "A male student makes a vulgar remark about your breasts? Don't slink off to whimper and simper with the campus shrinking violets." She concludes that "when a real rape occurs, [a woman] should report it to the police" and that "complaining to college committees is ridiculous" (Paglia 1992, p. 53). In "No Law in the Arena," she argues that the "sex education of white middle-class girls . . . produces young women unable to foresee trouble or to survive sexual misadventure or even raunchy language without crying to authority figures for help" (Paglia 1994, p. 27). Paglia not only provides trivial examples but describes feminists and their acolytes in ways that suggest their claims are completely unbelievable. Wolf lets her examples make her argument for her and does not overtly question anyone's mental health or ability to discern reality, but her stories are no less carefully chosen to make her characters look misguided and overwrought.

Women Who Cry with the Wolves

An additional theme that can be found in each of the books is that of women who falsely report being raped, an inversion of the rape myth ideology that the antirape movement had earlier drawn upon to such good effect. In *The Morning After,* Roiphe devotes several pages to two fabricated rape stories. Her presentation of these stories implies that they are not isolated and casts doubt on all of them. For example, she begins by saying "students are willing to lie" and says of the first woman's tale: "What's interesting is that her account didn't really stand out; she sounded like everyone else at the speak-out. Her story could have been the blueprint. Whatever else anyone can say about her, Mindy could really talk the talk" (1993, p. 39). Roiphe provides all the graphic details reported by Mindy, which suggests that the other stories she has related may be similarly concocted. Roiphe then relates how the woman was found out and discusses her confession, calling the lies "fictions in the service of political truth." Upon noting that the liar claimed to be "swept up in the heat of the moment," she asks: "If Mindy's political zeal and emotional intensity blurred the truth of her story, one wonders how many other survivors experience a similar blurring" (1993, p. 41). Here, Roiphe is doing exactly what feminist activists fear most will happen when a false charge comes to public attention—taking it to cast doubt on all claims. Roiphe then bolsters her own point by telling the story of another woman "caught inventing a rape" and concludes:

> The line between fact and fiction is a delicate one when it comes to survivor stories. In the heat of the moment, in the confessional rush of relating graphic details to a supportive crowd, the truth may be stretched, battered, or utterly abandoned. It's impossible to tell how many of these stories are authentic, faithful accounts of what actually happened. They all sound tinny, staged. (1993, p. 42)

Roiphe then accuses the speakers of being in a "competition for whose stories can be more Sadean, more incest-ridden, more violent, more like a paperback you can buy at a train station" (pp. 42–43).

Wolf's description combines the notion of overreacting with false reporting:

> At a speakout at my alma mater a couple of years ago, I saw a worrying conflict of aims . . . once or twice through the hours that I listened—I was struck by a false note and felt a creeping unease. An anxiety began to waver under my thoughts. I tried to overlook it or banish it altogether, but I couldn't; there were one or two stories—out of hundreds—that were not quite right. In one of these moments, a grieving woman took the mike and recounted an episode that brought her shame, embarrassment, humiliation, or sorrow, an episode during which she was unable to vocalize "No." My heart went out to her because the event had felt like rape. . . . But I kept thinking that, as terrible as it is to be unable to speak one's claim to one's body, what the sobbing woman described was not rape. . . . Some women, for whatever unfortunate reason, cannot yet say no so that it can be heard. (1993b, pp. 192–193)

While Wolf is careful to qualify her "creeping unease," because only a few of the stories ring "false" to her, she notes that she thinks of "how appalled I would be if I had sex with someone whose consent I was certain of, only to find myself accused of criminal behavior." She worries that the rape crisis center injunctions to believe women's stories "become dangerous when they are translated without modification into the public realm" and tells the story of a teacher who committed suicide after being charged with sexual harassment for making an "inappropriate" remark to a student (1993b, p. 193).

Paglia, as one might suppose, is much less circumspect. In an essay in *Vamps and Tramps* called "No Law in the Arena," Paglia begins by positing false sexual harassment claims and extends her argument to rape. After saying that she supports "moderate sexual harassment guidelines" and had even lobbied for them at her university, she recalls:

> On the other hand, I was concerned about the possibility of false charges by grandstanding neurotics, with whom I'd had quite enough contact. . . . Every sexual harassment code should incorporate stiff penalties for false accusations, presently rarely mentioned. This is also a glaring omission from the national rape debate. (Paglia 1994, p. 48)

In one essay Paglia compares Catharine A. MacKinnon, the feminist legal scholar and activist against sexual harassment and pornography, to the nineteenth-century hatchet-wielding temperance advocate Carry Nation. MacKinnon is responsible for "fomenting the crazed sexual hysteria that now grips American feminism," Paglia says:

> Date rape has swelled into a catastrophic cosmic event, like an asteroid threatening the earth in a Fifties science-fiction film. Anita Hill, a competent but priggish, self-interested yuppie, has been canonized as a virgin martyr ruined by the depraved emperor—who never laid a hand on her. (1994, p. 108)

In "No Law in the Arena," Paglia calls Anita Hill "wily" (1994, p. 49). By juxtaposing sexual harassment and date rape, and simultaneously dismissing Hill's claims and suggesting they were calculated, Paglia, like Roiphe and—to a lesser extent—Wolf, implies that all such claims of victimization are questionable.

In sum, the three prominent social critics whom I am calling representatives of a countermovement similarly argue that feminist activists campaigning against sexual violence have gone too far. According to these detractors, the antirape movement has perpetrated what Best has called a "domain expansion" (1990; see also Jenness 1995) in which a category of victimization has been extended to include more than what it did in earlier constructions. They additionally suggest that the feminists they critique have granted women insufficient agency and failed to recognize women's strengths. In order to bolster this argument, each author more significantly provides images of particular kinds of dubious "victims," women who are wrongly claiming rape or sexual harassment. These women are referred to not only as dupes but also as especially *dupable,* because they are young, naive, and even childish.

And they are not just children, but spoiled children who have been sheltered, pampered, protected, and coddled. Or, they are susceptible to feminists' claims because they are neurotic or hysterical. These characterizations lay the groundwork for constructions of what I call the "pathetic victim"—victims who so violate the cultural code of agency that we no longer feel sympathy for them. Below are excerpts from stories in Roiphe (1993), Paglia (1992, 1994), and Wolf (1993b) that dramatize and personalize this victim "type." Also, consistent with their suggestions that women may have doubtful motives for claiming victimization, there are ironic stories about pathetic victims who turn out to be more villainous that virtuous, precisely because they wrongly claim to be victims. They are still pathetic, but even more disgusting because they take advantage of being pathetic, in this view.

Vocabularies of Victimism:
Representations of Pathetic Victims

Katie Roiphe, a graduate student in English at the time she wrote *The Morning After,* uses literature from the late 1800s to argue that women are *not* frail creatures easily coerced against their will. This interjects a melodramatic tone into her argument: "Some date-rape pamphlets," Roiphe says, "have actually begun to sound like Victorian guides to conduct" (1993, p. 66). So does Roiphe's description of the image created by Charlene Muehlenhard and Jennifer Schrag (in 1991, in a chapter in *Acquaintance Rape: The Hidden Crime,* an anthology about date rape edited by Andrea Parrot and Laurie Bechofer):

> This is a portrait of a cowering woman, knocked on her back by the barest feather of peer pressure. Solidifying this image of women into policy implies an acceptance of the passive role. By protecting women against verbal coercion, these feminists are promoting the view of women as weak-willed, alabaster bodies, whose virtue must be protected from the cunning encroachments of the outside world. The idea that women can't withstand verbal or emotional pressure infantilizes them. . . . We should not nurture this woman on her back, her will so mutable, so easily shaped; we should not support her in her passivity. (Roiphe 1993, pp. 67–68)

Roiphe follows this melodramatic description with another excerpt from Victorian literature, apparently to highlight the similarities to the anti-rape literature—although it is worth noting that Muehlenhard and Schrag's work (1991) is written in adherence to social scientific rather than literary conventions. Roiphe feels no such compunctions, as the following excerpts reveal.

The Naïf and the Whiner

For this section, I draw upon Roiphe's characterizations of women telling their stories at a Take Back the Night speak-out—which really is ironic. The very same kinds of stories that feminists used to construct the problem of rape and sexual violence are used by Roiphe to diminish, even mock, claims-makers. Here is one example:

> A short, plump girl who looks like she is barely out of high school cups her hands around the microphone. Her face is pink from the cold. She begins to describe a party at one of the eating clubs. Her words are slow, loud, deliberate. That night, she had more beers than she could remember, and she was too drunk to know what was going on. A boy she knew was flirting with her, he asked her to go back to his room—it all happened so fast. Her friends told her not to. They told her she was too drunk to make decisions. She went anyway, and he raped her. Later, she says, his roommates thought he was cool for "hooking up." She left her favorite blue jean jacket in his room. She finally went and got it back, but she never wore it again. She pauses. Later the boy apologized to her, so, she says angrily, he must have known it was rape. She stops talking and looks into the crowd. Everyone applauds to show their support. (Roiphe 1993, pp. 30–31)

Many elements of Roiphe's description here foster an image of childishness and naïveté—babies are "short" and "plump" and "pink," after all—in a way that I think seeks to discredit the storyteller, as somebody too young or stupid perhaps to know the difference between real rape and "bad sex." Apparently, at first at least, the "girl" is more worried about her jacket than her bodily integrity. The line about the boy apologizing suggests that this is the only means by which the girl could define the situation as rape, and the mention of her "look[ing] into the crowd" implies that the girl is merely seeking attention and approval. Roiphe follows this story immediately with this one:

> As the applause dies down, another girl stands up, her face shiny with tears, and brushes the blond hair out of her eyes. I wasn't going to speak out, she explains, because I wasn't a survivor of rape, but I too was silenced. A friend, she continues, someone I used to have a crush on, betrayed my trust. We were lying next to each other and he touched my body. She pauses, swallowing the tears rising in her throat, then goes on: I didn't say anything, I was too embarrassed to say or do anything. I just pretended I was asleep. Distraught, confused, she talks in

circles for a while, not sure where her story is leading her, and finally walks away from the microphone. (1993, p. 31)

Again, Roiphe highlights elements of the speaker and her speech that delegitimize her claims. Crying is a sign of weakness, as is being distraught and confused and unable to tell a clear story. But more important, even though the woman is not claiming that she was raped, the offense is one that most people would be likely to see as trivial indeed, and most people would probably wonder why the woman did not just say something—the image is of extreme passivity as well as overreaction.

Here is how Roiphe characterizes the general effect of the Take Back the Night marches:

Although the march is intended to celebrate and bolster women's strength, it seems instead to celebrate their vulnerability. The marchers seem to accept, even embrace, the mantle of victim status. As the speakers describe every fear, every possible horror suffered at the hands of men, the image they project is one of helplessness and passivity. The march elaborates on just how vulnerable women are. . . . *Drained, beleaguered, anxious,* and *vulnerable* are the words women use to describe how they feel as they walk away from the march. (Roiphe 1993, p. 44; emphasis in original)

Given that the march is collective action in the context of a social movement, the collective identity Roiphe is constructing is jarring. It is as if she is asking us: Why would anyone want to be seen as, or identify as, "vulnerable" (used three times in the paragraph excerpted above), "helpless," and "passive"? And while she blames this imagery on the activists, those who "intended to celebrate and bolster women's strength," it is Roiphe who so artfully paints this portrait, adding vivid brush strokes with each new anecdote.

Here are two excerpts, presented pretty much back-to-back, that illustrate through highlighting pathetic victims' fear of the trivial. The first is from the story I related above in which "nothing happened."

Thank God, [the sophomore] tells her friend over her plastic cup of red punch, but it scares me to think of what could have, it scares me to think that I trusted him after I knew how he felt about me. Yeah, the other one agrees, you have to stay in public places in situations like that. (Roiphe 1993, p. 57)

A young woman asks a male friend to walk her three blocks back to her dorm at eight o'clock in the evening. Half of all women are raped in their lifetime, and she cannot walk outside at night without that thought hovering in the windblown leaves, the shadowy corners, the empty cars. She says she is glad they have those blue lights all over campus, although she adds firmly, they may not do any good. (Roiphe 1993, p. 58)

These stories do not flatter their protagonists. They drink "red punch" like little girls at a child's birthday party, and they are afraid to venture out after dark, even a few blocks, even well before the witching hour. Should we think the latter fear reasonable, Roiphe earlier has told us, "Myself, when I used to walk over the golf course to the graduate college, I was more afraid of wild geese than rapists" (1993, p. 45).

And here is Roiphe critiquing an image of a date rape victim on television:

The date-rape victim . . . is a virgin who sleeps with a stuffed animal in her bed. This is not an arbitrary characterization: the portrait of innocence defiled, [she is] the standard representation of a date-rape victim. Again and again, the rape-crisis movement peddles images of gender relations that deny female desire and infantilize women. (Roiphe 1993, p. 65)

Neither are Roiphe's own characterizations "arbitrary." She constructs a kind of cultural dupe every bit as infantile as the images she critiques.

Here is another Roiphe anecdote, this one about sexual harassment:

A student tells me that she first experienced sexual harassment when she came to college. She was at a crowded party, leaning against a wall, and a big jock came up to her, placed his hands on either side of her head, and pretended to lean against her, saying, So, baby, when are we going out? All right, he didn't touch me, she says, but he invaded my space. He had no right to do that. (Roiphe 1993, p. 98)

Like the other images I have transcribed, this one discounts the social problem by representing triviality and overreaction—even though narrow definitions of sexual harassment probably do not require that women be physically accosted. Here is one final story in the same mold, this one describing a young woman undergraduate who claimed to be victimized by pornographic images appearing on the library computers. Roiphe watches her walk off after the MacKinnon lecture and wonders, "Where was she going, and what did her room look like, pale blue bedspread sprinkled with flowers or bare futon on the floor? Did she sleep with the light on?" (1993, p. 162). While the mention of the futon connotes a type of asceticism or frigidity, clearly, the bedcovers and the light left on allude to little girls, afraid of the bogeyman under the bed.

Camille Paglia's narrative contributions to pathetic victim imagery are, like Roiphe's, initially framed in literary terms. For example, she refers to a "shrill feminist melodrama . . . straight out of nickelodeon strips of mustache-twirling villains and squealing maidens tied to train tracks" (Paglia 1994, p. 25). Later, in the same essay, she gets more specific and begins to talk again about her students:

> As a teacher, I have seen time and again a certain kind of American middle-class girl who projects winsome malleability, a soft, unfocused, help-me-please persona that, in adult life, is a recipe for disaster. These are the ones who end up with the string of abusive boyfriends or in sticky situations with overfamiliar male authority figures who call them "honey." (Paglia 1994, p. 36)

Like Roiphe, Paglia frequently uses the term *girl,* which linguistically diminishes the credibility (and likeability) of those who would claim violation. Here is a little story she tells, a few pages later. After castigating political discussions characterized by "whining and shrewishness," Paglia says this discourse

> cannot help the very pretty, too "nice" girl being pursued and shoved around by an oafish fellow she has dropped—a scene I witnessed as a student in a Harpur College parking lot. Several of us had to intervene, as the boy began breaking icy snow-chunks over her head. Even then, I was struck by the girl's maternal patience and melancholy affection, as she made no effort to fend off the blows but simply huddled, weeping, against the hood of a car. (1994, p. 46)

Although Paglia tells this story to illustrate women's power rather than their powerlessness (the "girl" recognizes her ex-boyfriend's "wounded desperation and helplessness"), because she links it on the next page to women's inability to "*terminate the fantasy*" and their ineffectual "wavering, dithering, or passive hysterical fear," the cumulative effect is one of women who "panic" and who are "pleading" to no avail (1994, p. 47; emphasis in original).

It is Paglia's scathing description of Andrea Dworkin, however, that is most expressive of the construct I am attempting to illustrate. Paglia's chapter is "The Return of Carry Nation," originally published in *Playboy* in 1992. The essay is about Dworkin and Catharine MacKinnon and their campaign against pornography, and in it, Paglia refers to both as "victim mongers, ambulance chasers, atrocity addicts" (1994, p. 110).

But listen to how Paglia portrays Dworkin, a radical feminist who had published extensively on topics of rape and pornography. After discussing her "mental instability" and "inability to cope with life," Paglia says:

> Dworkin, wallowing in misery, is a "type" that I recognize after twenty-two years of teaching. I call her The Girl with the Eternal Cold. This was the pudgy, clumsy, whiny child at summer camp who was always spilling her milk, dropping her lollipop in the dirt, getting a cramp on the hike, a stone in her shoe, a bee in her hair. In college, this type—pasty, bilious, and frumpy—is constantly sick from fall to spring. She coughs and sneezes on everyone, is never prepared with tissue and sits sniffling in class with a roll of toilet paper on her lap. She is the ultimate teacher's pest, the morose, unlovable child who never got her mama's approval and therefore demands attention at any price. (1994, p. 109)

This is a vivid and compelling image of the woman Paglia calls a "glutton for punishment," an image that is not only childish, but petulantly so. That she is "unlovable" signifies one of the most important characteristics of pathetic victims—the way in which we withhold sympathy, or sympathy is overwhelmed with pity verging on contempt. Moreover, Paglia intentionally constructs a "type," as she tells us, and then extends it to victims more generally: "Let's get rid of Infirmary Feminism, with its bedlam of bellyachers, anorexics, bulimics, depressives, rape victims, and incest survivors. Feminism has become a catch-all vegetable drawer where bunches of clingy sob sisters can store their moldy neuroses" (1994, p. 111). As controversial as Paglia is, and despite the furor that these vitriolic kinds of statements aroused at the time, she creates images that resonate widely even as they infuriate. They do so because agency is privileged in the cultural code and those who lack it are stigmatized. As Goffman (1963) argues, there is a discrepancy between "virtual" and "actual" identities, between the normative expectations embedded in our individualistic, Declaration of Independence society (and emphasized by women's "liberation" movements asserting our equality) and any kind of failure to embody them. The rape victim and the incest survivor share this stigma with the "Girl with the Eternal Cold," simply because we do not value victims and we do not honor victimization.

There is another way in which the "power feminists" draw on the cultural code to create pathetic characters, and with which I conclude this section before turning to some responses to their framing and claims. This last strategy is to show that some victims, while argued by feminists to lack agency, do in fact have choices. If they have choices, they can be held responsible for their actions. If they are responsible, they are not victims. And in some cases, they are all the more despicable because they fake their victimhood. These last are pathetic, then, but it is pathos of their own creation, and because it is, their "moral worth" (Loseke 2003) can be contested.

The Victim as Villain After All

Earlier in this chapter, I noted that Katie Roiphe tells the stories of two women who, seduced by the drama of the speak-outs and the privileging of victimization, lie about being raped. The first student, Mindy, was caught when her account was published in the campus newspaper, and "the facts could be checked." Because Mindy told "fictions in the service of political truth," as Roiphe puts it, without giving any thought to how "the boy [she] accused was in a terrible position until she set the record straight" and because "in the twisted justice of the grapevine no one is considered innocent until proven guilty" (1993, pp. 40–41), Mindy ultimately comes across as callous and calculating.

After commenting that "some may say, as an editorial in the *Daily Princetonian* did, that Mindy's false accusation was 'an isolated incident'" (1993, p. 41, citing the *Daily Princetonian* of May 22, 1991), Roiphe proceeds immediately to tell the story of another liar, a student from a different university—a juxtaposition suggesting that the telling of falsehoods is far from "isolated." Here is Roiphe's second "liar" story in its entirety:

> At George Washington University a few years ago, another student was caught inventing a rape. Mariam, a sophomore who worked in a rape-crisis center, told a story about "two muscular young-looking black males" in "torn dirty clothing" raping a white student. She later admitted to fabricating the story and wrote in a letter of apology that "my goal from the beginning was to call attention to what I perceived to be a serious safety concern for women." As the black student organization at George Washington pointed out, the fabricated rape was not just a lie, but a lie promoting racist stereotypes. (1993, pp. 41–42, citing the *Chronicle of Higher Education* dated December 19, 1990)

Because Mariam worked in a rape crisis center, Roiphe can make her duplicity representative: as she acerbically puts it, "when it comes to survivor stories . . . the truth may be stretched, battered, or utterly abandoned." Because Mariam is "promoting racist stereotypes," she becomes utterly unsympathetic and by extension, so may many of her fellow storytellers. Roiphe says that it is "impossible" to determine "how many of these stories are authentic, faithful accounts of what actually happened" and, further, that "they all sound tinny, staged" (1993, p. 42).

Paglia's villainous victims are a little different. In an interview with Sonya Friedman of CNN in 1991, Paglia was asked her view of William Kennedy Smith's acquittal that year of date rape. The case had been highly publicized, primarily because William Kennedy Smith was a nephew of the Kennedy brothers, who had themselves been associated with sexual improprieties (President John Kennedy's rumored affairs and the reputedly womanizing and adulterous Senator Edward Kennedy's abandonment of pretty young Mary Jo Kopechne to drown in waters near Chappaquiddick Island in 1969). After Paglia defines "real rape" as "either stranger rape or the intrusion of overt sex into a nonsexual situation," the following exchange took place:

> *Paglia:* Oh, I think that was an *appalling* case, because that girl [Patricia Bowman, Smith's accuser] had her own private agenda—
> *Friedman:* How do you know that? What an assumption on your part—
> *Paglia:* Trying to glom onto the Kennedy *glamour*! Puh-*leez*! Going back there in the middle of the night! She's a party girl! (Paglia 1992, pp. 69, 73; emphasis in original)

And in an interview with David Talbot of the *San Francisco Examiner* in 1992, Paglia said of Bowman:

> The girl in the Kennedy rape case is an idiot. You go back to the Kennedy compound late at night and you're surprised at what happens? She's the one who should be charged—with ignorance. Because everyone knows that Kennedy is spelled S-E-X. Give me a break, this is not rape. And it's going to erode the real outrage that we should feel about actual rape. (Paglia 1992, p. 58)

In the first interview, Paglia impugns Bowman's motives; in the second, her intelligence. Paglia's overarching argument is that women who engage in "provocative behavior" (1992, p. 72) should know that they are risking unwanted sex, but that this is not rape. For example, she says: "A girl who lets herself get dead drunk at a fraternity party is a fool. A girl who goes upstairs alone with a brother at a fraternity party is an idiot. Feminists call this 'blaming the victim.' I call it common sense." A few pages later she adds, "Blaming the victim makes perfect sense if the victim has behaved stupidly" (Paglia 1992, p. 51, 56). This essentially makes "ignorance" no excuse.

But Paglia reserves some of her most unappealing characterizations for her discussions of battered women. Here is an early characterization, from Paglia's 1991 interview with Celia Farber for *Spin:*

> You know what makes me sick and tired? The battered-woman motif. It's so misinterpreted, the way we have to constantly look at it in terms of male oppression and tyranny, and female victimization. When, in fact, everyone knows throughout the world that many of these work-ing-class relationships where women get beat up have hot sex. They ask why she won't leave him? Maybe she won't leave him because the sex is very hot. . . . We can't consider that women might have kinky tastes, can we? (Paglia 1992, pp. 65–66)

Although Paglia certainly does not disapprove of "kinky" sex, this vari-ation of her "some women like to flirt with danger because there is a siz-zle in it" theme (1994, p. 65) denies that battered women are victims because it casts them as choosing to stay despite, or even because of, the violence.

Paglia also decries what I call "pathetic" victim constructions, say-ing in "No Law in the Arena" that she "detest[s] the rhetorical diminu-tion of woman into passive punching bag, which is the basic premise of the 'battered woman syndrome.'" In her view, "any woman who stays with her abuser beyond the first incident is complicitous with him," and she refers again to the violence as "sexually exciting." Then, Paglia "conjectures" thus:

> She goads in her own way, little needling assertions of her territory and her rule over him. She implies he is inept, incapable of caring for himself without her. When he postures and demands, she is vague, vacillating; he can't reach her. He finds her serene self-containment intolerable. . . . Until it is recognized that women in these relationships are exerting their own form of aggression, battering will remain an enigma. (1994, pp. 43–44)

Paglia also uses the terms *mutual war game* and *sadomasochism* to describe what is "concealed by the judgmental term 'battered woman syndrome'" (1994, p. 44).

Paglia is able, not surprisingly, to use another notorious case, that of the Bobbitts, to illustrate how victims "are exerting their own form of aggression." In 1993, Lorena Bobbitt severed her sleeping husband's penis, testifying later that he had fallen asleep after raping her, had abused her for years, and had forced her to have an abortion. Feminists rallied to her defense. During the trial, Paglia joined Susan Estrich, a well-known rape survivor, antirape activist, and author of *Real Rape* (1988), and Susan Milano, a battered women's activist (whose own father had murdered her mother in 1989), on *CNN & Company*. After hearing that Lorena Bobbitt was reported to have battered her husband, Paglia says:

> I have to say I am not surprised at this new evidence. I have *always* regarded the Bobbitt relationship as a sadomasochistic one *on both sides*—both physically and psychologically. And my opinion remains that . . . Lorena Bobbitt committed a cruel and barbarous act, and a cowardly one, by attacking her husband while he was asleep. I reject *any* prior claim of victimization. . . . I do not excuse Lorena Bobbitt for what she did. I think it is criminal and she must go to prison! (1994, p. 419; emphasis in original)

Then, after talking about some women's "*addiction* to a certain kind of s&m relationship—that I believe is going on here," Paglia furiously rejects claims that women stay in violent relationships because they are financially dependent on their husbands as a "bunch of *malarky!*" (1994, p. 420, emphasis in original). The interview excerpt concludes:

> A woman who stays after she has been battered—*as* in this case—is psychologically addicted to that relationship. *She* was getting something out of it too! . . . There was a love relationship going on here—a *love-hate relationship* of ambivalence. She was *not* a pure victim! (Paglia 1994, p. 421; emphasis in original)

Although the comments of Estrich and Milano are not included in the excerpt, at one point Paglia says that she agrees with the former that this is "vigilantism," suggesting that Estrich, a lawyer, might see Bobbitt as somewhat less than the pure victim as well. But it is clear that Paglia means her analysis to apply beyond this dramatic case. She says that the case is a "*wonderful* demonstration . . . of the inadequacy of the normal victimization rhetoric of feminism" and that it shows that "*women* are as aggressive in sexual relationships and as vengeful as *men!*"—thus generalizing in a way that rejects helpless, innocent victim imagery and replaces it with that of the kitchen knife–wielding "*not* a pure victim" (Paglia 1994, p. 420; emphasis in original).

Lest we think that Paglia rejects pathetic victim imagery entirely, remember her descriptions of her "whimpering" and "pathetic" students cited above and her portrait of Andrea Dworkin as "The Girl with the Perpetual Cold." But it is Naomi Wolf who really manages to work deftly with the cultural code of agency. In a chapter in *Fire with Fire* (1993b) titled "Victim Feminism's Recent Impasses," Wolf uses some sensational criminal cases to argue that "victim feminism" confers so much "prestige" on victims some women will fabricate their own victimization. This makes these women pathetic without conferring true victim status on them. She also contends that victim feminism is blind to women's ability to be violent and ultimately, blind to their ability to choose. Here, the seemingly pathetic victim turns out to be not a true victim either.

Under the heading "Prestige Through Victimization," Wolf tells the story of Azalea Cooley and Susan Soen, a biracial lesbian couple in Portland, Oregon, who committed hate crimes against themselves in 1992 as part of what Wolf refers to as a "tragic hoax" (1993b, p. 203). After detailing the crimes and the rallying of activists to the couple's cause, Wolf describes an antihate rally and a parade, during which Portland police officers searched the couple's home and found the materials used to commit the crimes. Although acknowledging that Cooley, a "poster child," was mentally ill, Wolf castigates "victim feminists" for responding to her the way they did. "It is easy to see, in retrospect," she says, "how the identity of 'perfect victim' provided more support and recognition than might an identity of successful coping. . . . The worse her afflictions, the greater, she found, was her prestige." Wolf comments that the "fashionable lapse in logic among the left right now is that you can't identify *with* victims of oppression unless you identify *as* a victim" (1993b, pp. 202–203; emphasis in original).

Perhaps it is because Wolf is arguing against identifying "as" victims that she constructs victims "with" whom it is so hard to identify. Adding to Cooley's pathetic victim-as-villain status is Wolf's description of her telling her friends she had brain cancer: "She even shaved her head and eyebrows to maintain the illusion" and "confined herself to a wheelchair, claiming that the brain tumor had metastasized to affect her spine" (1993b, p. 203). In telling the reader this story, of a woman who is manufacturing her own illness and disability in addition to her victimization, Wolf provides a characterization of victims who are not really victims but pretend to be or are thought to be weaker than they are, who present the illusion of being trapped but who are in fact agents of their own destiny. Wolf does this to show that sympathy is misplaced; she knows, apparently, that cultural feeling rules require blamelessness and makes certain to attribute blame as she thinks we ought.

This is clearer yet in Wolf's discussion of Jean Harris, the "impeccably coifed" mistress of Scarsdale diet doctor Herman Tarnower, whom she shot and killed in 1980. Again, Wolf begins with a story detailing the crime itself: after driving to the doctor's house "hoping, as she claimed later, to kill herself. . . . Instead, Mrs. Harris shot him four times and left him dead." Framing Harris's story as "claimed" and reporting how many times Tarnower was shot suggests that Harris was a liar and that the crime was methodical. But, according to Wolf, Harris's "supporters, the mainstream press, and Harris herself collaborate perfectly in enshrining the killer as a victim" (1993b, p. 197). Then she asks:

> Whence the notion that Harris was not aggressor but victim? There was a suggestion that Dr. Tarnower had hit Harris, though she did not use that allegation as part of her defense. Harris was also suffering from drug withdrawal the night of the murder. But the real reason was that Harris was seen as helplessly in love, trapped, in her words, in a "magnificent obsession." Obsessive love and drugs or alcohol are the two most common reasons abusive men offer for murdering their wives or girlfriends. (Wolf 1993b, pp. 198–199)

Wolf asserts that "Jean Harris's character or culpability are not [her] subjects," but in the excerpt above, defining Harris as a victim is a "notion"—a term that, according to dictionary.reference.com, is often used to convey "a fanciful or foolish idea, a whim" or just "an opinion, view, or belief" rather than a fact. Harris *may* have been hit (real victimization that might require sympathy) but *was* a drug addict (sympathy is more tenuous). And she was only *seen as* "helplessly" obsessed, a "reason" that along with drugs is the excuse of murderers; thus Wolf's language explicitly and implicitly transforms Harris into a liar and a murderer who seeks to capitalize on public perceptions of her helplessness.

Wolf makes it very clear that Harris is not a victim because she is an agent. When she complains about "the way the popular mind turned somersaults to see [Harris] as an innocent victim," she asserts that as a consequence: "instead of seeing Mrs. Harris as a woman who had a wealth of options compared with other women who kill, victim feminism turns her into a mirror-image Mother Teresa figure, a hapless perfect lady to whom bad things happened" (Wolf 1993b, pp. 199–200). Like Azalea Cooley, in Wolf's telling of the story, Harris only pretends to be infirm ("hapless") and dupes the public. Wolf uses the phrase "perfect lady" because she makes much of how the press depicted Harris as such and of Harris's own presentation of herself as a "perfect Lady Bountiful" in prison. Like Cooley, Harris is all the more despicable because her weakness is contrived. And when Wolf says that victim feminists' "reluctance to assign women responsibility for their actions, evil as well as good, mirrors the opposition's traditional claim that women are children" (Wolf 1993b, p. 201), she draws upon the cultural code that joins together responsibility and respect.

Finally, Wolf compares the Harris case to the case of Amy Fisher (the Long Island girl who shot and disfigured her married lover's wife in 1992). Wolf says:

> Both women's actions were violent and destructive. But Harris, with her self-effacing femininity, became almost a victim-heroine and was granted clemency, while Fisher, with her assertive sexuality and her badness, found her bail set at $2 million and went off to an eighteen-year sentence . . . she remains, to date, insufficiently chaste or pathetic, unredeemable and unredeemed. (Wolf 1993b, p. 201)

Although Harris may not have been chaste (after all, she was Tarnower's mistress), Wolf refers to her earlier as the "archetypal wife" and says that compared to Tarnower's "curvaceous" new mistress, "the matronly Mrs. Harris was seen as sexless" (1993b, p. 199). Above, Wolf implies that it is her "self-effacing femininity" that makes her "pathetic," which absolves her of responsibility in the public, and victim feminist, perspective.

Perhaps the most extreme example Wolf uses to argue that some women are wrongly characterized as victims is that of Hedda Nussbaum, adoptive mother of a little girl, Lisa Steinberg, who died in 1984 at the hands of Nussbaum's severely abusive husband, Joel Steinberg. The crime, and Nussbaum's failure to protect her daughter, made the case national news, and it was widely discussed by feminists at the time (Hammer 2002). Because Nussbaum "stood by while her child slipped into unconsciousness and did not call for help" (Wolf 1993b, p. 208), Wolf questions her victim claims.

Here, it is interesting to note, she first uses the words of Nussbaum's supporters to help her construct Nussbaum as pathetic, which Wolf phrases as the "psychological underpinnings of the deterioration of her will" (1993b, p. 208). Wolf quotes a friend of Nussbaum's who refers to a "gentle nature," "sensitive soul," and "self-doubts." Wolf says: "These traits allowed her lover to overwhelm her psychologically and convince her that she was worthless to everyone but him, so that winning his approval became all important." She also references Nussbaum's doctor, who said: "She was a slave, totally submissive to this man, with no ability or will to save her own daughter" (1993b, p. 209).

In the next paragraph, Wolf begins to subtly shift her representation of Nussbaum toward a more clearly unsympathetic depiction. Here is what she says:

> Her lawyers stressed that Steinberg's domination left Nussbaum physically and psychologically incapable of committing any crime. The man had attained "Svengali-like control" over her. She described the months after he ruptured her spleen as "the best of the relationship and of my whole life." As for the night their daughter died, Nussbaum explained, she didn't call for help because she believed that Steinberg would supernaturally heal the child, and "I didn't want to show disloyalty or distrust for him." She was alone with the child for several hours. Seeing that the girl was unresponsive, Nussbaum spent the time rearranging Steinberg's files. She admitted lying to police to cover up for Steinberg when they came to investigate the bruises on Lisa's body. (Wolf 1993b, p. 209)

By quoting Nussbaum's attorneys, who clearly have a vested interest in mitigating her responsibility, Wolf casts doubt on the claim of incapability, reinforcing a skepticism she engenders with her description of a woman calm (and callous) enough to ignore her daughter and do clerical work while the child was dying. When Wolf says that Nussbaum "admitted" lying to police, she uses a term that references guilt and therefore, responsibility. Further, Wolf quotes Nussbaum in such a way as to suggest misplaced priorities and denial rather than trauma-induced immobility.

Then Wolf makes the following argument, after discussing the public support for Nussbaum and the feminist debates regarding her "culpability":

> The Hedda Nussbaum conundrum is at the heart of our dilemma now: What is choice; what is coercion? Where does volition begin? Where must we see that a woman is denied options? . . . Nussbaum had what other women do not have: access to some money; some credibility; her educated middle classness. For many women, most of the time, battering is exactly like enslavement; but not for all women, all the time. We can never waive a woman's moral responsibility for another life entirely . . . we should be wary of a moral exoneration that seals the tomb on a woman's will in the name of compassion. (Wolf 1993b, pp. 210–211)

I read this to say that Nussbaum is not really an innocent victim, pathetic though she may be portrayed by her supporters. Wolf is clearly distinguishing between agency and victimization (what she calls "volition" and "coercion") and conferring the former on women "like Nussbaum." Wolf cites the factors suggesting that Nussbaum, by virtue of her social class, did in fact have choices, made choices, chose her husband over her child. When she says, "we can never waive a woman's moral responsibility," she draws directly on a cultural narrative in which, no matter how "coercive" those forces are, women ultimately have "volition" (Wolf 1993b, p. 211). Women sympathize with Nussbaum ("wish to see [her] as will-less, and hence blameless") because they know that they (and by implication, Nussbaum) "might be tempted to *choose* themselves and their lovers over their children" (Wolf 1993b, p. 211; emphasis in original).

Once again, an image is carefully and artfully constructed that counters representations of women as victims. Whether it is Roiphe's fabricator, Paglia's sadomasochist, or Wolf's unfit mother, in each case, these spokeswomen for their brand of "power feminism" reinforce the cultural ideology that assumes choice regardless of the circumstance. At the same time, they create typifications (Best 1995) that seem designed to move audiences beyond sympathy, beyond pity, all the way toward contempt and disgust. Because we take the freedom to choose for granted, we scorn those who claim they have no choice, especially if we can show that the claim is calculated and false. How then might the "victim feminists" respond?

The Legacy of the Movement: "Realizing" Victims as Empowering Them

The cultural critics of "victimism" painted pictures of women as the naive dupes of feminist hysteria, as women who falsely "cry rape" for reasons of their own, and as women who did not know the difference between real rape and bad sex. In arguing against these kinds of constructions, feminists (and the social scientists whose research had been discounted) bolstered the facticity of date rape as rape, provided reasons why women might not be inclined to make false claims, and contested accusations of naïveté. Feminists who had been charged with promoting "victim theory" took care to reconstruct themselves in ways that highlighted their rationality rather than their emotionality, or their sexuality rather than their prudery.

Real Rape

In responses to an excerpt from Katie Roiphe's *The Morning After* (1993) published in the *New York Times Magazine* shortly before the book's release, two of her exemplary "rape crisis feminists" argued against the idea that attention to date rape was "hysteria." Psychiatrist and antiviolence educator Sonya Rasminsky had written a play titled "Calling It Rape" while an undergraduate in English and American literature at Harvard. Roiphe presented the play, based on interviews with rape victims, as confusing "coercion" with "coyness," rape with "misunderstanding" (1991, p. A27). In a letter to the editor of the *New York Times*, Rasminsky says that she interviewed "many strong and articulate women who had been physically threatened and forced into sex by men they knew" and that their voices are "conspicuously missing. . . . Had Roiphe been willing to listen to women's stories, she might have learned that bad things happen to strong, pro-sex feminists" (Rasminsky 1993, p. SM4). Not only does Rasminsky talk about incontestably "real" rape (involving physical force), but she implicitly constructs "real" women at the same time.

On the same page of the *New York Times*, Naomi Wolf professes that she is "astonished" to find herself characterized as one of the people "'finding' this rape crisis" and disputes the claim that the crisis is a fiction by providing what she calls "more accurate data" than Roiphe's on the prevalence of rape, citing several university studies and Department of Justice statistics (1993a, p. SM4). Susan Faludi, another well-known feminist, journalist, and author of the best-selling book *Backlash: The Undeclared War Against American Women* (1991), had the cover story in a *Newsweek* issue in 1993, "Whose Hype?" In it, she casts Roiphe and Neil Gilbert (whom Roiphe cites, but whom Faludi claims "has never actually done any research on rape") as "date-rape revisionists" and decries the lack of media "coverage that viewed acquaintance rape as legitimate" (Faludi 1993, p. 61).

Like Rasminsky, Faludi complains that Roiphe and others "never interview any real rape victims" and argues that women's sexual victimization is a "reality" (1993, p. 61). She faults the National Crime Survey data used by Gilbert for "undercounting rape" and points out that the research Gilbert characterized as done by "radical feminists" was funded by the National Institute of Mental Health. Katha Pollitt, in a 1993 *New Yorker* article, "Not Just Bad Sex," charges Roiphe with not having done her "homework" on rape and sexual harassment, asking: "Don't they teach the students at Harvard and Princeton anything about research anymore?" Roiphe misrepresents the legal analysis of Susan Estrich, according to Pollitt, who says Roiphe fails to acknowledge the obstacles rape victims face "in the real world" (Pollitt 1993, p. 221).

It is interesting that Pollitt argues that "the only time Roiphe discusses an actual court case it is to argue that the law veers too far to the victim's side." She then tells the story first as Roiphe presents it, followed by her own version, in a perfect example of image/counterimage. Here is Roiphe's version:

> In 1992 New Jersey's Supreme Court upheld its far-reaching rape laws. Ruling against a teenager charged with raping his date, the court concluded that signs of force or the threat of force is [sic] not necessary to prove the crime of rape—no force, that is, beyond that required for the physical act of penetration. Both the plaintiff and the defendant admitted that they were sexually involved, but the two sides differed on whether what happened that night was rape. It's hard to define anything that happens in that strange, libidinous province of adolescence, but this court upheld the judgment that the girl was raped. If the defendant had been an adult he could have gone to jail for up to ten years. Susan Herman, deputy public defender in the case, remarked, "You not only have to bring a condom on a date, you have to bring a consent form as well." (Roiphe 1993, p. 61, cited in Pollitt 1993, p. 221)

As we have seen, this is in fact a good example of what Pollitt calls "Roiphe's general portrait of date-rape cases: the hypersensitive female charging an innocently blundering male with a terrible crime for doing what came naturally and doing it without a peep from her" (1993, p. 221). Clearly, Roiphe's characterization of the case disputes that a "real rape" occurred; the "far-reaching" rape laws overreach, real rape requires the use of force, adolescents are too young to distinguish, if the defendant had gone to jail for ten years it would have been a miscarriage of justice, the consent requirement has become absurd—all these are implied in the passage above.

Here, then, is Pollitt's retelling of the same story, constructing a vocabulary of victimization and revealing it as a true rape:

> Roiphe should know better than to rely on a short item in the Trenton Times for an accurate account of a complicated court case, and she misrepresents even the sketchy information the article contains: the girl was not the boy's "date," and they did not both "admit" they were "sexually involved." The two, indeed, disagreed about the central facts of the case. The article does mention something Roiphe chose to omit: the girl was fifteen years old. . . . The offender, it turns out, was dating another girl living in the house where the rape took place, and not the victim, who, far from passively enduring his assault, did what Roiphe implies she did not: she slapped him, demanded that he withdraw, and, in the morning, told her mother, whereupon they went immediately to the police. (1993, p. 222)

As we know from reading rape stories in Chapter 2, Pollitt's victim is an "ideal victim" (Christie 1986): young, vulnerable by circumstance, and one who fought back and "immediately" reported the crime. Further, Pollitt, like Faludi, debunks Roiphe's efforts to "debunk statistics." She counters with data from studies "conducted by the Crime Victims Research and Treatment Center at the Medical University of South Carolina, working under a grant from the National Institute of Drug Abuse" and dismantles Roiphe's criticisms of the Koss research first published in *Ms.* in 1985 (1993, p. 222). And finally, she counters Roiphe's argument that if so many of her friends were being raped "wouldn't [she] know about it?" by noting what she knows of her "own circle of acquaintances":

> eight rapes by strangers (including one on a college campus), two sexual assaults (one Central Park, one Prospect Park), one abduction (woman walking down street forced into car full of men), one date rape involving a Mickey Finn, which resulted in pregnancy and abortion, and two stalkings (one ex-lover, one deranged fan); plus one brutal beating by a boyfriend, three incidents of childhood incest (none involving therapist-aided "recovered memories"), and one bizarre incident in which a friend went to a man's apartment after meeting him at a party and was forced by him to spend the night under the shower, naked, while he debated whether to kill her, rape her, or let her go. (Pollitt 1993, p. 223)

Like the story of the girl in New Jersey, all of the women on this list are unambiguously victims, as well as constituting a counter anecdote to Roiphe's "impressions." The only potentially questionable incident, the date rape, involves a drugged victim and terrible consequences, in stark contrast to Roiphe's and Paglia's easily offended, pampered coeds.

In response to stories of false claims of victimization, feminists counter with stories of what happens to real rape victims who seek help. After Roiphe's "Date Rape Hysteria" opinion piece came out (1991), Carol Sanger, then a visiting professor at Stanford Law School, wrote a letter to the *New York Times* in which she pointed out that consent "is what legally distinguishes date sex from date rape" and that juries as well as dates assess whether consent is given in a culture of "profound ambivalence." She castigates Roiphe's "obliviousness to the social and legal settings in which we act" (Sanger 1991, p. A34). Pollitt admonishes: "Nowhere does Roiphe acknowledge that . . . in the real world women who have been raped face enormous obstacles in obtaining justice in the courts or sympathy from their friends and families" (1993, p. 221).

Real Feminists

In addition to talking about real rape in the real world, feminists responded to images of themselves as naive, faint-hearted, and prudish with stories about their own experiences, of feminism and of sex. In 1992, Naomi Wolf engaged in debate with Camille Paglia in the pages of *The New Republic,* first arguing that far from being "prudish" and "puritanical,"

> feminism, like no other revolutionary movement except gay liberation, is sparked, driven, and fueled on the combustion of sexual desire. . . . The great feminists have been women of passionate impulses, sensuous beauty, and intense sexual magnetism. . . . Abstract principles can enlist our loyalties, but they can't fire the blood; political commitment often comes from intense physical experience. (Wolf 1992, p. 24)

Wolf goes on to say:

> I became a feminist because when I was 15, I was given the essential feminist gift: a safe loss of virtue unmarked by social ostracism; an orgasm that was pure heat and light, unshadowed by the specter of death from septicemia on a basement gurney. I became a feminist because a kindly young intern in a white lab coat at Planned Parenthood handed me, with no lectures or questions, a rubber disk and a trial-size tube of gel. No one made me sign a release that it would be used for non-threatening, egalitarian, unphallocentric activity. It—and hence my body—were [sic] mine to do with what I pleased. That is feminism, and that's why it's sexy. (1992, pp. 23–25)

Then, in ironic contrast to Paglia's frequent references to her own sexually charged, male-dominated rock and roll personae, Wolf says that she is listening to "new music" on her own radio; "raunchy, witty, crashing, humming, flirting, roaring . . . songs about women, and nothing like them has ever been sung before . . . urgent and scary and sweet" (1992, p. 25).

Thus, it is no surprise that in Wolf's "Date Rape Debate" letter to the editor excerpted above, part of her "astonishment" results from her perception that she was being accused by Roiphe of trying to "roll back the sexual revolution." She refers to her earlier (1990) bestseller, *The Beauty Myth,* and claims that in it, she "celebrates sexual pleasure throughout. . . . If anything, my enthusiasm for the female sexual yes borders on the fulsome" (Wolf 1993a, p. SM4). Wolf takes care in both her letter and her essay to show that she knows the difference between rape and sex: in 1992 she says that "it is to the extent that many feminists love sex that we hate rape" (1992, p. 25), and in 1993, quoting herself in *The Beauty Myth,* she says that she has enjoined women to "seek out the sex we want and fight fiercely against the sex we do not want" (1993a, p. SM4).

Near the conclusion of her *Newsweek* cover story, Susan Faludi wonders where "date rape revisionists" are finding the young women that "wallow in victimhood," given that "at least 84 percent of rapes go unreported." Then, in a manner similar to Wolf's, she offers a contemporary image of feminists countering Roiphe's. The "hordes of victim-emoting gals" are *not* to be found

> in feminist circles where the most striking recent development has been a massive influx not of hanky-clutching neo-Victorians but of such stand-tall feminist groups as Riot GRRRL, Guerrilla Girls, WHAM, YELL, and, my personal favorite, Random Pissed Off Women. These new feminists use wit, not whining, megaphones, not moping, to deliver their point. (Faludi 1993, p. 61)

A little less dramatically, Katha Pollitt makes much the same point:

> The point [Roiphe] misses is that it was not the theories of academics or of would-be Victorian maidens masquerading as Madonna fans that made sexual violence and harassment an issue. It was the movement of women into male-dominated venues. . . . If Roiphe's contention that focusing on "victimhood" were right, the experience of Anita Hill [who testified before Congress in 1991 about being sexually harassed by her former colleague and then Supreme Court nominee Clarence Thomas] would have sent feminists off weeping, en masse, to a separatist commune. Instead, it sparked a wave of activism that revitalized street-level feminism and swept unprecedented numbers of women into Congress. (1993, p. 224)

Pollitt also expresses some ironic dismay at Roiphe's lack of attention to "female pleasure" in descriptions of her and her peers' rebellious sexual escapades, saying that it would be "wonderful to hear from women who are . . . retaining the vital spark of sexual adventure" (1993, p. 224).

In all of these descriptions, women face real victimization, but do not make a "career" or "vocation" or "identity" (Wolf 1993b) out of being a victim. None of these images are pathetic; rather, they refute pathos, pity, contempt. They are images of women who are "raunchy," who "fight fiercely" and "stand tall," are "revitalized" and "sexually adventurous." And they are, importantly, agents whose victimization

takes place, when it does, in a "real world" with real rapists and real
structural and cultural obstacles. Kio Stark (a graduate student at Yale at
the time), who wrote a critical review in 1994 of Roiphe's *The Morning
After* and Wolf's *Fire with Fire* for *The Nation,* put it this way:

> The much-minced distinction between physical and emotional coer-
> cion (the warfare by anecdote that animates debate over definitions of
> both rape and harassment) is finally not the salient issue. Far more
> pressing are the ways in which these instances of coercion are also
> enabled by social and economic structure rather than gender alone.
> (1994, p. 138)

By emphasizing the reality of all these forms of "coercion," the feminist
counterargument returns once more to the cultural code of agency. Stark
argues that, according to Wolf, "if women don't earn their equality, 'it
will be because women on some level have *chosen* not to exert the
power that is our birthright'" (Stark 1994, p. 138, citing Wolf 1993b;
emphasis in Wolf). Once again, in order to account for victimhood,
activists deny women's untrammeled freedom to choose.

In conclusion, in analyzing cultural critics' claims of "victimism" in
the women's movements against rape and battering, we have seen that
the counterimages of victims they create, just like typifications of victims created by the antirape and battered women's movements, draw
upon cultural feeling rules (Hochschild 1979) determining sympathy
(Clark 1997). The vocabularies of victimization of "victim feminists"
explain how victims are trapped in order to prevent us from blaming
them, because they (and their advocates) know that we assume they
make choices unless we are shown otherwise. The vocabularies of victimism of the "power feminists" create victims who are pathetic when
they claim they do not have choices, because these storytellers know
that we not only *assume* choice, but we also *devalue* those who do not
possess it, and then we blame them for the lack of it.

In Stark's review, she makes another comment regarding what a
"nuanced feminist exploration of the anti-date-rape movement" would
include. She calls our attention to "history," arguing that "the learned
outrage about violence against women galvanized the women's movement in the 1970s; embracing one's victimhood became empowering
when one took on the name 'survivor'" (Stark 1994, p. 138). This link-
age of empowerment with the identity of "survivor" is the topic of
Chapter 6. In it, I show how one response to the dilemma of constructing (and being) a blameless victim without being a pathetic victim is a

different kind of imagery, one in which victims become, ultimately, heroic. To illustrate this, I turn to another kind of victimization, clergy abuse, and the aptly named group at the forefront of the movement against it, the Survivor's Network of those Abused by Priests, or SNAP. Here, we will see constructions of empowered victims and also explore what happens when "typical" victims are not portrayed as women.

6

Survivors of Clergy Abuse and Admirable Victims

In the preceding chapters, I have examined vocabularies of victimization, beginning with those I found in the stories women told at the first speak-out on rape, which were picked up and retold by antirape activists in the women's movement and which set out to dispel the myth of the "precipitating" victim. These vocabularies accounted for all the many actions and reactions toward rape for which women could be blamed or their stories discredited and their victimhood denied. Storytelling in the battered women's movement and social science research on domestic violence drew on language that similarly addressed how women in violent relationships were true victims, even if they sometimes failed to leave them.

Then, in the hands of a critical few, anecdotes and other tales about victims of rape, sexual harassment, and battering yielded images of pitiful and even contemptible not-really-victims-after-all. In some ways, the last set of constructions can be seen as following from earlier ones; in order to show that victims were blameless, activists had to show their helplessness. Unfortunately, helplessness is not a valued or desirable attribute to possess and is easily exploited by people arguing the illegitimacy of victim claims or seeking to preempt sympathy. These last spring from a new vocabulary, which I call a "vocabulary of victimism."

This can pose something of a dilemma, both for victims and for the social movements telling their stories. In what follows, I show one way a victim identity can be reframed in a more positive light and can negotiate the tension between being blameless and being helpless, between sympathy and pity, between identification and distancing. In some contemporary tellings and retellings, vocabularies of victimization facilitate stories of struggle, of coping, and of the courageous disclosure of shameful secrets. These are "survivor" vocabularies, which construct brave and resourceful victims for whom we can feel respect and even admiration, despite their victimization.

The images in the stories themselves counter pathetic victim constructions and also account for how *men* can be victims in a society that stigmatizes them for being helpless even more than it does women. Below, I examine excerpts from the stories of and about survivors of abuse by clergy, to show how they too reflect and respond to the cultural code of agency and the feeling rules associated with it. First, however, I will set the stage with a brief discussion of the emergence of child sexual abuse as a problem, followed by some consequences of the explosion of media attention to this kind of victimization. The dominant image of a clergy abuse *victim* is of a child (for reasons I will discuss in a minute). Thus, it is not possible to understand the issues facing survivors, who for the most part did not disclose the abuse they endured as children until they were adults, without considering how the incest/child sexual abuse survivor movement "ripened" (Plummer 1995) audiences for the story of clergy abuse.

An additional factor is that some victims were adults when they were abused, a special circumstance necessitating a particular vocabulary of victimization. It is much easier to bring children into conformity with the cultural code of agency, because we allow children the inability to consent—consenting being what we assume adults can always do. But whether they were children or adults during their abuse, victims of clergy abuse face potential stigma as adults—the stigma associated with being a victim (Clark 1997; Holstein and Miller 1997). This has only been exacerbated by "what happened when women said incest," the subtitle of Louise Armstrong's (1994) look back at the incest survivor movement. For this reason, I touch on this as well before examining survivor rhetoric in the accounts of victims of clergy abuse.

Accounting for Victimization: Incest Survivors' Responses to the Cultural Code of Agency

As I indicated in Chapter 2, Florence Rush, a feminist and psychiatric social worker, discussed incest early in the history of the antirape movement, speaking on the topic at the 1971 New York Radical Feminists' two-day conference on rape that followed the original speak-out and appearing in Connell and Wilson's *Sourcebook for Women* that chronicled these events in 1974. But it probably wasn't until Louise Armstrong published *Kiss Daddy Goodnight: A Speak-Out on Incest* in 1978 that incest victim narratives (Davis 2005b) entered popular culture.

Armstrong tells of being sexually abused by her father and presents the stories of other victims in order to "rescue the subject from both hysteria and denial" (1978, p. 241). The book presages her later work in some ways, because she argues against defining women by their victimization, even as she allows and encourages respondents to her call for stories to dwell on the "grisly details" (as she puts it). She seems to anticipate the problem of the pathetic victim, one of her foci in her reflection on the movement and the media, *Rocking the Cradle of Sexual Politics: What Happened When Women Said Incest* (1994).

Like the narratives in antirape speak-outs and explanations of why battered women "stay," many of the stories Armstrong relates in *Kiss Daddy Goodnight* have elements of accounts. As in the earlier movements, victims' explanations of what happened to them remediate social-scientific and popular images of precipitating victims resulting in victim-blaming and condemnation. Armstrong tells stories that portray little girls and young women (including herself) as innocents and that explain why they did not resist, leave, or tell anyone.

Thus, there are numerous places in the stories that function to create "ideal victim" images, using vocabularies of victimization that emphasize the youth and innocence of the narrators. Perhaps because there is more moral ambiguity in cases where victims and offenders are known to one another than when they are not intimates (Christie 1986), and almost certainly because of the emphasis of the women's movement on the propensity of "society" to blame women for their victimization, Armstrong takes pains to characterize incest victims as *children*. Consider the following, an account of her own incest experience:

> But did I know what was in my mind? What I wanted? No. Or at least I didn't know then the important thing in my mind, which was that (at fourteen) I wanted to be held—by my daddy. The way six-year-olds are. But surely, at fourteen, I should have been capable of escaping, of preventing that. Of screaming, perhaps? Or, as one psychiatrist put it, of *biting?* Damn right. And I would have been, too, you bet, if I hadn't so carefully preserved a portion of my kid-self, wrapped nicely in tissue paper. That portion which held as tightly to a belief in the magical powers of fathers as to a stuffed animal. (Armstrong 1978, p. 7; emphasis in original)

This excerpt shows how tightly agency and sympathy are intertwined. To foster compassion rather than blame, Armstrong emphasizes her youth, the characteristic of the ideal victim, when she says "I wanted to be held—by my daddy. The way six-year-olds are." At the same time, she describes her lack of resistance (a problematic feature given her actual age at the time) from the perspective of outsiders posing questions, who imply thereby that she is somehow culpable or precipitating. To remedy this, she eloquently reframes herself as yet a child (her "kidself"). She concludes a chapter, too, by saying that "the funny thing about it, daddy, is many, many of us weren't fourteen when it happened" (1978, p. 15).

Many of the narrators refer to their young ages at the time of the incest, and Armstrong comments: "Age three. Age four. Age five. So. A great many of these sexual insults were directed at little kids, not at plump and juicy (if poorly adjusted) sex objects like I was. At little, little kids" (1978, p. 18). And just in case there is any chance an audience might still judge them, Armstrong argues that:

> But little kids are needful, dependent creatures. When you sexualize them, and sexualize affection for them, it is something you are doing to them. You cannot say they wanted it—no matter how you elevate the importance of childhood sexuality. If they depend on you for their ring binders and their Band-Aids, they're going to do anything you say. (1978, p. 117)

From today's perspective, it almost seems like overkill, that Armstrong should find it necessary to frame victims as "little kids" and highlight their weaknesses, evoking their innocence with vivid childhood images. That she does suggests either the actual force of the agency cultural code or, at least, Armstrong's perception of its power to shape attributions.

"Frances," one of the women who wrote to Armstrong, articulates and contests the unspoken assumption that she and her fellow victims had choices:

> I think a young teenage girl—never mind an eight-year-old—feels very cut off and isolated in this situation. And trapped. I felt so trapped. That's the thing I keep coming back to. I was reacting to the power a lot. . . . I didn't like, as a kid, the feeling that I had to let this man do this to me because he was my father. And I had no choice. . . . Whether or not you like it, you're going to do it. And I kept saying, "If you don't have the freedom to say no, then it doesn't mean anything when you say yes." (Quoted in Armstrong 1978, p. 218)

These kinds of statements, like the stories rape victims relate about why they did not fight back, or battered women tell about why they did not leave, account for inaction on the part of victims and respond to cultural expectations that victims could act on their own behalf. These expectations are also reflected in the ubiquitous appearance of explanations of not "telling," in which incest victims say things like the following: "Nobody I felt I could tell. Because at that time I felt everybody would condemn me. That if I told anybody, they would think I was really bad—because it was my fault and not my father's" (Pamela, quoted in Armstrong 1978, p. 41). Pamela's reason is that she fears she will be blamed. Others do not think they will be believed, in addition to feeling responsible:

> So what occurred to me if I thought of telling anybody was that nobody's going to believe me—a child against a parent. People are going to say the child was making it up. These are respectable people. Why would they do a thing like that? . . . And I must be a very terrible person—otherwise this wouldn't be happening to me, see? (Frances, quoted in Armstrong 1978, pp. 216–217)

Barbara, like some of the rape and battering victims, presents justifiable fear as a constraint against telling anyone, in addition to the unlikelihood of being believed.

> See, I never told because—I just knew my parents. I knew them. I knew there was no way, even as a small child, there was just no way I was going to ever have been believed if I went to them. Plus the fact that I couldn't go because he said he would get me one way or the other, eventually. I mean I was just afraid of him, real frightened. (Quoted in Armstrong 1978, p. 171)

Frances brings together all of these reasons below:

> And I got very trapped. Because somehow even when I was thirteen, I had a feeling that if I told my mother she would see me as the other woman. Or maybe nobody would believe me and maybe he would beat up on me. And I couldn't risk either of those things, so I didn't say anything to her—and there wasn't anybody else I could talk to. (Quoted in Armstrong 1978, p. 213)

The fear of blame, of not being believed, and of further violence all contribute to being "trapped" and explain "not telling." Of the hundreds of letters Armstrong received when she was writing her book, she says, "in virtually every one was the fact that they had never told anyone before" (1994, p. 25). Although Armstrong does not consider this beyond its significance for the radical nature of what she and the other survivors were doing *by* telling, from the perspective I am taking here, each element that excuses or justifies, is a response to the presumption of agency—the cultural code in the larger culture that casts even little children as agents and requires them to account for their "decisions." Here is one more account, which brings together all of the above and forms a vocabulary of victimization:

> I didn't yell. I kept all that inside, you know. I didn't tell because I was too terrified. It was, why me? Because I felt guilty, you see. I mean, I had agreed to it. Because he was so big. . . . I still have a little bit of the guilt. Because even though I've been *told* that I wasn't accountable for it, that I was a child—the fact is that I agreed to it, you see. He'd say, "Do you want to play doctor?" And I'd say yes. And I really didn't at all. I just wasn't assertive enough. I mean, there weren't any assertiveness training classes for three-year-olds, for six-year-olds. . . . But *playing* doctor implies that you were playing it equally. And that's the guilt. That I did agree to it. But when you stop and think that I was only a little kid. How could I stand up to this great big brother and say no? I think that would have been a lot for a little kid that age. I wish that I had stood up to my brother. But I agreed. But I didn't like it. I really hated it. (Tess, quoted in Armstrong 1978, pp. 159–160; emphasis in original)

Tess's story weaves together her justifiable fear ("he was so big") and her other reasons for agreeing (she was not "assertive enough," but she was also "only a little kid").

The use of horrific, graphic details of incidents of incest and the detailing of the physical and emotional damage fathers and other male relatives inflicted on child-victims should have produced sympathy, and did, and the movement generated tremendous public interest as a result (Armstrong 1994). A latent consequence, however, was the provision of more fodder for the "victimism" mill, associated with what Armstrong describes as the "infantilizing" of incest victims (1978, 1994). Another was the emergence of "false memory syndrome" as a social problem; this sprang from organizations formed by parents of children claiming to have "recovered" repressed memories of childhood incest. Here, we find yet more pathetic victim constructions and another source of skepticism and potential discrediting of victims coming forth as adults (Goldstein 1992; Loftus and Ketcham 1994). Both the fears of Armstrong and the false accusation claims of parents were linked to therapeutic constructions of victimization (and healing from victimization), and it is partly in this context that I situate "survivor" imagery.

Vocabularies of "Victimism":
More Representations of Pathetic Victims

In *Kiss Daddy Goodnight,* Louise Armstrong notes the melodramatic nature of the stories she presents and the desire she shares with many of the storytellers not to be known as victims. It was not until the mid-1990s, however, that the image of the incest victim began to take on a character similar to that of the rape victim in Katie Roiphe's manifesto and of battered women in Camille Paglia's and Naomi Wolf's renditions. In *Rocking the Cradle,* Armstrong critiques a therapeutic culture that has served to "infantilize massive numbers of women, emphasizing their fragility, securing their helplessness, isolating them from the larger universe" (1994, p. 3). This is much akin to my own arguments, which link stigma to the weaknesses and lack of agency necessarily associated with victimization. Crucial to Armstrong's argument is the claim that constructions of harm have led to the idea that women are "forever damaged" (1994, p. 31), because this makes women forever *victims.*

For Armstrong, the quintessential "infantilized" woman is, perhaps, the dubiously victimized women of *Confabulations* (Goldstein 1992). *Confabulations* is about "false memory syndrome," a term used by the False Memory Syndrome Foundation (FMSF) to describe the situation when people in therapy are susceptible to suggestions of therapists and "recover" recollections of events that did not actually occur—most significantly, of incest. As with so many books about victims, it offers first-person narratives to dramatize the social problem at hand. In the case of false memory, the stories are those of parents who claim that they, as well as their adult children, are victims of overzealous or unscrupulous therapists and the twelve-step recovery movements. It is interesting to note that, as a way of accounting for the inexplicable behavior of falsely accusing parents of horrific crimes, parents construct their daughters as dupes.

For example, here is part of a letter written by a mother about her daughter, in which the arguments she makes are quite similar to those of the cultural critics and "power feminists":

> Susan went to a therapist when she was vulnerable. Could she have been especially susceptible to suggestion in those circumstances? Research is full of examples of how people are influenced by the expectations of the people they are with and by the way that questions are posed. To be against child sexual abuse is a "politically correct" position, especially for activist women. To be a "victim" of something is almost a social necessity on college campuses. . . . I have come to

believe that our very sad situation happened because my daughter's mental stress happened at this particular time and place in history. (Susan's mother, quoted in Goldstein 1992, pp. 54–55)

Not only is this an explanation constructing a "vulnerable" and "susceptible" victim (Susan), but it implicitly charges feminists with the promotion of victim self-identifications.

Also like Roiphe and Paglia, parents (and Goldstein) create child-like victim images. The mother of "Amy," an accusing daughter, says: "When we last saw our daughter, she may have been an adult according to the law, but emotionally she was like a fragile and extremely dependent ten year old" (quoted in Goldstein 1992, p. 103). Goldstein attended an event featuring John Bradshaw, a tremendously popular "recovery movement" therapist and public speaker. "The audience," Goldstein reports, "numbered five or six hundred and hung on to every word," adding that a "woman nearby had a teddy bear under her chair and was petting it as if it were a dog" (Goldstein 1992, p. 270). Goldstein also has this to say about the crowd: "Many of the people in the room have had problems coping with life: unable to form a relationship; addicted to drugs, alcohol, food, love, sex; unexplained feelings of fear, sadness, anger, panic" (Goldstein 1992, p. 274).

These are not particularly complimentary characterizations; the problems of these people reside in their *own* deficiencies. It is not their circumstances (or their parents) that victimize them, but their own "problems coping."

Some of the parents' descriptions simply cast their daughters as vulnerable: "Our daughter is very suggestible, trusting, and believing. We feel that she was talked into those things easily, at a time when she was already burned out and depressed" (a mother, quoted in Goldstein 1992, p. 70). The next construction clearly absolves the daughter of blame and places responsibility on, in this case, an unscrupulous therapist:

Our daughter is the victim of a "Great Cosmic Con." Her mind has been kidnapped and raped! Unfortunately people often conclude that mind-control victims must be "sick," "stupid," or "crazy." Our daughter was none of these. Most people do not understand the subtlety, complexity, and insidiousness of psychological manipulation. (A father, quoted in Goldstein 1992, p. 89)

There are stories in which the daughters themselves, however, begin to take on some of the attributes of the pathetic victims I showed in the previous chapter. For example, one parent received a videotape of her daughter's deposition in the civil suit against him and concluded "that either our daughter was very, very sick or had been duped by some very methodical brainwashing" (quoted in Goldstein 1992, p. 143). This is a little more ambiguous than the description of the "mind-control victim" above.

But here is another story, in which the image is somewhat more distasteful:

> We began to notice Jeanette becoming obsessed with her minor physical problems and decided she was becoming a hypochondriac and she was able to financially afford any and all kinds of treatments, which she utilized well over the next ten years. (Jeannette's mother, quoted in Goldstein 1992, p. 84)

Although hypochondria is a mental disorder, it is associated with false beliefs, with illnesses that are not real or are exaggerated—just as is the sexual abuse, in the parent's framing. The daughter is also an agent, because she "utilizes" her resources to indulge her "obsessions."

Here is one more parent's description, of "Jennifer":

> Moreover, she has a problem, no doubt about it. Otherwise she wouldn't be so susceptible to "remembering" sexual or any other form of abuse that never happened. However, until she uncovers the real roots of her unhappiness and low self-esteem, she will never be able to move ahead. She will forever be locked in an emotional time warp. (Jennifer's mother, quoted in Goldstein 1992, p. 155)

Jennifer's mother moves beyond vulnerability, beyond susceptibility, to some kind of flaw in her daughter's character (the "real roots" of the problem).

In *Rocking the Cradle*, Armstrong may well have these kinds of stories in mind when she notes talk shows presenting "therapists taking control of women's minds" and the "building of treatment centers for a predictably endless supply of the wounded who, in their public display of anguished neediness, are taken to suffer from diminished capacity—to be humored and offered warm milk and medication" (1994, pp. 204, 211).

This is an evocative counterimage, to say the least. Armstrong calls the survivors "entirely marginalized" (1994, p. 211). She goes on to imply that some people are susceptible to "the lure of the therapeutic ideology" (1994, p. 215) and might falsely recover memories. She has a scathing discussion of the "reification" of the inner child (1994, pp. 217–218) and an equally biting dissection of multiple personality disorder, which brings her again to false memory syndrome. Of this she says, tellingly:

> In all of the stories, in all of the megatons of material put out about the issue, survivors themselves were never blamed. Always, it was the therapists, who had programmed them, hypnotized them, and preyed on their suggestibility, who were held to be at fault and who were, collectively, held to be "cult-like." The women themselves were portrayed as vulnerable, gullible, *infantile* . . . and at the mercy of Craftier Forces. (1994, p. 226; emphasis in original)

This is a nice description of the social construction of the pathetic victim, she who evokes more negative feelings in audiences than purely sympathy. These are the victims I have described as "defined" by their victimization, in Louise Armstrong's terms, infantilized and pathologized, or lumped in with the "culture of victims" crowd, or deluded by recovered memory therapy into falsely believing themselves to be victims—victims of therapy, instead.

In the end, it is the pathetic victim whom Armstrong worries the most about. Even in 1978, this was a concern for her. In an interview, a woman she calls Eleanor discusses a radio program about incest in which

> *E:* the girls are just—damaged.
> *L:* Victims.
> *E:* And I don't want to be seen like that.
> *L:* No. Neither do I. Neither do I.
> (Armstrong 1978, p. 209)

Armstrong recognizes that to be a victim is to be disparaged, "damaged," and potentially stigmatized as a result. When discussing the women she interviewed for *Kiss Daddy Goodnight,* she says:

> I do concede some bias against playing into that need for melodrama, for "victims," which I sense in the world. . . . Melodrama is a definite pitfall for this subject. Already we have seen walking, talking incest victims silhouetted on our TV screens, their voices distorted, being asked whether they feel they were scarred forever. Making sexual abuse seem unearthly: making those of us who've experienced it seem "passed over," as though we were speaking to you from the other side. Or as though we were somehow doomed to a permanent lachrymose state. It is odd, this—that we are prone to look for retribution against the object of the broken "taboo," rather than looking for that retribution against the offender. Eleanor did not want to be known as a victim. Neither would Frances or Maggie or Barbara or Jenny. Neither do I. Better, I think, to speak of the fathers as victims—of their own sexu-

ality, their promiscuity with power. We were only incest objects. Chipped, maybe. Or chipped and mended. *But still with value and integrity.* (Armstrong 1978, pp. 232–233; emphasis added)

Thus, long before Roiphe and her kind were to make "victims" the object of derision, Armstrong speaks of herself and the women she interviewed in ways that directly contrast images of the damaged, weepy, worthless, and false.

This is the overarching cultural context for the emergence of clergy abuse victims as "survivors"—vocabularies of victimization emphasizing that victims are only little children, and therefore innocent, and vocabularies of victimism that disparage victims if they are *too* childlike or otherwise in possession of insufficient agency and autonomy. Some survivors of clergy abuse ironically though, are not children when they are victimized. In order to show their innocence, then, they must show how, like children, they were not "consenting." This is the source of the final set of victim typifications I discuss before turning to survivors: the "vulnerable adult."

More Accounting for Victimization: Clergy Abuse Survivors' Responses to the Cultural Code of Agency

Although the predominant image of clergy abuse survivors is of male children (Bonavoglia 2008), all of the survivors in the following excerpts are women who were adults when they had sexual relationships with their pastors. It is apparent from their stories that they feel that it is necessary to explain why they neither resisted nor told someone what was going on—given their presumed ability to do so. To start, here is a quotation from the Reverend Marie M. Fortune's Foreword to *Victim to Survivor* (Poling 1999), in which she defines the word *victim*. Fortune is an expert on clergy abuse and a cofounder of a church-based organization that was then called the Center for the Prevention of Sexual and Domestic Violence.

In this volume you will read about women who see themselves as *victims*. To be a victim is to be made temporarily powerless by the actions of another or by a natural disaster. Each of these women at some point was a victim, although there was nothing natural about these disasters. The women were deprived of their usual resources for discernment, good judgment, and action by the behavior of a trusted helper. (Poling 1999, p. x; emphasis in original)

By framing the storytellers this way, Fortune recognizes our expectation that adult women can tell right from wrong and choose accordingly and aligns their deviation; the women were *made* "powerless" and *deprived* of their agency by someone who, like a parent, they should have been able to trust. By taking away their adult capabilities, Fortune explains their complicity and restores their childlike innocence.

All of the women describe their vulnerability; many do so in ways that mirror the vocabularies of victimization in the stories of child sexual abuse I excerpted above. "Et Al," who introduces herself in part by saying that in 1951 she was "the only black child in [her] hometown to get polio," begins with the story of her drunken, physically and sexually abusive father. She never told anyone about the abuse, blaming her polio and the "accompanying financial problems" for his behavior, until she finally confided in a priest. After describing her low self-esteem and loneliness at the time, followed by her confusion when her father died, Et Al says that she turned to the priest for counsel.

> Looking back, I can see that's when he began to exploit my vulnerability. He was interested in the sexual details of incest but didn't want to hear about the shame I felt. . . . He began to give me prolonged hugs, supposedly to comfort me when I cried about the pain of incest. He patted my leg when I told him about being bewildered by my father's touch during my hospitalization with polio. . . . With trusting innocence, I turned to him for advice when I entered delayed puberty. It was the summer before my junior year in college, and I didn't understand my sexual stirrings and interest in a classmate. The uneasy feelings and fantasies sent me running to my "father figure." . . . He listened to my naïve report of self-touching, which I didn't learn until years later was called masturbation. . . . He began to kiss me, laughing at my inexperience when I didn't know what to do with his tongue in my mouth. (Quoted in Poling 1999, pp. 22–26)

Et Al tells a story here in which she places her experience of child sexual abuse and clergy abuse parallel to one another and thus emphasizes how the latter mirrors the former. Even as she tells him of being abused, he enacts the same abuse, violating her when she tells him of incest, taking advantage of her just as her father did when she was most helpless (in the hospital, crippled). And Et Al describes herself like a child: trusting, innocent, naive, and inexperienced.

Another woman who tells her story in the same collection, "Lindsey," begins by describing the "factors" that made her susceptible to abuse: the "deep, primitive need" to relieve others' suffering, growing up in a "culture that did not value women," the "judgmental theology" of her childhood, and her "unsatisfying" relationship with a cold and absent husband. These "vulnerabilities" made her an "easy target," she explains (quoted in Poling 1999, p. 103). After a sexual relationship that lasted for years and had many repercussions, Lindsey says:

> A turning point in my life occurred the day I told my therapist about the affair I had had with my pastor. "It wasn't an affair," she told me. She explained my relationship with [the pastor] as being something like a father's abuse of a child. . . . Having previously thought of it as consensual, I now saw the imbalance of power. [He] had power not only because of his role as pastor but also because he was male and big. (Quoted in Poling 1999, p. 110)

Although Lindsey uses the therapist's comparison rather than explicitly making it herself, she confirms it with the comments that follow, implicitly characterizing herself as unable to consent because she was female and small (like a little girl).

The next excerpt comes from one of the 2007 SNAP "Stories for Living" that members submitted to the organization in a contest held in 2007 and 2008 for "most inspiring" story. In this story, titled "He Was My Minister," a woman begins by repeating: "He was my minister. I was eighteen. I was a virgin. When he seduced me, I succumbed. To his advances, to his charm, to his position of power." This beginning sets up the power imbalance and establishes the narrator as an innocent and submissive teenager at the time of the abuse. Then, a little later in the story, this survivor speaks, perhaps, to her reasons for starting this way:

> Being victimized as an adult is really hard. It is difficult to admit that "no" you were not a child. And as an adult [you are] expected to take full responsibility—every bit of it. And he knew that. . . . He now calls it "dating" but that is a lie. Dating is not secretive. If he had not held the position of Minister, and my counselor, I would never have. . . . Well, you know. It is like being in no-mans land . . . that no one cares or understands. (Survivors Network of those Abused by Priests 2007–2009, 2007 Story No. 31)

She also says that her therapist helped her to understand that people "can be victimized at any age." Her story thus begins with an account, just like those of victims of rape and of battered women, that explains why she is *not* responsible for what happened. And the "expected" she refers to is the assumption that adults always have choices—so she will be perceived as being in a relationship that her minister (and others might also) characterize as consensual ("dating"). A "most inspiring" story from the 2008 SNAP contest begins the same way: "I am an adult survivor of clergy abuse. . . . Adult abuse can be complicated to understand, but because of the power differential, the relationship is never consensual" (Survivors Network of those Abused by Priests 2007–2009, 2008 Story No. 6).

Another story starts: "I am a 36 year old vulnerable adult, who three years ago, was repeatedly assaulted by Father X" (Survivors Network of those Abused by Priests 2007–2009, 2007 Story No. 45). Above, Katy used the same term *vulnerable adult* as the identity representing the person she no longer is, that is, a victim, so it appears that for some clergy abuse survivors, the terms are synonymous as well as exculpatory. In all of the stories told by adult victims, we can see that the emphasis is on weakness, rather than strength; on accounting for presumed agency, rather than remediating the stigma of lack of agency. The final vocabulary I examine is very different. This way of accounting and aligning with the cultural code of agency acknowledges victimization but refutes the negative connotations of victimism. I call this rhetoric a *vocabulary of surviving*.

Vocabularies of Surviving: Representations of the Admirable Victim

In their book *When Ministers Sin: Sexual Abuse in the Churches,* Australians Neil Ormerod (a theologian) and Thea Ormerod (a social worker and domestic violence advocate) have a chapter called "From Victim to Survivor" (1995, pp. 33–52). In it, the Ormerods say they will "explore more closely the process of moving out of being a victim to becoming a survivor," a phrasing that in its ordering implicitly privileges the latter and also indicates the necessity of doing this. After first discussing how victims may blame themselves for their own "vulnerabilities," the "burden of guilt and shame" related to being vulnerable, and the "betrayal of a sacred trust," the Ormerods argue that "these are all issues that must be dealt with as the victims shed their victimhood and become survivors" (1995, pp. 33–34). Here is how they describe the "shedding":

> Many survivors have experienced within themselves a definite movement whereby they begin to come to grips with their past experience of abuse. They begin to recognize that they were not responsible for being abused. . . . Paradoxically they can begin to take responsibility

for their present life precisely in disclaiming responsibility for their past sufferings . . . in acknowledging their previous experience of being victims of abuse people can begin to break out of the chains of victimhood. They are no longer victims but are becoming survivors, who begin to reclaim their dignity, their strength and their self-esteem. (1995, pp. 35–36)

The "paradox" here is the authors' attempt to simultaneously confer victim status but obviate its stigma, through making "victim" a temporary identity—one that is weak and undignified to be sure—but one from which a person can be freed through a "definite movement" (Ormerod and Ormerod 1995, p. 42). A man who introduces himself as "Matt Stevens" in one of the SNAP "Stories for Living" says that after realizing through counseling that he was an "innocent victim," he went on and "decided to relinquish the title of 'victim' and become a healed soul. Being a victim refers to my past, not my present, nor my future" (Survivors Network of those Abused by Priests 2007–2009, 2007 Story No. 5). The process is difficult and takes "courage and determination," warn the Ormerods, "but the alternative is often to slip back into being a victim" (1995, p. 42). That is, using my terminology, to lose once more the agency the cultural code assumes and prizes.

Below, from a selection of "Stories for Living" (Survivors Network of those Abused by Priests 2007–2009), I show how survivors distance themselves from victim identities in ways that reveal the need to do so to fend off stigma. I then look at how survivor identities are amplified when victims not only move "from victim to survivor" but continue onward to becoming people who "truly live" and who sometimes call themselves "thrivers" to reflect this transformation. I also consider how gender might be linked to vocabularies of surviving, before turning to the legacy of the clergy abuse survivor movement.

Distancing from Victimhood

"I am not a victim. I am a survivor" (Survivors Network of those Abused by Priests 2007–2009, 2007 Story No. 23). "I was given a chance to . . . reflect on me, to see myself finally not as a victim but as a survivor" (Survivors Network of those Abused by Priests 2007–2009, 2008 Story No. 10). The identities are so frequently juxtaposed; one transcends the other. Another man says:

I was sexually abused. This is one of the hardest things I had to admit to myself, let alone declare it to the multitudes. I would not be declar-

ing it at all, if I were alone. It all goes back to the meaning of victim
and survivor. In one sense, I am still a victim. I still suffer the depression, lack of self esteem, and nightmares associated with sexual abuse.
Yet on the other hand I have survived until now. After 26 years, I am
still alive, I still function, and I still support myself and a family. . . .
Many victims don't make it. Many can't face life anymore. Many just
give up and become lost. (Survivors Network of those Abused by
Priests 2007–2009, 2007 Story No. 27)

This story reflects this man's concern about "admitting" abuse, as if it
were something to be ashamed of, and suggests that the distinction
between "victim" and "survivor" is important to his sense of self as a
person who did not "just give up."

The following quote is the passage in Reverend Marie M. Fortune's
Foreword immediately following her definition of the narrators in
Poling (1999) as *victims:*

Some of the authors refer to themselves as *survivors*. This means that
they have begun their journey toward healing and wholeness; they are
regaining their sense of self and the ability to act on their own behalf.
In short, they have survived against great odds. (1999, p. x; emphasis
in original)

This in itself does not really suggest the stigma associated with victimization, but consider the next paragraph from the Foreword:

Still other authors refer to themselves as *thrivers*. This means that they
see themselves as having moved beyond having survived the victimization, truly regaining themselves, and getting on with their lives.
While they will never forget what happened, it no longer serves as a
defining, limiting experience. They take away lessons learned and turn
their energies to other parts of their lives. (1999, p. x; emphasis in
original)

Like Armstrong (1978, 1994), Fortune speaks of women who do not
allow themselves to be "defined" by their victimization—we can also
read this as not allowing themselves to be defined *as* victims.

"Katy" begins her story like this: "Admitting my vulnerability is
hard. I hate it when people react with sympathy. I want no sympathy. I
am a survivor" (quoted in Poling 1999, p. 41). Then, after telling about
how she finally decided to disclose the abuse she suffered at the hands
of "Pastor Cool," Katy says:

Disclosure became the first in a series of incidents leading to what I
consider a remarkable recovery from everything that ailed me. For the

first time in my life, I was confronting my worst fear—admitting the vulnerabilities that led me to become a victim. I was giving others permission to look behind the tough exterior I frequently put up. (Quoted in Poling 1999, p. 54)

That Katy's "worst fear" is admission of weakness, and that she has lived her life presenting the opposite to the world, is a testament to the undesirability of "vulnerability" as an attribute. As Katy concludes her story, she asserts: "I am not a vulnerable adult anymore. . . . Obviously I have the will to survive. Believe me when I say I have survived in the grandest style" (quoted in Poling 1999, pp. 58–59).

Like Katy, a man who was abused by priests during the time he lived at a Catholic boys' school begins his story by distancing himself from the despised identity: "Those priests and religious brothers are exploiters and opportunists; they have the problems. I am not—and never was—the eternal victim handing out cards saying 'I'm yours for the taking'" (quoted in Ormerod and Ormerod 1995, p. 137). One very angry man who titled his submission to the SNAP contest "Explosion of Rage" tells of reimagining his experience as a young boy sexually abused by a seminarian: "So I compose a story. In my story, I am no victim. I kill the —— " (Survivors Network of those Abused by Priests 2007–2009, 2007 Story No. 24).

Another woman in the Ormerod and Ormerod collection writes that telling her story "might help me reclaim some of my own integrity, self-worth and dignity." A little later, she uses the vocabulary of surviving more directly, saying: "There is a new anger in me, an anger that is enabling me to take charge of my life, to decide what is right for me, to take risks in letting people know my story, to continue moving from victim to survivor" (quoted in Ormerod and Ormerod 1995, pp. 118–120).

For many, the shift from victimization to agency is itself framed as a choice. Like Matt Stevens, the man described earlier who "decided to relinquish" his victim identity, the author of another story submitted to the "Stories for Living" contest in 2007 (and voted one of the ten "most inspiring" by SNAP members) also describes this kind of decision. It is called "Hope Offered" and is written in the third person. The woman who wrote it tells of her vulnerability, the "skeletons of her past," and of being "alone with the heartache . . . alone with the disappointment." She also describes being "groomed" by her pastor for a sexual relationship, and in another statement indicating her relative powerlessness, says that she "loved him like a father, and would do anything to please him . . .

she would dance like the puppet he created her to be." Finally, after she "cut the strings," she says that she found a good priest and his wife who helped her:

> They listened. They advised. They offered hope. And with one state-ment, they turned her life around. They said, "You can choose to see yourself as a victim, OR, you can see yourself as a survivor and move on with your life." She didn't want to be a victim anymore. She had survived, and it was time to live like she was standing on that truth. In grasping this, she was truly free. His hold on her was over. She is a survivor . . . and with the strength of a survivor, she now holds out her arms to embrace the hurts of others, who need to hear, "You, too, are a survivor!" (Survivors Network of those Abused by Priests 2007–2009, 2007 Story No. 2)

Another "most inspiring" storyteller uses the same language to describe his own experience: "I learned that I was not a victim unless I chose to be and I could release myself from the past and heal my wounds" (Survivors Network of those Abused by Priests 2007–2009, 2007 Story No. 41).

Here are parts of a story that show why some people disidentify as victims, how victim identities are framed as temporary, and how victims perceive identity change as within their own power:

> I have walked a similar path to other victims during my life. I under-stand weakness, fear, and shame. I had ownership of these emotions. . . . Every victim can blame there [*sic*] past on the abuse. I did. But I made a decision. I wasn't going to be a victim anymore. I wasn't going to move forward in life as a victim. I choose to live my life. Not live the past. (Survivors Network of those Abused by Priests 2007–2009, Story No. 46)

Another woman does not use the terms *victim* or *survivor* but makes an identity claim similar to that in "Hope Offered" and to that of the man in the excerpt directly above:

> During this whole process [of remembering and disclosing the abuse] I also found an outstanding therapist. Through her guidance she helped me to take ownership of my abuse, accept it, and live with it . . . to understand that I can move ahead, and be able to accept that being abused actually helped me to mold me into the person I am and to own the fact that I am in charge of my own life! (Survivors Network of those Abused by Priests 2007–2009, 2007 Story No. 29)

This woman's story was also one of the ten "most inspiring" in the 2007 contest, an indication that her message is one with which many members could identify. She uses the language of "mov[ing] ahead," which implies "leaving behind." Her conclusion further distances her from a person who does not have any power and reconstructs her as someone who does (who "owns" and is "in charge").

Here is yet another "most inspiring" member who compares his or her experience with SNAP to a "roller coaster" and says that "with every ride, I grow a little more, become more enlightened, stronger, and braver" (Survivors Network of those Abused by Priests 2007–2009, 2007 Story No. 3). And another man says: "Today I am a successful teacher in the very area that I was abused in. Like a phoenix rising from the ashes, I am here as a true survivor" (Survivors Network of those Abused by Priests 2007–2009, 2007 Story No. 34).

Beyond "Just" Surviving

For some, even the term *survivor* is inadequate, interestingly, for creating the distance from "victim" they seek to establish, as Fortune's earlier description of "thrivers" indicates. A contributor to the "Stories for Living" describes a therapeutic trip to the woods with a group of "victims/survivors" during which the women threw eggs at rocks, shouting and cheering together. "We had become cheerleaders for one another," the storyteller says, "on our healing journey from victim to survivor to celebrant" (Survivors Network of those Abused by Priests 2007–2009, 2007 Story No. 17). This idea of celebration is also captured in a phrase I read in a couple of different stories: "Life is not about waiting for the storm to pass, it is about learning to dance in the rain" (Survivors Network of those Abused by Priests 2007–2009, 2007 Story No. 38).

One woman in the Poling collection, Hope, starts her tale of abuse with the following epigraph (each of the narratives in this book begins with a similar epigraph, which presumably is a statement or description that the narrator or Nancy Poling thought representative of the tale that follows):

> I was tired of patting myself on the back because I hadn't committed suicide. I was tired of protecting my abusers and feeling all the guilt and shame. I wanted to give my children more, and I wanted to protect them from being victimized someday. I decided to deal with the issue head-on. Being a survivor wasn't enough for me anymore. I wanted to thrive. (Quoted in Poling 1999, p. 61)

Hope separates her story into three sections: "The Victim's Story," "The Survivor's Story," and "The Thriver's Story," encapsulating her identity journey. Hope says that "the biggest difference came when I told the truth to a group of people," and finally "truth moved me from being a survivor to being a thriver." Her words are echoed by Mikki, who reflects on her own experience and relates:

> Sometimes I want to scream, "Yes, I am a victim of clergy sexual abuse!" Yes, it did happen to me. . . . But in many ways I am no longer a victim. I don't even want to use the word "survivor," because I don't want just to survive. I want to live and thrive. And I am thriving—despite what happened, despite the pain, despite the shame I feel, despite the secret. . . . I will not let the victimized part of my life own me, define me, or kill me. (Quoted in Poling 1999, pp. 78, 98–99)

Mikki's words reflect the tensions between victimization and agency that I have been delineating. In a society where all too many people question, discredit, or deny victim identity claims on the basis of an assumption and ideology of choice no matter what the circumstances, men and women like Mikki "want to scream" to make their voices heard and believed. At the same time, despite feeling somehow responsible (as her use of the word *shame* suggests), she works to redefine herself as a person who "will not let" things happen to her—that is, as an agent.

Like those in others' stories, the vocabularies I have excerpted here accomplish or seek to create new identities that acknowledge victim identities but construct them as transient (albeit necessary to recognize and "own" in order to transcend). When storytellers distance themselves from their hard-fought victim selves, "moving" from being victims to survivors and even "thrivers," they simultaneously divest themselves of the stigma that so easily attaches to any identity that evokes the pathetic. Next, I consider how gender complicates these processes, a topic about which another book could easily be written and which I touch on only briefly here before concluding.

A Reflection on Gender and the Cultural Code of Agency

There are four sets of claims or frames of interest when thinking about how survivors of clergy abuse are gendered. First, there are the claims that dominant images of victims are of children, especially little boys. Second, feminists claim women are the "invisible" victims of clergy abuse. Third, although social scientists report that there are more male victims than female victims (e.g., Rossetti 1995), feminists argue that the statistics may be misleading. Despite the notion that men are less likely to disclose abuse (because of homophobia and masculinities that steer men away from seeking help), women are *more* afraid of telling than men because they know they are likely to be blamed. Fourth, feminists and others assert, people are less sympathetic toward female victims, both because the abuse of little boys and male adolescents is seen as more heinous and because people do think of women, even very young women, as "seductive" and "participating."

In the first "wave" (Lytton 2008) of media attention to clergy abuse, Jason Berry, who was later to write *Lead Us Not into Temptation* (1994), wrote an article in 1985 about Gilbert Gauthe for the *Times of Acadiana*, the newspaper for the region in Louisiana where Gauthe had molested at least thirty-seven children (possibly twice as many). It was Berry's article a month later in *The Catholic Reporter* that triggered national media attention (Jenkins 1996). Although Gauthe abused girls as well as boys, the image Berry constructs in the *Times of Acadiana* is of "mostly boys," and Gauthe "drew most of his victims from the ranks of altar boys" (Berry 1985, pp. 19–20).

One of the earliest cases of clergy abuse to become widely publicized in the second wave, chronicled in the best-selling *A Gospel of Shame: Children, Sexual Abuse, and the Catholic Church* (Burkett and Bruni 1993), was the story of Catholic priest James Porter, who admitted to molesting dozens of children over thirty years beginning in the 1960s. The victim who set out to find other victims was Frank Fitzpatrick, and the first television appearance was made by Fitzpatrick, six other men, and two women, with all the men but Fitzpatrick shown with their faces "masked in shadow" (Burkett and Bruni 1993, p. 13). Thus, one of the earliest representations of clergy abuse, the group that came to call itself the Survivors of Father Porter, pictured mostly men, almost all of whom did not want to show their faces. The problem could be seen as male victimization, and victimization as shameful.

Despite this widespread typification, a number of claims-makers argue that women are also abused but have been ignored as victims of clergy abuse. Linked to this is the claim that the abuse of young boys generates more outrage than that of girls. Moreover, however shameful being a victim is for boys, activists assert that they remain more likely to disclose abuse (Bonavoglia 2008) and suggest that this may be because women and even girls are held more accountable. That women were not initially conceived of as victims is suggested in David Arnold's 1993 article in the *Boston Globe* (which later investigated and reported on the cover-up of abuse initiating the second wave of public attention in early 2002). The article, headlined "Panel on Abusive Clergy May

Hear from Women, Too," reports that according to then-cardinal Bernard Law, the Boston Archdiocese review board investigating clergy abuse "will hear allegations brought by women as well as minors" and that new pastoral policy procedures "also will be followed should charges be made by women." We should not make too much of the implication that this last is not likely; in the same article Law stated that he and his staff had reviewed "all charges of sexual abuse against minors" and that "*one* resulted in a preliminary finding of behavior that he deemed 'inappropriate'" (Arnold 1993, p. 71; emphasis added).

In an article in the feminist social work journal *Affilia,* Katherine van Wormer and Lois Berns claim that: "A great deal of attention has been devoted of late to the sexual abuse of boys by their priests. . . . The focus in media accounts and the limited scholarly research on the topic has been on the harm done to boys and young men" (2004, pp. 53–54). They refer to findings from a large random sample of Catholics that "about twice as many boys as girls" were victims (Rossetti 1995) as "controversial." Then, in a section titled "Are Boys Victimized More Often Than Girls?" van Wormer and Berns review "the assumption that victimization by priests is largely a violation of male youths" and provide some counterarguments. They note the argument that priests had easier access to boys, that older girls and their parents may be "not so likely to be repulsed by heterosexual acts that boys and their parents may be at homosexual acts" (van Wormer and Berns 2004, p. 56), and that an emphasis on homosexuality has allowed the church to scapegoat gay men. They seem to agree with the contention that "the plight of female victims of priest sexual abuse has been largely overlooked by the media and that this form of victimization has been trivialized" (van Wormer and Berns 2004, pp. 56–57, citing Tolbert 2003).

In her 2008 book *Good Catholic Girls: How Women Are Leading the Fight to Change the Church,* Angela Bonavoglia (a well-known journalist who published an article about clergy abuse in *Ms.* in 1992) has a section in her chapter "Sex, Priests, and Girlhoods Lost" called "Girl Victims Invisible." She begins it thus: "When the clergy sex abuse crisis burst onto the scene in 2002, the abuse of girls by Catholic priests remained invisible or, at most, a footnote." She discusses how many of Father John Geoghan's 148 victims were girls (twenty-three) and argues that the 19 percent of victims who were girls reported by the often-cited John Jay College of Criminal Justice survey of priests and ordained deacons in 2004 comes from questionable self-report data (Bonavoglia 2008, pp. 62–64).

Mary A. Tolbert, whom van Wormer and Berns cited (as mentioned above), is a professor of biblical studies at the Pacific School of Religion and the Graduate Theological Union in Berkeley, California, and executive director of their Center for Lesbian and Gay Studies in Religion and Ministry (CLGS). In a 2003 article on the CLGS website titled "Where Have All the Young Girls Gone?" she argues that the absence of young girls in media debates on clergy abuse "begs for explanation." She attributes the lacunae to a heterosexist attitude exemplified by the remark of Cardinal Francis George of Chicago, whom she quotes as saying:

> There is a difference between a moral monster like [the Rev. John] Geoghan [who engaged in sex with boys] and someone who perhaps under the influence of alcohol engages with a 16- or 17-year-old young woman who returns his affection. That is still a crime . . . so the civil law does not distinguish. But in terms of the possibility of reform of one's life, there are two very different sets of circumstances. (George is quoted in Sennott 2002, p. A1, cited by Tolbert 2003, p. 1)

In Sennott's article that Tolbert quotes, Cardinal George had termed Geoghan a person who "preys upon little children and does so in a serial fashion" (Sennott 2002, p. A1). But for Tolbert, the issue is that if the sixteen- or seventeen-year-old had been *male,* that even if the teenager had consented, it would be as abhorrent as what Geoghan had done.

In Donileen Loseke's terms, the harm done to boys is perceived as greater and their victimization as occurring "through no fault of their own" (2003, p. 79). In an article in the *Philadelphia Inquirer* at the height of the second wave, when the Boston cover-up was "engulfing the world's most powerful church," Jane Eisner says that the young age of victims is one factor,

> but there's another reason for the outrage and disgust: Most of the Catholic priests' victims are boys. "And when it happens to boys, it's a bigger deal," says Marie Fortune, a minister who heads the Center [for the Prevention of Sexual and Domestic Violence] in Seattle. "The sexual abuse of boys is treated as a more grievous act," adds Gary Schoener, a clinical psychologist [and expert witness]. . . . "The damages awarded to boys are much, much higher than when girls or women are involved. There's harm to both sets of victims, but we tend to pay more attention to the boys." (2002, p. A19)

Eisner continues, this time shifting to issues of victim-blaming and, implicitly, revictimization:

> Inevitably with girls there's the accusation—directly made or vaguely implied—that she was somehow responsible. But, Schoener says, "I've never heard anyone accuse a 10-year-old boy of being seductive. I've never even heard of anyone accusing an adolescent boy of being

seductive." The implication that the female is an active player—but the male can never be—is not confined to clergy abuse cases, unfortunately. (2002, p. A19)

Females as "active players" are the polar opposite of females as "passive victims," and perhaps Eisner quotes Schoener to suggest why fewer women come forward. If I am right about the cultural code of agency, that it always queries victims, women abused by clergy would not only blame themselves but expect to be treated in the way Gary Schoener is quoted as saying they are. What is most interesting is that the boys, even when they are "adolescent," are not held to the same victimization standard.

Later in 2002, *USA Today* published Janet Kornblum's article titled "85% of Church Abuse Victims Are Male, Research Finds." Kornblum quotes SNAP founder Barbara Blaine, who says that although SNAP has as many women members as men, this is because "women are more inclined to join support groups than are men" and also because when only boys were serving at the altar, and nobody questioned whether they should be chaperoned on trips by priests, they were simply more accessible (Kornblum 2002, p. 6D).

Kornblum also comments, however, that "for some abusers gender doesn't even matter" and adds presciently:

> And some point out that adult women have also been victimized by priests. Susan Archibald of the victims' group The Linkup was 18 when she went to a priest for counseling. Instead, she says, she ended up in a relationship. Unfortunately, she adds, it's an all-too-common story. "Whether the victim is 12 or 16 or 20, the priest still has the responsibility to say no." But it is up to the victim to come forward. And it may be that women tend to publicly accuse their abusers less often than men. (2002, p. 6D)

Why not? Kornblum posits that this may be because men find disclosure more "empowering" (quoting Jason Berry), or because victims come forward when they see others like themselves in the media, or because "stories about priests abusing boys are inherently more sensational" (quoting David Clohessy, director of SNAP). Then Kornblum makes an argument very similar to Eisner's, as given above, that "male and female victims are treated differently," and goes to the same source:

> "Most of the females who try to come forward gave up because they were treated as if they somehow seduced a priest," says Sheila Poettgen, 31, . . . who says she was abused by a priest when she was 10. . . . "If you're dealing with an adolescent girl, the likelihood that she'll be cast as seductress is virtually certain," says Gary Schoener,

executive director of the Walk-In Counseling Center in Minneapolis and a frequent expert witness in abuse cases. "I've never yet had a boy, even in a deposition, accused of seducing a pastor," he says, but "girls are accused regularly. It's a given. They're going to be asked if they enjoyed it, if they have orgasms." (Kornblum 2002, p. 6D)

This argument is echoed more recently by Angela Bonavoglia, who argues under the heading "Little Eves" that the fact that the "vast majority" (an estimated 95 percent) of victims who brought suit against the Boston Archdiocese were male "may have less to do with the actual incidence of abuse than with the reluctance of women to come forward, and that has to do with how women victims are treated and seen" (2008, p. 64).

Like Eisner (2002) and Kornblum (2002), Bonavoglia turns to Schoener and his observations of how women and girls are treated in court. She repeats his claim that girls will always be called seductive and that boys never will be and quotes him as saying, in addition: "The issue of holding the woman accountable or blaming her, that's there. It's lurking just below the surface, and it presents a tremendous obstacle to overcome." Bonavoglia also quotes an unnamed "activist survivor" who says the abuse of girls by clergy is looked at "much the same way as rape has been viewed in the past" (2008, p. 64).

To illustrate the issue of "female culpability," Bonavoglia begins with the story of Nancy Sloan, molested at age eleven by a priest whose monsignor reportedly told Sloan and a victims' advocate that "if she were a male child, he would have taken stronger action" (2008, pp. 64–65).

She also tells the story of Rita Milla, who was

> held responsible by some for having been turned effectively into a prostitute by Father Santiago Tamayo, who had begun to groom her at the age of sixteen. When she later confessed to a priest about her involvement with Tamayo, hoping for absolution and help, instead, she reports, "The priest gave me this lecture on how some women enjoy making priests sin. I thought, I must be one of those women." (Bonavoglia 2008, pp. 65–66)

Like Talbot, Bonavoglia quotes Cardinal George's comment about the difference between a "moral monster" and the priest who acts inappropriately with the young woman (like Talbot, Bonavoglia edits out "preys upon little children" and instead substitutes the phrase "Boston's serial pedophile," which is also gender-neutral). She critiques George for seeing the girl he describes not as a minor, but as

> a consenting adult, wholly capable of a clear-eyed assessment of the risks and benefits of involvement with a priest and the ability to decide

to go ahead anyway. While there may be a teenager here or there who could do that, the laws forbidding sex with minors have been written to protect the vast majority who cannot. (Bonavoglia 2008, p. 67)

In each of these stories, Bonavoglia emphasizes the youth of the victims: Sloan was eleven when she was molested, Milla sixteen when she was "groomed." The hypothetical teenager is *not* capable of consent, *not* an adult. So once again, a vocabulary of victimization emerges in which the cultural code of agency requires that victims be children in order to be innocent. What is most interesting, perhaps, is that this is necessary accounting for girls, but not for boys, if these claims-makers are correct in their depictions.

Last, there is a way in which the cultural code of gender penetrates the cultural code of agency that is important for understanding victimization, victimism, and surviving. The qualities we necessarily associate with victimization are some of the very same qualities we stereotypically associate with femininity (Rader 2008). In an article I retrieved from a link on the activist website BishopAccountability.org, the author writes about male sexual abuse, claiming that "it is easier for society to perceive women as victims than it is for them to see men in the same light," after beginning with the statement: "It is hard for our society to accept boys as powerless" (Morretti 2007). I argue that we rank *both* victim and female identities low, in normative and gender systems of stratification. Because of this, men who claim victimization risk "feminization" as a consequence, an unwelcome additional stigma. Victims are deviant by definition (Clark 1997; Dunn 2005, forthcoming). Women are *also* deviant by definition (Schur 1984). Herein lies an additional advantage of being "survivors"—their courage, strength, capability, and competence (that is, their agency)—belies their traditional (demeaning) femininity. It is possible that the existence of a vocabulary of surviving has enabled more men to disclose the victimization they experienced as little boys and perhaps, some day, will facilitate telling about adult victimization as well.

The Legacy of the Movement: Identity Transformation and Domain Expansion

In this chapter, I have examined the ways in which victims of child sexual abuse and clergy abuse and their advocates negotiate the demands of a society inclined toward blame. As with rape and battering, this is a tricky business. I began with vocabularies of victimization in narratives of child sexual abuse drawn from Louise Armstrong's speak-out in print, *Kiss Daddy Goodnight* (1978). I showed that much like the accounts of rape victims and battered women, incest stories employ vocabularies of victimization deflecting responsibility and accomplishing innocence (Holstein and Miller 1997). Incest victims and advocates emphasize youth and innocence and explain why little girls do not resist, leave, or tell anyone. The apparent necessity of doing so, even for *children,* attests to the power of the cultural framework presuming choice, the cultural code of agency. The resulting images are of *ideal victims,* like those in Chapter 4.

It is tricky because of some consequences of the "success" of claims-making about child sexual abuse. There is the phenomenon Armstrong later calls the "infantilization" of women (1994, p. 3) and the emergence of the FMSF and its claims of a different kind of victimization, the duping of vulnerable women by unethical or overzealous therapists, feminists, and recovery groups. Some of these women bear a strong resemblance to the *pathetic victims* created by the cultural critics and "power feminists" of Chapter 5 and provide additional examples of vocabularies of victimism. And although Armstrong herself says that the term *survivor* has been "debased" and "hijacked" (1994, p. 30), my belief is that the label and the identity it confers emerged in opposition to the pity, contempt, and stigma associated with the pathetic. From early on, in the battered women's movement and feminist discourse on sexual violence, "survivor" connotes agency, strength, resistance, and the overcoming of shame.

The "Stories for Living" of members of SNAP (and other sources using vocabularies of surviving), many of which are told by men, construct "survivors" who leave behind victim identities and "reclaim their dignity, their strength and their self-esteem" (Ormerod and Ormerod 1995, p. 36). The stigma of victimization reveals itself in the ways in which narrators distance themselves from this identity, and agency itself becomes a choice. The message for victims, their advocates, and scholars of collective and individual identity is that "survivor" is a transformative identity (Taylor and Whittier 1995) and one that aligns the deviance of victimization with the normative expectation of agency.

Another legacy of the clergy abuse survivor movements is what Best (1990) calls "domain expansion," which is here linked to the gendering of clergy abuse. Domain expansion occurs when claims-makers constructing a social problem "offer a new definition, extending the problem's domain or boundaries, and find new examples to typify just what is at issue" (1990, p. 65). Clergy abuse survivors have expanded the domain of child sexual abuse in two ways. First, through constructing victims as mostly little boys, they have broadened the category of victimization. Researchers discussing the time prior to the "discovery" of clergy abuse claim that "male victims of sexual abuse received little attention" (Ganzevoort 2002, p. 313) and that "most of the research on [childhood sexual] abuse survivors focuses on adult females" (Fater and Mullaney 2000, p. 282). Given that the qualities (weakness, helplessness, dependence, and passivity) we associate with victims are so much more stereotypically feminine than masculine, it is possible that it is only through the availability of survivor identities that men have been able to tell their stories of abuse.

Second, the stories of clergy abuse survivors and activists show that they perceive victim-blaming as gendered; that is, that women, especially adult women, are more likely to be held to account. Through the use of vocabularies of victimization that show how victims who were not children at the time of their abuse are "vulnerable adults," the category of "clergy abuse victim" now includes women as well as children. In what I have encountered thus far, this seems to be gendered as well; heterosexism and homophobia may restrict adult male victims from telling this kind of story (cf. Tolbert 2003).

Both kinds of domain expansion could, as Best puts it, give clergy abuse claims-makers a "competitive advantage in the social problems marketplace" (1990, p. 78). Certainly it is a social problem that has garnered tremendous attention in successive waves in the early parts of three successive decades. There is another benefit, however; the survivor stories that make it possible for men to also be victims and for adults to be the moral equivalent of children resolve some dilemmas adhering to cultural feeling rules for victimization and agency. The stories engage outrage at the abuse of boys and sympathy toward women we look at in a different way. The *admirable victim* and even the "vulnerable adult" provide new possibilities for the social construction of victims and how we judge them. I turn now to a reflection on all the identity work processes I have illuminated here and to new possibilities for scholarship, policy, and self-awareness.

7

The Vanguard of Victimology: Survivors, Identity Work, and Cultural Change

In the opening paragraphs of this book, I make the argument that victimization presents an identity dilemma. This holds for people who *must* claim to be victims and for the social movements and individuals who advocate for them, because victims need compassion and the help that goes with it, but the identity of "victim" is not one we value very much. Moreover, we have a cultural predisposition toward blaming victims, effectively denying them this identity and our sympathy. Because of this tendency, which links to what I call the cultural code of agency, we judge victims, and mostly we judge them not to be victims after all. But if we do allow them their claims, we pity them, we back away, we stigmatize. It is the problem Edwin Schur, referring specifically to women as victims, calls being "deviant-either-way" (1984).

Because one of the tasks of a social movement is to get us to care about the victims of a social problem, the stories members tell to engage our feelings inform us about this dilemma and its resolutions, if there are any. This storytelling has been a historical process, a succession of speak-outs in public auditoriums, books, and now on the Internet, that build on, respond to, counter, and reframe different kinds of images of victims. These "typifications" (Schutz 1954; Best 1995) take different, almost archetypal forms that I have identified as *blameworthy, ideal, pathetic,* and *admirable.* Using social constructionist notions of "feeling rules," "deviance," "stigma," and "identity work" as lenses through which to view both how victims explain themselves and how social problems claims-makers create typical and (they hope) sympathetic victims, I looked at images of victimization in survivor movements.

First I looked at the antirape movement, born of the stories women told each other in consciousness-raising groups and then, more publicly, in the speak-outs. Here, "myth-debunking" (Plummer 1995) is the goal of the movement. To show that the myths that accompany the cultural code are in fact pervasive and powerful, I examined victims' vocabularies of victimization in stories they told about being raped. These stories take the form of accounts that reflect victims' understandings of how they deviate from what we expect of them. Thus, they explain their "choices" as not really choices at all. Women explain why they did not scream, that they tried to fight but were overcome, that they were afraid if they resisted they would be killed.

Using the first speak-out transcripts and other early stories of rape, I then looked at how activists used vocabularies of victimization to construct images of *blameworthy* victims, mythical victims. They did this to foreground their opposite and show that rape is never the victim's fault. This is a strategy that recognizes and even amplifies the cultural code of agency, in order to argue against it. The cultural code implies that women are, like everyone always, agents who cannot therefore be raped "against their will." The antirape movement vocabularies maintain that this is not true and show the many ways in which rapists and circumstances rob rape victims of any *free* "will." I also showed that *blameworthy* victims appear in other survivor movement stories, suggesting their broader necessity and utility.

In contrast to the blameworthy victim is the *blameless* victim, a type of victim I have illustrated by using vocabularies of victimization from the battered women's movement and social science research on battering. The cultural code is the source of the ubiquitous "valuative inquiry" (Scott and Lyman 1968): "Why do battered women stay?" The problem for victims and advocates is that staying in or returning to violent relationships looks like a choice to us, and if so, the victim is not really a victim. Just as the antirape movement did for rape victims, the battered women's movement provided accounts that dispelled the notion of agency. Activists countered the question with explanations of the dangers of leaving, the structural and economic barriers women face, and battered women's justified fear, despair, and culturally induced guilt. The vocabularies of victimization of battered women themselves, like the vocabularies of rape victims, mirror these accounts and similarly counter the cultural code.

There are latent potential consequences, however, of blameless constructions, of constructing battered women as so entrapped and passive. Here, I turn to the other "way" of "deviant-either-way," the stigma of being passive when only being active has value, of being powerless when powerful is the cultural ideal. In the critique of "victimism" and "victim feminism," I find images of pseudovictims that also depend on the cultural code of agency for their resonance. Because we privilege autonomy and responsibility, it is easy to evoke contempt for women who are portrayed as gullible, hysterical, overreacting, or irresponsible or as denying responsibility. These victims are *pathetic,* and when held up as a model, tell us what we do *not* want to be. They also foreground the cultural code by throwing it into relief. And despite the efforts of feminist and survivor movements to counter these counterimages, I believe they yet constitute a powerful archetype that has led to the widespread embracement of an alternative to the victim identity, that of the "survivor."

Although the antirape and battered women's movements are (rightly) also called survivor movements these days, it is collectivities of clergy abuse survivors, expanding the domain of incest and child sexual abuse, who have perhaps most popularized the term and all that goes with it. If we direct blame toward precipitating victims, sympathy toward the trapped, and contempt toward the pathetic, the emotion that we can feel toward survivors is *admiration.* This identity constructs victimization but makes it temporary; when people "move from victim to survivor" they regain their agency.

Here, I have tried to show that constructions of incest victims as pathetic set the stage. In their efforts not to be defined by their victimization, for reasons I argue are inextricable from the disregard in which we hold victims, victims of child sexual abuse and especially of clergy abuse call themselves "survivors." Possibly partly because of this reframing, consistent with the cultural code, men as well as women disclose and organize and adopt this transformative collective identity. Also consistent with the cultural code, women who have "affairs" with clergy redefine themselves as "vulnerable adults" and as survivors too.

In the next section, I consider what my "story about stories" adds to contemporary feminist sociological "survivor discourse" (Alcoff and Gray 1993). Then, I return to the social constructionist understandings of deviance, personal identity, social problems, social movements, and collective "identity work" that I used to introduce this research, to consider where the study fits into these varied and interrelated substantive areas. I also talk a little about culture as a source and resource for all of these. I ponder what my research contributes to the discipline of victimology and then reflect a little on how it might help victims and survivors.

The Emergence and Establishment of "Survivors"

Feminists have been writing about survivors for as long as they have been writing about victims, although the widespread use of the former term is more recent. The groundwork for activists' use of the term *survivor* may have been laid by Del Martin in 1976, in the chapter in *Battered Wives* called "Survival Tactics." In it, she discusses "physical fitness," "mental fitness," and divorce. Others frame battered women's *deviance* as survival tactics. Thus Lenore Walker, in disputing the myth that "battered women are crazy" to stay in violent relationships, argues that

> Battered women's survival behaviors have often earned them the misdiagnosis of being crazy. Unusual actions which may help them to survive in the battering relationship have been taken out of context by unenlightened medical and mental health workers. . . . I wonder how many other women who have been mislabeled as mentally ill were really attempting to cope with a batterer. After listening to their stories, I can only applaud their strength in retaining their sanity. (1979, p. 21)

Here Walker not only attempts to contextualize the unexpected behavior but recasts it as a virtue, a form of "strength." Kathleen Barry, in *Female Sexual Slavery,* uses a similar framing, in which women are "active and doing," but "often they are or appear to be complicit with their enslavement as a means of survival, a way of staying alive and coping" (1979, p. 39). This is the core of survivor discourse; it simultaneously normalizes deviance and elevates the moral standing of the deviant. Moreover, it does so by conferring agency on battered women even as it excuses them from responsibility for their deviance, thus balancing the tensions created by the helplessness and entrapment of victims.

Liz Kelly, author of *Surviving Sexual Violence* (1988), claims that "within feminism" the term *survivor* began to replace the term *victim* in the early 1980s. Kelly says: "Just as we are not passive victims at the time of assaults nor are we passive victims in relation to the consequences of abuse" (1988, p. 159). This foreshadows the complaints of later activists such as Esther Madriz, who notes that early feminist studies "tended to disregard the resistance strategies used by many women who struggle against their powerlessness" (Madriz 1997, p. 73). In Kelly's chapter "Victims or Survivors? Resistance, Coping and Survival," she focuses on women "as decision-makers and actors at the centre," noting that her book's

> focus on resistance and survival reflects the experiences of the women [she] interviewed; it draws attention to the strength women display

despite their experiences of victimization through shifting the emphasis from viewing women as passive victims of sexual violence to seeing them as active survivors. . . . The term "victim" . . . makes invisible the other side of women's victimization: the active and positive ways in which women resist, cope and survive. (1988, p. 163)

Kelly then warns that "without this perspective, and given the extent of sexual violence, women can be presented as inherently vulnerable to victimization and as inevitable passive victims" (1988, p. 164). Sharon Lamb discusses the connotations of the word *survivor*, noting that a "quality that the term *survivor* evokes is one of heroic adaptation" (1999a, p. 119; emphasis in original). More recently, Amanda Konradi explains how she will refer to the women participating in rape prosecution that she studied:

I use "survivors" and "women" in this text when I refer to the participants in my study, as these terms separate the experience of being sexually violated—victimization—from what women do about it. While "victim" is often heard and read as passive, survivor is more open, and because agency is the focus of my investigation, I prefer this term. (Konradi 2007, p. 13)

Konradi's discussion here is interesting not only because she says she uses "survivor" to avoid the "passive" connotations of "victim" but also because she tells us that she is focusing on agency. This makes her entire project a means of countering some of the negative characterizations I have been describing.

Other feminists offer similar accounts, all of which implicitly or explicitly recognize problems adhering to early constructions of victims and posit more active social actors in their stead. To illustrate the idea that radical feminism and psychology produce different "discourses" of victimization, Chris Atmore argues that "the radical feminist discourse . . . uses the term *survivor*, in contrast to the more common, psychological use of *victim*, even those two words alone implying significant difference" (Atmore 1999, p. 189; emphasis in original). Vera Taylor and Nancy Whittier similarly argue that "one of the visions of feminism has been to reconstitute the experience of victimization. Thus, women who have been battered or raped or have experienced incest or other forms of abuse are termed 'survivors' to redefine their experiences as resistance to male violence" (Taylor and Whittier 1992, pp. 119–120). A little later, in a chapter about the culture of the women's movement, the same authors discuss how the speak-out, along with other practices, is a place where "ritual is used to evoke and express emotion, dramatize inequality and injustice, and emphasize the way that women's individual experiences are connected to their disadvantaged status as a group" (1992, p. 178).

Explicitly, they discuss "testimony" as a way of transforming "feelings of shame over past events into pride over having survived such ordeals":

> The antirape movement relies heavily on rituals that downplay the fear, guilt, and depression women experience following victimization, emphasizing instead emotions that empower women. . . . The ritual of "taking back the night" by marching in all-female groups through urban areas and the use of the term *survivor* to refer to victims of rape, incest, or battering explicitly legitimate women's experiences and encourage participants to recognize women's collective strength. (1992, pp. 178–179; emphasis in original)

This contrasting of the shameful emotions of victimization with the "empowering" attributes of claiming a survivor identity delineates the "significant difference" between passivity and agency and shows how the latter framing remediates the stigma associated with the former. And like the other sources I have cited, Taylor and Whittier show how activists appropriated a term signifying an identity that counters the constructions I have called "pathetic."

When thinking about the persistence and, now, pervasiveness of "survivor" as a new and more positive way of constructing victimization, it is also important to consider the role of therapeutic and self-help or "recovery" influences—ironically, despite the cultural critique of these as fostering a "cult of victimhood" (Tavris 1993). In Joseph Davis's analysis (2005a) of how the women's movement produced childhood sexual abuse narratives that have become part of how we now understand victimization, he talks about the very stories I have searched for the vocabularies I presented. He argues that when victim narratives were told publicly in speak-outs and in consciousness-raising and self-help groups and were printed in collections, they became a powerful new "collective story."

These "accounts of innocence" not only absolve adult survivors of blame for their childhood victimization but also explain "debilitating features of their lives in the intervening years." Because the stories "made the basis for the [new] common identity not simply past victimization but a present state of having moved beyond it," they result in "widely adopted" self-labeling as "survivors" (Davis 2005a, pp. 104, 107). Then, Davis shows, this collective story became the basis for the psychological trauma model of effects of child sexual abuse and "helped to depathologize and destigmatize the adult survivor's symptoms and experiences by explaining them as necessary coping responses" (2005a, p. 134).

Finally, according to Davis, therapists using the model transmit the new identity to their clients, as part of the healing and recovery process. Clients come to recognize their "survivor strength" and learn that they are not responsible for their symptoms. Integral to this process is participation in the self-help "movement," through books and groups in addition to therapy, all of which are intertwined. Together, they provide a "pathway" to the survivor identity (Davis 2005a, pp. 148–149, 154). Most significantly for my own argument, Davis characterizes this process as one of the "narrative repair" of "tarnished identities" (2005a, p. 175, following Nelson 2001). Or as Lamb puts it, "victims resist being called 'victims' . . . because no matter what therapists tell victims, they feel that they have been weak, and weakness is shameful in our culture" (1999a, p. 120).

In this brief review of how other scholars have written about survivors, it is clear that for the most part, we see its embracement by victims as reparative, if not transformative. To use a vocabulary of surviving is to accomplish an identity profoundly different than "victim," one that reclaims self-respect and the respect of others, as my title suggests. In the next section, I reflect a bit on what my research adds to the symbolic interactionist literature on the work of reclaiming respect, otherwise known as "identity work." While doing so, I also situate the processes I have been describing in the sociology of emotions.

Deviance, Identity Work, and Emotions

Throughout this book, I have taken a social constructionist approach toward deviance in which I assume that it is a "label" (Becker 1963) rather than anything inherent in a person or situation. It is a meaning people ascribe to other people, just as "victim" is an assignation (Holstein and Miller 1997). What I have done is join the labels, showing how the latter is inextricable from the former. That is, people we think of as "victims" are people we think of as "deviants," usually without even being aware of it. There are two ways in which this book illustrates the deviance of victims. We see the first way in vocabularies of victimization that reveal "what people think" and how victims and their advocates worry about this. These are the accounts that show that even though a victim *violates* our feeling rules for sympathy, her appearance of being somehow responsible for or choosing victimization is false.

Erving Goffman, in *Stigma* (1963), asserts that we hold expectations of the people we encounter, based on our stereotypes, and if people violate those, we rank them low and treat them, unthinkingly, as "not quite human" (1963, p. 5). The "normative expectations" for stereotypical victims are that they be "morally good people [who] are greatly harmed through no fault of their own" (Loseke 1999, p. 77). If a woman is "promiscuous," or even just "sexually active," she lacks the moral worthiness to be a rape or clergy abuse victim. If she foolishly hitchhikes, wears scanty clothing, or drinks alcohol, and she does not yell and scream and physically resist, we do not judge her experience as rape. If she stays in a violent relationship, or returns to one after leaving, she may be battered but we call her a "participant."

If she claims she had no choice when we think she really did, she loses our sympathy. If what she calls "rape" is really "bad sex," then she is not greatly harmed, and so she is *not* actually a victim. The use of vocabularies of motive as data in the form of accounts, like all analyses of the "aligning actions" (Hunter 1984) that bring identity and behavior into conformity with cultural norms, indicates to us the nature of those norms and the culture that provides and enforces them. This study adds to our understanding of the myriad ways in which victims may fall short, which has thus far come mostly from research outside the literature on deviance (Stanko 1982; Frohmann 1991; Dunn 2001, 2002; Konradi 2007).

The second way we see victims as deviant is like the expectation that they not have brought their victimization on themselves, because it is closely linked to the overarching cultural code of agency. This set of ideals presumes and privileges exactly the attributes victims *cannot* possess. We see virtually everyone as agents, but victims, by definition, are not. "Agent" is what Goffman calls a "virtual identity," the person we all ought to be, and "victim" is the "actual identity" that is discrepant and thus the source of stigma (1963, p. 2). When clergy abuse survivors so emphatically distance themselves from their victimization, and then vehemently articulate the choices they now have, they reveal the deviance inherent in simply being a victim.

Candace Clark argues that because people "receive sympathy only when something goes wrong," even innocents can be blamed when people think in terms of a "just world" (Clark 1997, p. 46, citing Lerner 1980). Victims are people whose experience is "not 'normal' or 'routine' . . . people in plights may slip in others' estimation for the mere fact of undergoing them" (Clark 1997, p. 197). James Holstein and Gale Miller earlier alluded to this when they spoke of the "debilitating" aspects of victimization (1997, p. 43) and in their discussion of the early feminist concerns (e.g., Barry 1979) about the consequences of successful application of the victim label that I have explored in some depth. This "deviance by definition" is empirically reinforced in the vocabularies of surviving and theoretically bolstered by linking it to the cultural code of agency.

Another area to which this study adds, which is often treated as a topic in the sociology of deviance and identity, is the idea of "identity management" (Goffman 1963), accomplished through the use of situated vocabularies of motive (Mills 1940), "accounts" (Scott and Lyman 1968), and various kinds of what Snow and Anderson call "identity work" (1993). The way survivors narrate their "moving" away from being victims is certainly an example of the "role distancing" they describe, and becoming a survivor could be seen as a kind of "role embracement." But when Snow and Anderson write about the homeless men whose "identity talk" they discerned in the stories the men told, they are especially concerned with how stigmatized people "attempt to generate identities that provide them with a measure of self-worth and dignity" (Snow and Anderson 1987, p. 1336).

We have seen that victims, like people who are homeless, are subject to the loss of self-esteem associated with feeling powerless and the guilt that comes from blaming themselves. Like the homeless, they tell stories that not only align their deviance (in this case, from ideal victim expectations) but also "salvage" self from the disdain accorded people for being victims in the first place. That is, they tell stories to others but also to themselves. Davis has identified two traditions in the sociology of accounts: the "interactionist" emphasis on accounting for the deviant or problematic "in the context of a social predicament" and the research in "social psychology" he sees as broader in scope. In this tradition, "account-giving is more than an interaction ritual or remedial practice; it is an effort to understand, to find meaning, to reestablish coherence and biographical continuity" (Davis 2005b, pp. 531–532).

The accounts in this book are of both types, and they suggest linkages between them. Davis says that "self-explanatory accounts" help people feel as if they have more control over what has happened to them. He also discusses the "increasingly common shift in self-description from 'victim' to 'survivor'" due to the "personal stigma" of being "damaged, passive, and powerless" (Davis 2005b, p. 544, citing Best 1997, p. 13). My research makes visible the stigma we attach to lack of control and shows how survivor vocabularies account to others for the deviance of victimization and provide new ways for victims to understand their experience and themselves. If power were not so privileged, powerlessness would not be so despised, and thus victim vocabularies perhaps *necessitate* the identity work survivor vocabularies accomplish.

Linked to all of this are emotions, a topic of increasing interest to sociologists over the years as we divest ourselves a little of our cognitive biases when studying "passionate processes" (Gould 2004). We know that emotions have a social basis, that is, we learn through enculturation which of them to feel and show, when, how deeply, and toward whom (Hochschild 1979). In the case of victims, I am not the first to point out that the feeling rules for sympathy articulate so neatly with the rules for defining victimization; Donileen Loseke says they spring from the same "cultural coherence system" (2000, p. 49). The coherence system they share is the cultural code of agency, because to feel sympathy for a person and to define a person as a victim both require that the person be innocent of responsibility.

What my work adds to this discussion is empirical illustration of *other* emotions related to victimization and the code: blame, pity, contempt, admiration. They are different feelings stitched together by the same cultural thread. It is our ideas about choice and free will that lead us to blame victims who are "responsible," pity those who are "helpless," despise those who are "hysterical," and admire those who can *choose* to move on "from victim to survivor." The range of emotions and the "behavioral expressions" they evoke (Loseke 2000, p. 49) that are governed by this particular cultural code are greater than has been previously shown. And just as the feeling "sympathy" follows from and reaffirms the label "victim," these other emotions hook up with different kinds of identities and identity work. From this, we can surmise that identity work is sometimes emotion work. This last notion can provide conceptual leverage for the study of collective identity as well.

Survivor Movements and Collective Identity Work

Identity work is also something people in social movements do, as part of *collective* identity construction. Here, it refers to the "range of activities in which movement actors engage to construct, promote, and maintain their identities, both as individuals and as members of a collective" (Einwohner 2005, p. 41, citing Snow and McAdam 2000). In previous analyses of the use of survivor terminology to describe battered women

(Dunn 2004, 2005), I have argued that collective identities sometimes also need the kind of identity work that Snow and Anderson (1987) described as "salvaging" or what I have termed reparative—first, if constructing victim agency is problematic, and then, if successfully constructing the lack of agency necessary to establish victimization has unintended consequences.

If movements' identity work is strategic impression management for audiences but *also* the "work done by individuals to align the personal sense of self with the collective" (Einwohner 2005, p. 41, citing Snow and McAdam 2000), then survivor movements constructing victim collective identities must contend with all the reasons people might not want to so identify. Although we do not know the intention of Barbara Blaine and her peers when they called their group the *Survivors* Network of those Abused by Priests, we can see this naming as an important instance of social movement identity work of each of the types Einwohner describes.

It is not just the use of terms such as *survivor* that constitute survivor movement identity work, however. *All* of the vocabularies, of victimization, victimism, and surviving, that activists, feminist researchers, and "backlash" cultural critics choose and reproduce and use to construct the "typical" are part of this identity work. That so many of them are of the first type—the dramaturgical, strategic, reparative, reconstructive stories that refashion the stigmatized for those who judge them—suggests that the scholarship of "new social movements" can benefit from more attention to the efforts activists make *before* collective and individual identities can merge and that sometimes "modification" of the former must occur instead of the latter (Broad 2002, p. 319). Either way, the accounts I have retold negotiate the blameless in opposition to the blameworthy, the admirable against the pathetic, and thus are identity management strategies (Goffman 1963) very like the kind so often studied in the sociology of deviance. They are aligning actions, just writ a little larger.

Vocabularies of Victimization, Formula Stories, and the Cultural Code of Agency

The preceding discussion brings me to another consideration, suggesting as it does that social movement "identity workers" make use of the stories people tell when they are engaged in processes of creating and recreating themselves. Identity narratives, as Loseke has recently pointed out, "are produced at cultural, institutional, organizations, and individual levels of social life." She goes on to argue that these different types of narrative are "reflexively related . . . [and] much could be learned by bringing an examination of these reflexive relationships into the forefront of analysis" (Loseke 2007, p. 662). We can use the narrative identity work of victims and survivors, and even their detractors, to explore some of these relationships. To do so, I return once more to the idea of vocabularies of motive and accounts, bring them into a discussion of social movement "formula" stories, and argue that their content in the contemporary United States is always determined by the cultural code of agency.

The beginning, a point that is somewhat arbitrary (Loseke 2007, p. 663) given the reflexivity, or recursivity, of narratives at different levels, is the article C. Wright Mills wrote in 1940, "Situated Actions and Vocabularies of Motive." These vocabularies provide the mostly verbal explanations of behavior that are appropriate in *particular* circumstances, lingual forms that "vary in content with historical epochs and societal structures" (Mills 1940, p. 913). They are learned along with language; they are part of Mead's "generalized other" (what "people think"). They cue us to the values and expectations of an era and a place, because they "link [an act] to situations, integrate one [person's] actions with another's, and line up conduct with norms" (Mills 1940, p. 908). That is, we can infer from victim and survivor vocabularies, in this case, what Hochschild calls the "feeling rules" (1979) for sympathy, which Loseke argues are coterminous with the "cultural coherence system producing 'victims'" (2000, p. 49).

Mills characterized the ethos of his time as dominated by "individualistic, sexual, hedonistic, and pecuniary vocabularies of motive" (1940, p. 911). If we are to believe the cultural critics discussed in Chapter 4, we now live in a historical and cultural moment in which a "vocabulary of *victimism*" is particularly salient. People such as Rieff (1991) and Sykes (1992) claim we use our victimization to excuse any and all deviations. The "power feminists" accuse "victim feminists" of creating a "cult of victimhood" and of then wallowing in it (e.g., Wolf 1993b). Although I would argue that the deviance and the stigma that result from being victimized are more powerful incentives to *deny* victimization than to claim it, there are ways in which social movements beginning at least as early as the "rights" movements of the 1960s have contributed to new ways of thinking about a variety of violations and the harm they cause.

Joseph Davis, for example, points out some "positive implications" of claiming victim identities. In the case of "retractors," people who come to believe that their memories of childhood sexual abuse are induced by therapists, what Davis calls the "formula story" of false memory syndrome "narrativizes the experience of the sufferer-victim of the condition" (2005b, p. 537). This has value for both the retractors and the "secondary victims" for understanding their strange and humiliating experience and repairing familial relationships as well as aligning deviance. In his more extended analysis of child sexual abuse narratives as a "collective story" (aptly titled *Accounts of Innocence*), Davis shows that the trauma model of abuse arising out of the incest survivor movement helps people to make "sense of confusing and troublesome experience and . . . [restore] the basic goodness of the self" (2005a, p. 6). Here is how he explains it:

> As formulated, the trauma model supported the coherence of the condition-category of sexual abuse and the innocence of victims by locating harm in the conditions of the sexual experience itself. . . . It explained enduring victim harm by providing a causal model, with an associated biology, that encompassed a very wide range of distresses, disabilities, somatic symptoms, and life problems as trauma aftereffects. It helped to depathologize and destigmatize the adult survivor's symptoms and experiences by explaining them as necessary coping responses . . . in the trauma model, no aspect of the harm could be construed as self-inflicted. (Davis 2005a, p. 134)

There is a way, then, in which a vocabulary of victimization enables new, more positive self-constructions, when it encompasses the qualities we despise and locates their source not in us, but in what happened to us.

A vocabulary of victimization also allows us to consider factors beyond the individual and shifts attention to the sociological, as the "victim feminists" have pointed out (see Atmore 1999; Berns 1999; Lamb 1999a). This particular vocabulary is thus a crucial component of all social problems claims-making directed toward social change and all social movements' framing, when there is any question where responsibility lies. The language of the social structures, social forces, oppression, domination, coercion, threat, and violence—all the things that "determine" or, more specifically, "trap" people and rob them of choice—is the foundation of the "new" social movements and the "old" ones too. So although victims as individuals may have to deal with the micropolitical consequences of calling themselves victims (and the vocabularies of surviving suggest one way in which they do), social movements cannot do without them and must frame them in ways that establish their innocence.

For this reason, activists and claims-makers tell "formula stories," such as the "accounts of innocence" Davis illuminates at the institutional level and I have used to show how individual victims of rape, battering, incest, and clergy abuse account for victimization—and their advocates do too. Formula stories are "narratives of typical actors engaging in typical behaviors within typical plots leading to expectable moral evaluations" and they construct "cultural identities" (Loseke 2007, p. 664). Loseke argues that all social problems formula stories share the "stock character" of a victim and that this character is *always* morally worthy and blameless within the "cultural coherence system" (2000, p. 48). If so, then it follows that the prevalence of formula stories in social problems claims-making, including within social movements, has led to the relatively new cultural identity of "victim." The vocabularies I have identified lend support to this notion; further, they suggest that this identity is perpetually contested and potentially problematic. They expand the formula story cast of characters to include victims who are blameworthy as well as blameless, and contemptible as well as estimable. There is more than one stock victim, or she appears in more than one costume. This study reveals that different survivor movements, as well as their critics, have drawn on each of her permutations—all of which are formulaic.

What makes them formulaic is what they have in common. The personal stories in which people construct themselves as victims and survivors, the vocabularies of victimization and surviving that inform their accounts, the pathetic victim vocabulary of victimism, and the formula stories that provide the settings, plots, and scripts from which victims, advocates, and critics choose are all undergirded by what Mills has called an "ethos" or a "*typal vocabulary of motive*" or even a "milieu" (1940, pp. 909–910; emphasis in original). This is the cultural code of agency, and it is a defining characteristic of the contemporary, capitalist, individualist, US culture.

The code of agency is the formula for the formula story, the foundation of a larger cultural narrative that insists that all humans have free will and equal opportunity in all situations unless proven otherwise. It is the source of victim-blaming and thus the origin of *blameworthy* victim constructions and survivor movements' use of them as a foil, a means of arguing against the cultural code, which they *must* do to engender sympathy. It provides the reasons and the rules for constructing *blameless* victims; women and even children must show that their attackers were bigger, stronger, older, more powerful, had weapons, tricked them. Victims must explain that they had no place to go, no resources, no help, no way out, no hope. That no one would believe them, so they did not tell. That they were vulnerable, like children. That they did not *consent*, because consent is a choice and they had no choice.

The cultural code is also the resource for the vocabulary of victimism that produces the story of the *pathetic* victim, because it is a hierarchical narrative as well as a normative one. As Goffman says about stigma, we need "a language of relationships not attributes" (1963, p. 3) to understand why we discredit, deny, and even despise victimization and the "victim" label. In addition to telling us that we *have* choices, our culture tells us that if we think we do not, or tell others that we do not, there is something wrong with *us*. This makes it easy to tell stories about overreacting, cowardly, infantile, dopey, immature, self-pitying, stupid, idiotic, pathetic, naive, passive, drippy, unassertive, pitiful, dependent, childish, debilitated, incompetent women who shirk responsibility because they are so easily duped. These descriptive terms are part of a "symbolic repertoire" (Williams 2002), the power of which resides in the discrepancy between what the cultural code leads us to assume and the meaning we attach to deviance from that assumption.

Finally, we can look to the cultural code for the resonance of the *admirable* victim as well and according to the same hierarchical relationship between victimization and agency that makes the pathetic victim so (un)appealing. Although the logic of the cultural code decrees that a victim cannot be an agent and still be a victim (thus the emergence in survivor movements of the oppositional identity of the blameless victim), it also tells us not to respect people who lack agency, but to "look down" on them, to call them the kinds of names I listed above. In contrast, the survivor bifurcates her victim self and her agent self and *moves* from being a blameless but pitiable victim to becoming an admirable person who did what she had to in order to survive, but who is now in control of her own life, taking responsibility rather than shirking it, and leaving behind both victimization and its stigma. Although the blameless victim claims the cultural code is false (she did *not* have a choice), the admirable victim's claim of falsity is only temporary and ultimately reaffirms the assumption and privileging of choice.

Transgressions, Subversions, and Behavioral Expressions

In concluding this book, there are a few other things to think about. These have to do mostly with what happens when victims and survivors start telling their stories and with the role of vocabularies of victimization in these "consequential definitional processes" (Dunn, forthcoming). There is a down side to what Alcoff and Gray call the "confessional." These authors acknowledge the empowering character of disclosing trauma; telling people about it can enable victims to "make the transition from passive victim to active survivor" (1993, pp. 261–262).

Alcoff and Gray worry, however, about what they call the "co-opting" of survivor discourse, by the media and by "experts" who ultimately blame victims as they construct people needing their help. When this happens, the speak-outs have "unwittingly facilitated the recuperation of dominant discourse" (1993, p. 263). By 1994, when Louise Armstrong wrote about "what happened," she believed that the term *survivor* was no longer as useful as it had been. She writes that

> many of the women I spoke with were adamant that they not be seen as "victims." They saw themselves, and they wanted to be seen, as *survivors*. That word, which has now been thoroughly degraded and bankrupted, seemed fresh at the time. It allowed for the notion of serious injury without classifying the injury as necessarily permanently deforming. (Armstrong 1994, p. 30; emphasis in original)

She also says the word has been "hijacked and debased" (1994, p. 30). Armstrong's comment is interesting for a number of reasons; she recognizes the "debilitating" (Holstein and Miller 1997) consequences of claiming victimization, which she calls "deforming," and what she sees as the initially oppositional qualities of a survivor identity. The "hijacking" she refers to is that done by the media, primarily, and the "debasing" results from the extension of the label to all and sundry. In the process, "survivor" loses its "transgressive" effects, as Alcoff and Gray put it (1993, p. 267). In fact, according to Alcoff and Gray, when television talk shows become the primary venue for disclosure, "the survivors are reduced to victims, represented as pathetic objects who can only recount their experiences as if these are transparent, and who offer pitiable instantiations of the universal truths the experts reveal" (1993, p. 277).

Certainly, at the time that was written, this was a legitimate concern, a slippage of *survivor* back toward the meanings associated with *victims* and *victimization*. Since then, however, I believe there has been another shift, facilitated by the ways in which the clergy abuse survivor movement in general, and SNAP in particular, has come to public awareness. When a particular group's constructions of a phenomenon come to dominate public perceptions, that group can be said to have "ownership" of the problem (Gusfield 1980), and its definitions become, in a sense, part of the symbolic environment that shapes it. When the group has made strategic use of overarching cultural narratives, its framing of the problem has "cultural resonance" and thus appeals to broad audiences (Williams 1995; Benford and Snow 2000). Moreover, these ideas are related, because cultural resonance likely bolsters, if not actually results in, ownership. The group that "owns" a problem has framed it in such a way that its images, ideologies, and moralities have come to be widely accepted and even taken for granted at times.

Whether SNAP and other survivor movements now have ownership of the social problems of rape, battering, child sexual abuse, and clergy abuse is arguable, of course. My research and analysis suggest, however, that vocabularies of surviving may be more "subversive" than "hegemonic" (Ewick and Silbey 1995). Patricia Ewick and Susan Silbey argue for the foundational and the political character of narrative: "Stories people tell about themselves and their lives both constitute and interpret those lives" and give voice to the "silenced" (1995, pp. 198–199). Narratives are hegemonic when they "emphasize particularity, and when they efface the connection between the particular and the general." Alternately, they are subversive when they "bridge particularities and make connections across individual experiences and subjectivities" (Ewick and Silbey 1995, p. 200).

As I have, Ewick and Silbey argue that storytelling relies on conformity to cultural codes: "Even the most personal of narratives rely on and invoke collective narratives—symbols, linguistic formulations, structures, and vocabularies of motive—without which the personal would remain unintelligible and uninterpretable." Because of this, they may "reproduce existing ideologies and hegemonic relations of power and inequality" (Ewick and Silbey 1995, pp. 211–212), just as Armstrong (1994) and Alcoff and Gray (1993) feared. They can function as mechanisms of social control and become taken for granted in their conventionality, thus stifling alternatives.

Alternatively, they may make explicit the relationship between biography and history, "emplotting the connections between the particular and the general." This is done not by generalizing but by framing "particular experiences as *rooted* in and part of an encompassing cultural, material, and political world that extends beyond the local." It is important for my purposes here that subversive stories bridge the personal and political by *"locating the individual within social organization"* (Ewick and Silbey 1995, pp. 219–220; emphasis in original). In the case of the earlier survivor movements, the social organization was patriarchy, and the consciousness-raising groups and speak-outs created "both a common opportunity to narrate and a common content to the narrative, thus revealing the collective organization of personal life" (Ewick and Silbey 1995, p. 221).

In the survivor movements emerging today, there are many more opportunities to narrate, such as in the burgeoning number of forums on the Internet and via websites such as that sponsored by SNAP. In the case of SNAP and the other clergy abuse survivor movements, hierarchical religious institutions in which abuse occurred may provide a more tangible "social organization" within which survivors can locate themselves and a more specific institution from which to seek redress. As integral components of subversive stories, then, vocabularies of surviving may be quite powerful collectively as well as individually.

The last topic on my agenda for these concluding thoughts is related to what Loseke calls the "behavioral expressions" that accompany successful constructions of narrative identity (2000). In the case of victims, if we are sympathetic, the behavioral expression is help. But, worries Loseke, "survivor" may lead to different responses: "It might lead audiences to praise women for their strengths, but that does not lead necessarily to evaluations that such women need assistance" (2003, p. 137n.). In response to this concern, my answer takes a somewhat indirect form. I want to begin by looking at what this book can contribute to the subdiscipline within criminology that we call victimology. I do this for a couple of reasons. First, this academic domain has contributed to images of victims beginning with Amir's infamous discussion of "victim-precipitated rape" (1971). Second, some of the people who can make the biggest impact on cultural evaluations of victims are those who will be working directly with them in the criminal justice system and who might be reading this book in a course called "Victims of Crime" or "Victimology." This book is not much like any of the current texts available for such courses and has different things to offer this kind of audience (and, I hope, the people teaching these courses).

Victimology to date suffers from much the same theoretical dilemmas that characterized the study of social problems until social constructionism began to come into favor in the late 1970s and then established itself as the dominant sociological approach in the field. Until then, scholars had yet to develop general theoretical perspectives nor to move much beyond narrowly focused, separately considered, empirical descriptions of social problems (Best 2004). Sociologists have since successfully and fruitfully redirected the objectivist study of social problems, using analytical tools that transcend differences between particular problem conditions to reveal patterns in how conditions come to be subjectively apprehended *as* problems and attend to the implications of these claims-making and framing processes for social change.

Victimologists have recently argued that their field "lacks its own well developed theories of human behavior" (Karmen 2007, p. 19) and "still needs theoretical and conceptual development" (Shichor and Tibbetts 2002). The more sociologically inspired (e.g., Kennedy and Sacco 1998) have spoken of the need to place the study of victims' interactions with offenders and with the criminal justice system in larger social contexts. The study of victim and survivor vocabularies suggests some possibilities for how victimology can further engage history and culture and situate victimization. In addition, the social constructionist approach taken here can provide some of the theoretical coherence now lacking in the field, bringing as it does a focus on "generic social processes" (Schwalbe et al. 2000).

Holstein and Miller's (1997) "rethinking" of victimization draws on labeling theory in the sociology of deviance to show that victimization is not simply something that happens to people but is also a label. This makes victimization a process of identity construction that extends beyond the criminal event into its "aftermath." Accounts such as the ones excerpted in this book are an integral part of the identity work in which I have shown victims *must* engage. The use of vocabularies of victimization provides historically and culturally situated empirical examples of, especially, the "victim contests" Holstein and Miller articulate. Some victimologists have argued that victimization must be understood "in context" (Kennedy and Sacco 1998), and the "accomplishment of victimization" (Holstein and Miller 1997) I have illuminated in this study does not end with the individuals involved nor does it take place in a vacuum. My work directs attention to important components of this context: the vocabularies of victimization, formula stories, social movements, and cultural codes that victims and others employ.

Moreover, and for good reason, significant attention within victimology has been directed toward illuminating and explaining societal reaction to victims and victimization (Karmen 2007). Because identity work processes of victimization "deflect responsibility," "assign causes," and "specif[y] responses and remedies" (Holstein and Miller 1997, pp. 31–35), and because victim and survivor vocabularies are integral to how victimization is established, this research has clear implications for interactions between victims and criminal justice system actors, who must routinely decide whether the people they encounter in the course of their daily work should be assigned the label of "victim." How victims are treated is contingent on how compelling their stories are, on how well they account for the questionable, and on the degree to which their story is formulaic and consistent with feeling rules for sympathy. In a victim contest, we have begun to specify the rules of the game, through illustrating vocabularies of victimization and elaborating their roots in the cultural code of agency.

A number of victimologists (e.g., Karmen 2007; Kennedy and Sacco 1998; Weed 1995) have brought attention to the impact of survivor movements on public and criminal justice system perceptions of victims and victimization and, as a result, on how victims are treated. The perspective I have taken here, and the data, sheds light on this macrolevel "victim work" (Holstein and Miller 1997, p. 41). I have done this, once again, by elucidating the norms that shape victims' and audiences' social constructions. Victim and survivor vocabularies in victims' accounts can focus attention in victimology toward survivor movements' efforts to tell the right stories and examine the consequences of effective (and ineffective) storytelling within the organizations where victims seek sympathy and its behavioral expression of help.

A large body of feminist scholarship on victimization has shown how criminal justice system actors and others who work with victims define and label them, often on the basis of characteristics that go well beyond legalities. For example, a number of scholars have shown how typifications of "normal" victimization influence the perceptions and responses of police officers responding to battered women (Ferraro 1993), prosecutors rejecting sexual assault cases (Frohmann 1991), and shelter workers assessing battered women (Loseke 1992). Some researchers have examined the efforts of victims to convince others of their victimization (e.g., Konradi 1999; Dunn 2001, 2002). The study of victim and survivor vocabularies can contribute to this research as well, by locating these kinds of interactive processes within the larger cultural context this work articulates.

Many have explicated victims' suffering of what is sometimes referred to as the "second assault" as a function of audiences' need to or tendency to question victims' legitimacy (Holmstrum and Burgess 1983; Kerstetter 1990; Madigan and Gamble 1989; Martin and Powell 1994; Rose and Randall 1982; Stanko 1982). This study of victim and survivor identity work shows the parameters within which such *revictimization* takes place. In my previous research (Dunn 2001, 2002) on stalking victims' accomplishment of victimization in the prosecutor's office and courtroom, I argued that the pain and harm that victims endure after they become involved with the criminal justice system results from interactions with people who seek to discredit their victimhood. Police officers, prosecutors, judges, defense attorneys, and even victim advocates may ask questions that imply that victims are not who they say they are. Revictimization is the failure to achieve victimization. The vocabularies of victimization in this book reveal some of the sources of this failure.

A final consideration for victimologists that my research can address concerns the ways in which the discipline has been controversial; namely, the arguments that it has obscured the influence of power relations (e.g., gender) on victimization (Best 1999; Garcia and Clifford 2010) and that it has had a tendency toward victim-blaming (Weis and Borges 1973; Reiff 1979; Anderson and Renzetti 1980) or, conversely, that it has produced scholars more interested in reform than in real research (Karmen 2007). The first critique, that victimology glosses structure, is mediated to some degree by my approach because analyses of vocabularies of victimization, victimism, and surviving illuminate rather than hide the significance of inequalities. The characters in formula stories are highly gendered; people blame rape victims because they violate normative expectations for women, for example, and women involved with clergy must construct themselves as "vulnerable adults" lest they be seen as seductresses. Taylor and Whittier's (1995) discussion of the "culture of the women's movement" suggests that the cultural code of agency itself is male; the many ways in which women in this culture are constructed as pathetic and men as admirable lend support to this idea as well.

The approach I have taken here additionally offers an avenue out of the "blaming versus defending" debate (Karmen 2007), in that it takes the attribution of responsibility to victims as a topic for researchers to study rather than an activity in which to engage. My focus in presenting and analyzing victim and survivor vocabularies is on how victims come to be judged and on what fosters sympathy for them and aid, not whether they should be heeded or ignored, helped or hampered. Clearly, the data taken as a whole show victims and survivors facing tremendous obstacles as a consequence of having to tell their stories in the context of the cultural code of agency, and their pain and humiliation, self-blame and doubt, grief and loss resonate on every page. Even the "Stories for Living" (Survivors Network of those Abused by Priests 2007–2009) are not without distress. As a researcher, I do not judge victims. But my research may help others to judge victims differently, or not at all.

Related to this is the relevance of this work not only for rethinking victimology but also for fostering more humane and efficacious responses to victims and survivors. The outcomes of survivor movement and individual storytelling are most consequential when their meanings become shared by those with the power to effect social change, and social change is impossible without changing meanings. The domain expansion that included adult women in the category of clergy abuse victims has been essential for their ability to seek redress, and having defined themselves as victims, they have led the charge to change the church (Bonavoglia 2008). The availability of survivor identities in addition to, or instead of, victim identities has likely allowed more people to understand their experience in ways that help them let go of shame and self-blame. If we read the "Stories for Living" carefully, we might offer advocates and others who work with victims some tools to assist with redefinitions that obviate stigma.

Understanding the importance of vocabularies of victimization and surviving, and especially the logic of the cultural code of agency, also suggests ways in which to systematically improve criminal justice system interactions with victims. Law enforcement personnel can be trained to recognize when they begin to make assumptions about victims that discount the forces with which they must contend, during criminal events and afterwards. Prosecutors can perhaps find strategies for helping victims construct themselves for juries and (official) judges that emphasize victimization without robbing them of dignity. And finally, victim advocates in the criminal justice system, community-based organizations, and the academy could educate all of us who judge victims about the bases on which we do so.

Bibliography

Adams, Celeste. 2002. "Catholic Priests and the Sexual Abuse of Children with Barbara Blaine." *The Spirit of Ma'at* 2(12) (e-zine interview). Available at http://www.spiritofmaat.com (retrieved March 9, 2009).

Alcoff, Linda, and Laura Gray. 1993. "Survivor Discourse: Transgression or Recuperation?" *Signs* 18(2):260–290.

Alexander, Jeffrey C., and Philip Smith. 1993. "The Discourse of American Civil Society: A New Proposal for Cultural Studies." *Theory and Society* 22(2):151–207.

Altheide, David. 2006. *Terrorism and the Politics of Fear.* Lanham, MD: Alta Mira Press.

Amir, Menachem. 1967. "Victim Precipitated Forcible Rape." *Journal of Criminal Law, Criminology, and Police Science* 58(4):493–502.

———. 1971. *Patterns in Forcible Rape.* Chicago: University of Chicago Press.

Anderson, M., and C. Renzetti. 1980. "Rape Crisis Counseling and the Culture of Individualism." *Contemporary Crises* 4(3):323–341.

Andrews, Arlene Bowers. 1992. *Victimization and Survivor Services: A Guide to Victim Assistance.* New York: Springer Publishing.

Armstrong, Louise. 1978. *Kiss Daddy Goodnight: A Speak-Out on Incest.* New York: Hawthorne Books.

———. 1979. "Kiss Daddy Goodnight." *Cosmopolitan* 186 (February):168.

———. 1994. *Rocking the Cradle of Sexual Politics: What Happened When Women Said Incest.* Reading, MA: Addison Wesley.

Arnold, David. 1993. "Panel on Abusive Clergy May Hear from Women, Too." *Boston Globe,* January 16, p. 71.

Atmore, Chris. 1999. "Victims, Backlash, and Radical Feminist Theory (or, The Morning After They Stole Feminism's Fire)." Pp. 183–212 in *New Versions of Victims: Feminists Struggle with the Concept,* edited by Sharon Lamb. New York: New York University Press.

Barry, Kathleen. 1979. *Female Sexual Slavery.* Englewood Cliffs, NJ: Prentice-Hall.

Becker, Howard S. 1963. *Outsiders: Studies in the Sociology of Deviance.* New York: Free Press.

Bellah, Robert, Richard Madsen, William Sullivan, Ann Swidler, and Steven Tipton. 1985. *Habits of the Heart.* Berkeley: University of California Press.

Bem, Sandra Lipsitz. 1993. *The Lenses of Gender: Transforming the Debate on Sexual Inequality.* New Haven, CT: Yale University Press.

Bender, Loretta, and Abram Blau. 1937. "The Reaction of Children to Sexual Relations with Adults." *The American Journal of Orthopsychiatry* 7:500–518.

Benford, Robert D., and Scott A. Hunt. 1992. "Dramaturgy and Social Movements: The Social Construction and Communication of Power." *Sociological Inquiry* 62(1):36–55.

Benford, Robert D., and David A. Snow. 2000. "Framing Processes and Social Movements: An Overview and Assessment." *Annual Review of Sociology* 26:611–639.

Berger, Peter L., and Thomas Luckmann. 1966. *The Social Construction of Reality: A Treatise in the Sociology of Knowledge.* New York: Doubleday.

Berns, Nancy. 1999. "My Problem and How I Solved It." *The Sociological Quarterly* 40(1):85–108.

Berry, Jason. 1985. "The Tragedy of Gilbert Gauthe." *The Times of Acadiana* (Lafayette, LA), May 23, pp. 18–28.

———. 1994. *Lead Us Not into Temptation: Catholic Priests and the Sexual Abuse of Children.* New York: Doubleday.

Best, Joel. 1987. "Rhetoric and Claims Making: Constructing the Missing Children Problem." *Social Problems* 34(2):101–121.

———. 1990. *Threatened Children: Rhetoric and Concern About Child Victims.* Chicago: University of Chicago Press.

———. 1991. "'Road Warriors'" on 'Hair-Trigger' Highways: Cultural Resources and the Media's Construction of the 1987 Freeway Shootings Problem." *Sociological Inquiry* 61(3):327–345.

———. 1995. "Typification and Social Problems Construction." Pp. 3–10 in *Images of Issues: Typifying Contemporary Social Problems,* edited by Joel Best. New York: Aldine.

———. 1997. "Victimization and the Victim Industry." *Society* 34(4):9–17.

———. 1999. *Random Violence: How We Talk About New Crimes and New Victims.* Berkeley: University of California Press.

———. 2004. *Deviance: Career of a Concept.* Belmont, CA: Wadsworth.

BishopAccountability.Org. 2004. "Toledo Native Barbara Blaine Crusades Against Sexual Abuse in the Catholic Church." Retrieved October 20, 2009, from http://www.bishopaccountability.org/news2004_01_06/2004_04_29_Frogameni_ToledoNative.htm.

Blumer, Herbert. 1971. "Social Problems as Collective Behavior." *Social Problems* 18(3):298–306.

Bograd, Michele. 1988. "How Battered Women and Abusive Men Account for Domestic Violence: Excuses, Justifications, or Explanations?" Pp. 3–77 in *Coping with Family Violence: Research and Policy Perspectives*, edited by Gerald T. Hotaling, David Finkelhor, John T. Kirkpatrick, and Murray A. Straus. Newbury Park, CA: Sage.

Bonavoglia, Angela. 2008. *Good Catholic Girls: How Women Are Leading the Fight to Change the Catholic Church*. New York: Regan Books.

Britt, Lory, and David Heise. 2000. "From Shame to Pride in Identity Politics." Pp. 252–268 in *Self, Identity, and Social Movements*, edited by Sheldon Stryker, Timothy J. Owens, and Robert W. White. Minneapolis: University of Minnesota Press.

Broad, K. L. 2002. "Social Movement Selves." *Sociological Perspectives* 45(3):317–336.

Brownmiller, Susan. 1975. *Against Our Will: Men, Women, and Rape*. New York: Bantam.

———. 1999. *In Our Time: Memoir of a Revolution*. New York: Random House.

Burke, Kenneth. 1969. *A Grammar of Motives*. Berkeley: University of California Press.

Burkett, Elinor, and Frank Bruni. 1993. *A Gospel of Shame: Children, Sexual Abuse, and the Catholic Church*. New York: Viking Press.

Burt, Martha. 1980. "Cultural Myths and Supports for Rape." *Journal of Personality and Social Psychology* 38(2):217–230.

Burton, Lindy. 1968. *Vulnerable Children*. London: Routledge and Kegan Paul.

Butler, Sandra. 1978. *Conspiracy of Silence: The Trauma of Incest*. San Francisco: New Glide Publications.

Charmaz, Kathy. 1994. "Identity Dilemmas of Chronically Ill Men." *The Sociological Quarterly* 35(2):269–288.

Christie, Nils. 1986. "The Ideal Victim." Pp. 17–30 in *From Crime Policy to Victim Policy*, edited by Ezzat A. Fattah. New York: St. Martin's Press.

Clark, Candace. 1987. "Sympathy Biography and Sympathy Margin." *American Journal of Sociology* 93(2):290–321.

———. 1997. *Misery and Company: Sympathy in Everyday Life*. Chicago: University of Chicago Press.

Connell, Noreen, and Cassandra Wilson (eds.). 1974. *Rape: The First Sourcebook for Women by New York Radical Feminists*. New York: Plume Books.

Davidson, Terry. 1978. *Conjugal Crime: Understanding and Changing the Wifebeating Pattern*. New York: Hawthorn Books.

Davies, Jill, Eleanor Lyon, and Diane Monti-Catania. 1998. *Safety Planning with Battered Women: Complex Lives/Difficult Choices*. Thousand Oaks, CA: Sage.

Davis, Joseph E. 2000. "Accounts of False Memory Syndrome: Parents, 'Retractors,' and the Role of Institutions in Account Making." *Qualitative Sociology* 23(1):29–56.

———. 2002. "Narrative and Social Movements." Pp. 3–30 in *Stories of Change: Narrative and Social Movements*, edited by Joseph E. Davis. New York: SUNY Press.

———. 2005a. *Accounts of Innocence: Sexual Abuse, Trauma, and the Self.* Chicago: University of Chicago Press.

———. 2005b. "Victim Narratives and Victim Selves: False Memory Syndrome and the Power of Accounts." *Social Problems* 52(4):529–548.

Davis, Laura, and Ellen Bass. 1988. *The Courage to Heal: A Guide for Women Survivors of Child Sexual Abuse.* New York: Harper Perennial.

Dobash, R. Emerson, and Russell Dobash. 1979. *Violence Against Wives: A Case Against the Patriarchy.* New York: Free Press.

Dunn, Jennifer L. 2001. "Innocence Lost: Accomplishing Victimization in Intimate Stalking Cases." *Symbolic Interaction* 24(3):285–313.

———. 2002. *Courting Disaster: Intimate Stalking, Culture, and Criminal Justice.* New York: Aldine de Gruyter.

———. 2004. "The Politics of Empathy: Social Movements and Victim Repertoires." *Sociological Focus* 37(3):235–250.

———. 2005. "'Victims' and 'Survivors': Emerging Vocabularies of Motive for 'Battered Women Who Stay.'" *Sociological Inquiry* 75(1):1–30.

———. forthcoming. "Vocabularies of Victimization: Toward Explaining the Deviant Victim." *Deviant Behavior.*

Dunn, Jennifer L., and Melissa Powell. 2007. "Everybody's Got Choices: Victim Advocates' Constructions of Battered Women's Victimization and Agency." *Violence Against Women* 13(10):977–1001.

Einwohner, Rachel. 2005. "Identity Work and Collective Action in a Repressive Context: Jewish Resistance on the 'Aryan Side' of the Warsaw Ghetto." *Social Problems* 53(1):38–56.

Eisner, Jane. 2002. "Boys, Girls, and Church Sex Scandal." *Philadelphia Inquirer,* April 25, p. A19.

Elshtain, Jean Bethke. 1982. "The Victim Syndrome: A Troubling Turn in Feminism." *The Progressive,* June, pp. 42–47.

Estrich, Susan. 1987. *Real Rape.* Cambridge, MA: Harvard University Press.

Ewick, Patricia, and Susan S. Silbey. 1995. "Subversive Stories and Hegemonic Tales: Toward a Sociology of Narrative." *Law and Society Review* 29(2):197–226.

Faith, Karlene. 1993. *Unruly Women: The Politics of Confinement and Resistance.* Vancouver, BC: Press Gang Publishers.

Faludi, Susan. 1991. *Backlash: The Undeclared War Against American Women.* New York: Crown Publishers.

———. 1993. "Whose Hype?" *Newsweek,* October 25, 122(17), p. 61.

Fater, Kerry, and Jo Ann Mullaney. 2000. "The Lived Experiences of Adult Male Survivors Who Allege Childhood Sexual Abuse by Clergy." *Issues in Mental Health Nursing* 21(3):281–295.

Ferraro, Kathleen J. 1993. "Cops, Courts, and Woman Battering." Pp. 165–177 in *Violence Against Women: The Bloody Footprints*, edited by Pauline B. Bart and Eileen Geil Moran. Newbury Park, CA: Sage.

Ferraro, Kathleen J., and John M. Johnson. 1983. "How Women Experience Battering: The Process of Victimization." *Social Problems* 30 (3):325–339.

Fitzpatrick, Frank. 2009. *The Survivor Activist*. Available at http://survivor connections.net/ (retrieved March 11, 2009).

Fleming, Jennifer Baker. 1979. *Stopping Wife Abuse*. New York: Anchor Books.

Forward, Susan, and Craig Buck. 1978. *Betrayal of Innocence: Incest and Its Devastation*. Los Angeles: J. P. Tarcher.

Fried, Amy. 1994. "'It's Hard to Change What We Want to Change': Rape Crisis Centers as Organizations." *Gender & Society* 8(4):562–583.

Frohmann, Lisa. 1991. "Discrediting Victims' Allegations of Sexual Assault: Prosecutorial Accounts of Case Rejections." *Social Problems* 38(2):213–226.

Gagne, Patricia. 1998. *Battered Women's Justice: The Movement for Clemency and the Politics of Self Defense*. New York: Twayne.

Ganzevoort, R. Ruard. 2002. "Common Themes and Structures in Male Victims' Stories of Religion and Sexual Abuse." *Mental Health, Religion, and Culture* 5(3):313–325.

Garcia, Venessa, and Janice E. Clifford. 2010. *Female Victims of Crime: Reality Reconsidered*. Upper Saddle River, NJ: Prentice-Hall.

Garfinkel, Harold. 1964. "Studies of the Routine Grounds of Everyday Activities." *Social Problems* 11(3):225–250.

Gayford, J. J. 1975a. "Research on Battered Wives." *Royal Society of Health Journal* 95(6):288–290.

———. 1975b. "Wife Battering: A Preliminary Survey of 100 Cases." *British Medical Journal* 1(5951):194–197.

Gelles, Richard J. 1976. "Abused Wives: Why Do They Stay?" *Journal of Marriage and the Family* 38(4):659–668.

Gelles, Richard J., and Donileen Loseke. 1993. "Introduction." Pp. ix–xvii in *Current Controversies on Family Violence*, edited by Richard J. Gelles and Donileen Loseke. Newbury Park, CA: Sage.

Gilbert, Neil. 1991. "The Phantom Epidemic of Sexual Assault." *The Public Interest* 103(Spring):54–65.

Goffman, Erving. 1959. *The Presentation of Self in Everyday Life*. New York: Anchor Books.

———. 1963. *Stigma: Notes on the Management of Spoiled Identity*. New York: Simon and Schuster.

———. 1974. *Frame Analysis: An Essay on the Organization of Experience.* New York: Harper and Row.

———. 1983. "The Interaction Order." *American Sociological Review* 48(1):1–17.

Goldstein, Eleanor C. 1992. *Confabulations: Creating False Memories, Destroying Families.* Boca Raton, LA: SIRS.

Gondolf, Edward W. 1988. *Battered Women as Survivors: An Alternative to Treating Learned Helplessness.* With Ellen R. Fisher. Toronto: D. C. Heath.

Goode, William J. 1971. "Force and Violence in the Family." *Journal of Marriage & Family* 33(4):624–635.

Goodwin, Jeff, James M. Jasper, and Francesca Polletta. 2001. "Why Emotions Matter." Pp. 1–24 in *Passionate Politics: Emotions and Social Movements,* edited by Jeff Goodwin, James M. Jasper, and Francesca Polletta. Chicago: University of Chicago Press.

Gould, Deborah B. 2004. "Passionate Political Processes: Bringing Emotions Back into the Study of Social Movements." Pp. 155–175 in *Rethinking Social Movements: Structure, Meaning, and Emotion,* edited by Jeff Goodwin and James M. Jasper. New York: Rowman and Littlefield.

Griffin, Susan. 1971. "Rape: The All-American Crime." *Ramparts* 10(September):26–35.

Gusfield, Joseph. 1980. *The Culture of Public Problems: Drinking-Driving and the Symbolic Order.* Chicago: University of Chicago Press.

Hammer, Rhonda. 2002. *Antifeminism and Family Terrorism: A Critical Feminist Perspective.* Lanham, MD: Rowman and Littlefield.

Hentig, Hans von. 1948. *The Criminal and His Victim: Studies in the Sociobiology of Crime.* New Haven, CT: Yale University Press.

Herman, Dianne. 1984. "The Rape Culture." Pp. 20–39 in *Women: A Feminist Perspective,* edited by Jo Freeman. Palo Alto, CA: Mayfield.

Herman, Judith L. 1981. *Father-Daughter Incest.* Cambridge, MA: Harvard University Press.

Hidalgo, Myra L. 2007. *Sexual Abuse and the Culture of Catholicism: How Priests and Nuns Become Perpetrators.* New York: Haworth Maltreatment and Trauma Press.

Higgenson, Joanna Gregson. 1999. "Defining, Excusing, and Justifying Deviance: Teen Mothers' Accounts for Statutory Rape." *Symbolic Interaction* 22(1):25–44.

Hochschild, Arlie Russell. 1975. "The Sociology of Feeling and Emotion: Selected Possibilities." Pp. 280–307 in *Another Voice: Feminist Perspectives on Social Life and Social Science,* edited by M. Millman and R. Kanter. Garden City, NY: Anchor Books.

———. 1979. "Emotion Work, Feeling Rules, and Social Structure." *American Journal of Sociology* 85:551–575.

Hoff, Lee Ann. 1990. *Battered Women as Survivors.* London: Routledge.

Holmstrum, Linda L., and Ann W. Burgess. 1983. *The Victim of Rape: Institutional Reactions.* New Brunswick, NJ: Transaction Books.

Holstein, James A., and Gale Miller. 1997. "Rethinking Victimization: An Interactional Approach to Victimology." Pp. 25–47 in *Social Problems in Everyday Life,* edited by Gale Miller and James A. Holstein. Greenwich, CT: JAI Press.

Hunt, Scott A., and Robert D. Benford. 2004. "Collective Identity, Solidarity, and Commitment." Pp. 433–457 in *The Blackwell Companion to Social Movements,* edited by David A. Snow, Sarah A. Soule, and Hanspeter Kriesi. Oxford: Blackwell.

Hunter, Christopher H. 1984. "Aligning Actions: Types and Social Distribution." *Symbolic Interaction* 7:155–174.

Irvine, Leslie. 1999. *Codependent Forevermore: The Invention of Self in a Twelve Step Group.* Chicago: University of Chicago Press.

Jasper, James M., and Jane D. Poulsen. 1995. "Recruiting Strangers and Friends: Moral Shocks and Social Networks in Animal Rights and Antinuclear Protests." *Social Problems* 42(4):493–512.

Jenkins, Philip. 1996. *Pedophiles and Priests: Anatomy of a Contemporary Crisis.* New York: Oxford University Press.

Jenness, Valerie. 1995. "Social Movement Growth, Domain Expansion, and Framing Processes: The Gay/Lesbian Movement and Violence Against Gays and Lesbians as a Social Problem." *Social Problems* 42(1):145–170.

Johnson, John M. 1981. "Program Enterprise and Official Cooptation in the Battered Women's Shelter Movement." *American Behavioral Scientist* 24(6):827–842.

———. 1995. "Horror Stories and the Construction of Child Abuse." Pp. 17–31 in *Images of Issues: Typifying Contemporary Social Problems,* edited by Joel Best. New York: Aldine de Gruyter.

Kalven, Harry, and Hans Zeisel. 1966. *The American Jury.* Boston: Little, Brown.

Kaminer, Wendy. 1993. *I'm Dysfunctional, You're Dysfunctional: The Recovery Movement and Other Self-Help Fashions.* New York: Vintage.

Karmen, Andrew. 2007. *Crime Victims: An Introduction to Victimology.* Belmont, CA: Thomson Wadsworth.

Kelly, Liz. 1988. *Surviving Sexual Violence.* Minneapolis: University of Minnesota Press.

Kendrick, Karen. 1998. "Producing the Battered Woman: Shelter Politics and the Power of the Feminist Voice." Pp. 151–174 in *Community Activism and Feminist Politics: Organizing Across Race, Class and Gender,* edited by Nancy Naples. New York: Routledge.

Kennedy, Leslie W., and Vincent F. Sacco. 1998. *Crime Victims in Context.* New York: Roxbury.

Kerstetter, Wayne A. 1990. "Gateway to Justice: Police and Prosecutorial

Response to Sexual Assault Against Women." *The Journal of Criminal Law and Criminology* 81(2):267–313.

Konradi, Amanda. 1999. "I Don't Have to Be Afraid of You: Rape Survivors' Emotion Management in Court." *Symbolic Interaction* 22(1):45–77.

———. 2007. *Taking the Stand: Rape Survivors and the Prosecution of Rapists.* Westport, CT: Praeger.

Kornblum, Janet. 2002. "85% of Church Abuse Victims Are Male, Research Finds." *USA Today*, June 24, p. 6D.

Koss, Mary P., C. A. Gidycz, and N. Wisniewski. 1987. "The Scope of Rape: Incidence and Prevalence of Sexual Aggression and Victimization in a National Sample of Higher Education Students." *Journal of Consulting and Clinical Psychology* 55(2):162–170.

Kulka, R., J. Veroff, and E. Douvan. 1979. "Social Class and the Use of Professional Help for Personal Problems: 1957 and 1976." *Journal of Health and Social Behavior* 20:2–17.

Lamb, Sharon. 1996. *The Trouble with Blame: Victims, Perpetrators, and Responsibility.* Cambridge, MA: Harvard University Press.

———. 1999a. "Constructing the Victim: Popular Images and Lasting Labels." Pp. 108–138 in *New Versions of Victims: Feminists Struggle with the Concept,* edited by Sharon Lamb. New York: New York University Press.

———. 1999b. "Introduction." Pp. 1–12 in *New Versions of Victims: Feminists Struggle with the Concept,* edited by Sharon Lamb. New York: New York University Press.

Lasch, Christopher. 1979. *The Culture of Narcissism.* New York: W. W. Norton.

Lerner, Melvin J. 1980. *The Belief in a Just World: A Fundamental Delusion.* New York: Plenum.

Lichterman, Paul. 1995. "Beyond the Seesaw Model: Public Commitment in a Culture of Self-Fulfillment." *Sociological Theory* 13(3):275–300.

Loftus, Elizabeth F., and Katherine Ketcham. 1994. *The Myth of Repressed Memory.* New York: St. Martin's Press.

Lorber, Judith. 1993. "Believing Is Seeing: Biology as Ideology." *Gender & Society* 7(4):568–581.

Loseke, Donileen R. 1989. "'Violence' Is 'Violence' . . . or Is It? The Social Construction of 'Wife Abuse' and Public Policy." Pp. 191–206 in *Images of Issues: Typifying Contemporary Social Problems,* edited by Joel Best. New York: Aldine de Gruyter.

———. 1992. *The Battered Woman and Shelters: The Social Construction of Wife Abuse.* Albany: State University of New York Press.

———. 1999. *Thinking About Social Problems: An Introduction to Constructionist Perspectives.* New York: Aldine de Gruyter.

———. 2000. "Ethos, Pathos, and Social Change: Reflections on Formula Narratives." *Perspectives on Social Problems* 12:41–54.

———. 2001. "Lived Realities and Formula Stories of 'Battered Women.'" Pp.

107–126 in *Institutional Selves: Troubled Identities in a Postmodern World*, edited by Jaber F. Gubrium and James A. Holstein. New York: Oxford University Press.

———. 2003. *Thinking About Social Problems: An Introduction to Constructionist Perspectives*, 2nd ed. New York: Aldine de Gruyter.

———. 2007. "The Study of Identity as Cultural, Institutional, Organizational, and Personal Narratives: Theoretical and Empirical Integrations." *Sociological Quarterly* 48(4):661–688.

Loseke, Donileen R., and Spencer E. Cahill. 1984. "The Social Construction of Deviance: Experts on Battered Women." *Social Problems* 31(3):296–310.

Lytton, Timothy. 2008. *Holding Bishops Accountable: How Lawsuits Helped the Catholic Church Confront Clergy Sexual Abuse*. Cambridge, MA: Harvard University Press.

Madigan, Lee, and Nancy Gamble. 1989. *The Second Rape: Society's Continued Betrayal of the Victim*. New York: Lexington Books.

Madriz, Esther. 1997. *Nothing Bad Happens to Good Girls: Fear of Crime in Women's Lives*. Berkeley: University of California Press.

Mahoney, Martha. 1994. "Victimization or Oppression? Women's Lives, Violence, and Agency." Pp. 59–92 in *The Public Nature of Private Violence: The Discovery of Domestic Abuse*, edited by Martha Albertson Fineman and Roxanne Mykitiuk. New York: Routledge.

Martin, Del. 1976. *Battered Wives*. San Francisco: Glide Publications.

Martin, Patricia, and Marlene Powell. 1994. "Accounting for the "Second Assault': Legal Organizations' Framing of Rape Victims." *Law and Social Inquiry* 19:853–890.

Martin, Patricia Yancey. 1990. "Rethinking Feminist Organizations." *Gender and Society* 4(2):182–206.

Matthews, Nancy A. 1994. *Confronting Rape: The Feminist Anti-Rape Movement and the State*. New York: Routledge.

Mead, George Herbert, and Charles W. Morris (eds.). 1967. *Mind, Self, and Society: From the Standpoint of a Social Behaviorist*. Chicago: University of Chicago Press.

Medea, Andra, and Kathleen Thompson. 1974. *Against Rape*. New York: Farrar, Straus, and Giroux.

Meiselman, Karin C. 1978. *Incest: A Psychological Study of Causes and Effects with Treatment Recommendations*. San Francisco: Jossey-Bass.

Miller, Gale, and James A. Holstein. 1993. "Reconsidering Social Constructionism." Pp. 5–24 in *Reconsidering Social Constructionism: Debates in Social Problems Theory*, edited by James A. Holstein and Gale Miller. New York: Aldine de Gruyter

Mills, C. Wright. 1940. "Situated Actions and Vocabularies of Motive." *American Sociological Review* 5(6):904–913.

Moore, Donna M. 1979. *Battered Women*. Beverly Hills, CA: Sage Publications.

Morretti, Stefania. 2007. "Males Surviving Abuse: The Overlooked Victims." *London Topic*, August 20, 2007. Available at BishopAccountability.org (retrieved August 3, 2009).

Ms. Magazine. 2002. "Women of the Year." Winter Issue (December). Available at http://www.msmagazine.com (retrieved October 20, 2009).

Muehlenhard, C. L., and J. Schrag. 1991. "Nonviolent Sexual Coercion." Pp. 115–128 in *Acquaintance Rape: The Hidden Crime*, edited by A. Parrot and L. Bechhofer. New York: John Wiley and Sons.

National Institute of Justice. 1996. *Domestic Violence, Stalking, and Antistalking Legislation: An Annual Report to Congress Under the Violence Against Women Act*. Washington, DC: US Department of Justice.

———. 2009. *Violence Against Women and Family Violence Program*. Available at http://www.ojp.usdoj.gov/nij (retrieved October 17, 2009).

Nelson, Hilde Lindemann. 2001. *Damaged Identities, Narrative Repair*. Ithaca, NY: Cornell University Press.

Nevens-Pederson, Mary. 2006. "Groups Offer Support, Healing: Victims of Abuse by Clergy Find Help." *Dubuque Telegraph Herald* (March 11, 2006). Available at http://www.snap-greatplains.org (retrieved March 11, 2009).

New York Times. 1982. "Children of Alcoholics: A Troubled Heritage." October 17, sec. 1, pt. 2, p. 74. Available at LexisNexis (retrieved August 3, 2009).

———. 1992. "Battle of Sexes Joined in Case of a Mutilation." November 8, sec. A, p. 17. Available at http://www.nytimes.com (retrieved October 25, 2009).

Office for Victims of Crime. 2009. "History of Rape Crisis Centers." Office for Victims of Crime, Training and Technical Assistance Center, Sexual Assault Advocate/Counselor Training Module. Available at https://www.ovcttac.gov/saact (retrieved October 17, 2009).

Okun, Lewis. 1986. *Woman Abuse: Facts Replacing Myths*. New York: State University of New York Press.

Orbuch, Terri L. 1997. "People's Accounts Count: The Sociology of Accounts." *Annual Review of Sociology* 23:455–478.

Ormerod, Neil, and Thea Ormerod. 1995. *When Ministers Sin: Sexual Abuse in the Churches*. Alexandria, Australia: Millennium Books.

Pagelow, Mildred Daley. 1981. *Woman Battering: Victims and Their Experiences*. Beverly Hills, CA: Sage Publications.

Paglia, Camille. 1992. *Sex, Art, and American Culture: Essays*. New York: Vintage Books.

———. 1994. *Vamps and Tramps: New Essays*. London: Viking.

Parrot, Andrea, and Laurie Bechofer. 1991. *Acquaintance Rape: The Hidden Crime*. New York: John Wiley and Sons.

Peled, Einat, Zvi Eisikovits, Guy Enosh, and Zeev Winstok. 2000. "Choice and

Empowerment for Battered Women Who Stay: Toward a Constructivist Model." *Social Work* 45(1):9–25.

Picart, Caroline Joan (Kay) S. 2003. "Rhetorically Reconfiguring Victimhood and Agency: The Violence Against Women Act's Civil Rights Clause." *Rhetoric and Public Affairs* 6(1):97–126.

Pizzey, Erin. 1974. *Scream Quietly or the Neighbours Will Hear.* Harmondsworth: Penguin.

Plante, Thomas G. 1999. *Bless Me Father for I Have Sinned: Perspectives on Sexual Abuse Committed by Roman Catholic Priests.* Westport, CT: Praeger.

Pleck, Elizabeth. 1987. *Domestic Tyranny: The Making of Social Policy Against Family Violence from Colonial Times to the Present.* New York: Oxford University Press.

Plummer, Ken. 1995. *Telling Sexual Stories: Power, Change, and Social Worlds.* London: Routledge.

Poling, Nancy. 1999. *Victim to Survivor: Women Recovering from Clergy Sexual Abuse.* Cleveland, OH: United Church Press.

Polletta, Francesca. 2002. "Plotting Protest: Mobilizing Stories in the 1960s Student Sit-Ins." Pp. 31–51 in *Stories of Change: Narrative and Social Movements,* edited by Joseph E. Davis. New York: SUNY Press.

Pollitt, Katha. 1993. "Not Just Bad Sex." *New Yorker,* October 4, pp. 220–224.

Rader, Nicole E. 2008. "Gendered Fear Strategies: Doing Gender and Fear Management Strategies in Married and Divorced Women's Lives." *Sociological Focus* 41(1):34–52.

Rasminsky, Sonya. 1993. "Letter to the Editor 9—No Title." *New York Times,* July 4, p. SM4.

Reiff, R. 1979. *The Invisible Victim.* New York: Basic Books.

Richardson, Laurel. 1990. "Narrative and Sociology." *Journal of Contemporary Ethnography* 19(1):116–135.

Rieff, David. 1991. "Victims All? Recovery, Co-Dependency, and the Art of Blaming Somebody Else." *Harpers,* September, pp. 49–56.

Rieff, Phillip. 1966. *The Triumph of the Therapeutic: Uses of Faith After Freud.* New York: Harper and Row.

Roiphe, Katie. 1991. "Date Rape Hysteria." *New York Times,* November 20, p. A27.

———. 1993. *The Morning After: Sex, Fear, and Feminism on Campus.* Boston: Little, Brown.

Rose, Vicki McNickle. 1977. "Rape as a Social Problem: A Byproduct of the Feminist Movement." *Social Problems* 25(1):75–89.

Rose, Vicki McNickle, and Susan Randall. 1982. "The Impact of Investigator Perceptions of Victim Legitimacy on the Processing of Rape/Sexual Assault Cases." *Symbolic Interaction* 5(1):23–36.

Rossetti, Stephen J. 1995. "The Impact of Clergy Sexual Abuse on Attitudes

Toward God and the Catholic Church." *Child Abuse and Neglect* 19(12):1469–1481.

Rubin, Bonnie Miller. 2002. "Survivor Groups Gain Support Amidst Priest Scandal." *Chicago Tribune* (April 28). Available at http://www.snapnetwork.org (retrieved March 10, 2009).

Rush, Florence. 1974. "The Sexual Abuse of Children: A Feminist Point of View." Pp. 64–75 in *Rape: The First Sourcebook for Women,* edited by Noreen Connell and Cassandra Wilson. New York: New American Library.

———. 1980. *The Best-Kept Secret: Sexual Abuse of Children.* New York: McGraw-Hill.

Russell, Diana E. H. 1975. *The Politics of Rape: The Victim's Perspective.* New York: Stein and Day.

Russo, Ann. 2001. *Taking Back Our Lives: A Call to Action for the Feminist Movement.* New York: Routledge.

Rutenberg, Sharon. 1983. "Rape Trauma Syndrome: Doctors Detail Painful Recovery Process of Rape Victim." United Press International, March 8. Available at LexisNexis (retrieved August 2, 2009).

Ryan, William. 1971. *Blaming the Victim.* New York: Pantheon.

Sanger, Carol. 1991. "Society's Ambivalence Clouds Date Rape Issue." *New York Times,* December 6, p. A34.

Schechter, Susan. 1982. *Women and Male Violence: The Visions and Struggles of the Battered Women's Movement.* Boston: South End Press.

Schultz, Leroy G. 1960. "The Wife Assaulter." *Journal of Social Therapy* 6:103–112.

Schur, Edwin M. 1984. *Labeling Women Deviant: Gender, Stigma, and Social Control.* New York: Random House.

Schutz, Alfred. 1954. "Concept and Theory Formation in the Social Sciences." *The Journal of Philosophy* 51(9):257–273.

Schwalbe, Michael, Sandra Godwin, Daphne Holden, Douglas Schrock, Shealy Thompson, and Michael Wolkomir. 2000. "Generic Processes in the Reproduction of Inequality: An Interactionist Analysis." *Social Forces* 79(2):419–452.

Scott, Marvin B., and Stanford M. Lyman. 1968. "Accounts." *American Sociological Review* 33(1):46–62.

Seligman, Martin E. P. 1975. *Helplessness: On Depression, Development, and Death.* San Francisco: W. H. Freeman.

Sennott, Charles M. 2002. "Pope Calls Sex Abuse Crime." *Boston Globe,* April 24, p. A1.

Sheehy, Gail. 1971. "Nice Girls Don't Get into Trouble." *New York,* 4(7), pp. 26–30.

Shichor, David, and Stephen G. Tibbetts. 2002. *Victims and Victimization.* Prospect Heights, IL: Waveland.

Snell, John E., Richard J. Rosenwald, and Ames Robey. 1964. "The

Wifebeater's Wife: A Study of Family Interaction." *Archives of General Psychiatry* 11(2):107–112.

Snow, David A., and Leon Anderson. 1987. "Identity Work Among the Homeless: The Verbal Construction and Avowal of Personal Identities." *The American Journal of Sociology* 92(6): 1336–1371.

———. 1993. *Down on Their Luck: A Study of Homeless Street People.* Berkeley: University of California Press.

Snow, David A., and Doug McAdam. 2000. "Identity Work Processes in the Context of Social Movements: Clarifying the Identity/Movement Nexus." Pp. 41–67 in *Self, Identity, and Social Movements,* edited by S. Stryker, T. J. Owens, and R. W. White. Minneapolis: University of Minnesota Press.

Sommers, Christina Hoff. 1994. *Who Stole Feminism? How Women Have Betrayed Women.* New York: Simon and Schuster.

Spector, Malcolm, and John I. Kitsuse. 2001 [1977]. *Constructing Social Problems.* New Brunswick: Transaction.

Spillman, Lyn. 2002. "Introduction: Culture and Cultural Sociology." Pp. 1–16 in *Cultural Sociology,* edited by Lyn Spillman. Malden, MA: Blackwell Publishers.

Stanko, Elizabeth. 1982. "Would You Believe This Woman? Prosecutorial Screening for 'Credible' Witnesses and a Problem of Justice." Pp. 63–82 in *Judge, Lawyer, Victim, Thief,* edited by Nicole Rafter and Elizabeth A. Stanko. Boston: Northeastern University Press.

Stark, Kio. 1994. "I'm O.K., You're O.K." *The Nation,* January 31, pp. 137–140.

Steinmetz, George. 1992. "Reflections on the Role of Social Narratives in Working-Class Formation: Narrative Theory in the Social Sciences." *Social Science History* 16(3):489–516.

Stokes, Randall, and John P. Hewitt. 1976. "Aligning Actions." *American Sociological Review* 41(5):838–449.

Straus, Murray A. 1992. "Sociological Research and Social Policy: The Case of Family Violence." *Sociological Forum* 7(2):211–237.

Straus, Murray A., Richard Gelles, and Suzanne Steinmetz. 1976. "Violence in the Family: An Assessment of Knowledge and Research Needs." Paper presented at the annual meeting of the American Association for the Advancement of Science, Boston.

Stucker, Jan. 1977. "I Tried to Fantasize That All Fathers Had Intercourse with Their Daughters: The Story of Mary C." *Ms.,* April, p. 66.

Survivors Network of those Abused by Priests (SNAP). 2007–2009. "Stories for Living." Available at http://www.snapnetwork.org (retrieved on multiple occasions between December 2007 and March 2009).

Swidler, Ann. 1986. "Culture in Action: Symbols and Strategies." *American Sociological Review* 51(2):273–286.

Sykes, Charles J. 1990. *The Hollow Men: Politics and Corruption in Higher Education.* Washington, DC: Regnery Gateway.

———. 1992. *A Nation of Victims: The Decay of the American Character.* New York: St. Martin's Press.

Sykes, G., and D. Matza. 1957. "Techniques of Neutralization: A Theory of Delinquency." *American Sociological Review* 22(6):664–670.

Tannenbaum, Frank. 1938. *Crime and the Community.* Boston: Ginn and Company.

Tatum, Jeffery D. 2002. "Compassion on Trial: Movement Narrative in a Court Conflict over Physician-Assisted Suicide." Pp. 179–202 in *Stories of Change: Narrative and Social Movements,* edited by Joseph E. Davis. New York: SUNY Press.

Tavris, Carol. 1993. "Beware the Incest-Survivor Machine." *New York Times Book Review,* January 3, pp. 1–3.

Taylor, Verta. 1989. "Social Movement Continuity: The Women's Movement in Abeyance." *American Sociological Review* 54(5):761–775.

———. 1996. *Rock-a-by-Baby: Feminism, Self-Help, and Postpartum Depression.* New York: Routledge.

———. 2001. "Emotions and Identity in Women's Self-Help Movements." Pp. 271–299 in *Self, Identity, and Social Movements,* edited by Sheldon Stryker, Timothy J. Owens, and Robert W. White. Minneapolis: University of Minnesota Press.

Taylor, Verta, and Nancy E. Whittier. 1992. "Collective Identity in Social Movement Communities: Lesbian Feminist Mobilization." Pp. 104–130 in *Frontiers in Social Movement Theory,* edited by Aldon D. Morris and Carol McClurg Mueller. New Haven, CT: Yale University Press.

———. 1995. "Analytical Approaches to Social Movement Culture: The Culture of the Women's Movement." Pp. 163–187 in *Social Movements and Culture,* edited by Hank Johnston and Bert Klandermans. Minneapolis: University of Minnesota Press.

The Pulitzer Prizes. 2009. Available at http://www.pulitzer.org/awards/2003 (retrieved October 20, 2009).

Thomas, William I., and Dorothy Thomas. 1929. *The Child in America.* New York: Alfred Knopf.

Tierney, Kathleen J. 1982. "The Battered Women Movement and the Creation of the Wife Beating Problem." *Social Problems* 29(3):207–220.

Tobias, Sheila. 1997. *Faces of Feminism: An Activist's Reflections on the Women's Movement.* Boulder, CO: Westview Press.

Tolbert, M. 2003. "Where Have All the Young Girls Gone?" *Clergy Sexual Misconduct: Perspectives.* CLGS Special Report. Center for Lesbian and Gay Studies in Religion and Ministry. Available at www.clgs.org (retrieved October 24, 2009).

United States Department of Justice Office of Violence Against Women. 2009.

Available at http://www.ovw.usdoj.gov/regulations.htm (retrieved October 17, 2009).

van Wormer, Katherine, and Lois Berns. 2004. "The Impact of Priest Sexual Abuse: Female Survivors' Narratives." *Affilia* 19(1):53–67.

Voice of the Faithful. 2009. Available at http://www.votf.org (retrieved October 20, 2009).

Walker, Lenore E. 1979. *The Battered Woman.* New York: Harper and Row.

Wallerstein, Immanuel. 1997. "Social Science and the Search for a Just Society." *American Journal of Sociology* 102(5):1241–1257.

Warshaw, Robin. 1988. *I Never Called It Rape: The Ms. Report on Recognizing, Fighting, and Surviving Date and Acquaintance Rape.* New York: Harper and Row.

Weber, Ellen. 1977. "Incest: Sexual Abuse Begins at Home." *Ms.*, April, p. 64.

Weed, Frank J. 1995. *Certainty of Justice: Reform in the Crime Victim Movement.* New York: Aldine de Gruyter.

Weis, K., and S. Borges. 1973. "Victimology and Rape: The Case of the Legitimate Victim." *Issues in Criminology* 8(2):71–115.

Whittier, Nancy. 1995. *Feminist Generations.* Philadelphia: Temple University Press.

———. 2001. "Emotional Strategies: The Collective Reconstruction and Display of Oppositional Emotions in the Movement Against Child Sexual Abuse." Pp. 233–250 in *Passionate Politics: Emotions and Social Movements,* edited by Jeff Goodwin, James M. Jasper, and Francesca Polletta. Chicago: University of Chicago Press.

Williams, Gwyneth I., and Rhys H. Williams. 1995. "'All We Want Is Equality': Rhetorical Framing in the Father's Rights Movement." Pp. 191–212 in *Images of Issues: Typifying Contemporary Social Problems,* edited by Joel Best. New York: Aldine de Gruyter.

Williams, Rhys H. 1995. "Constructing the Public Good: Social Movements and Cultural Resources." *Social Problems* 42(1):124–144.

———. 2002. "From the 'Beloved Community' to 'Family Values': Religious Language, Symbolic Repertoires, and Democratic Culture." Pp. 247–265 in *Social Movements: Identity, Culture, and the State,* edited by David S. Meyer, Nancy Whittier, and Belinda Robnett. New York: Oxford University Press.

Winkler, Cathy. 2002. *One Night: Realities of Rape.* Walnut Creek, CA: AltaMira Press.

Wolf, Naomi. 1992. "Feminist Fatale." *The New Republic,* March 16, pp. 23–25.

———. 1993a. "The Date-Rape Debate." *New York Times,* July 4, p. SM4.

———. 1993b. *Fire with Fire: The New Female Power and How It Will Change the 21st Century.* London: Chatto and Windus.

Wuthnow, Robert. 1994. *Sharing the Journey: Support Groups and America's New Quest for Community.* New York: Free Press.

Yates, Joshua J., and James Davison Hunter. 2002. "Fundamentalism: When History Goes Awry." Pp. 123–148 in *Stories of Change: Narrative and Social Movements,* edited by Joseph E. Davis. New York: SUNY Press.

Index

About the Book

Dunn explores the shifting perceptions over time of victims as blameworthy, blameless, pathetic, or heroic figures. She also links those images to their real-world consequences, demonstrating that they dominate the ways in which people think about intimate violence and individual responsibility. Her analysis cuts to the core of fundamental issues at the center of debates about crime and deviance, victimization, and social problems.

Jennifer L. Dunn is associate professor of sociology at Southern Illinois University. Her book *Courting Disaster: Intimate Stalking, Culture, and Criminal Justice* received the Charles Horton Cooley book prize of the Society for the Study of Symbolic Interaction.